# The Spirit of Rewilding

## Steps toward a shamanic ecology

## Peter Taylor

In dedication to Alan Watson Featherstone and his team
for their inspiring work at Trees for Life, Findhorn, Scotland.

First published by Ethos in the UK in 2016
Copyright © Peter Taylor, 2016

ISBN: 978-0-9547064-4-9

Ethos Publications
Windmill Farm
Walton Hill
Somerset
England
BA16 9RD


A catalogue record of this book is available from the British Library

Printed and bound in the UK by Lightning Source, Milton Keynes. This company has received Chain of Custody certification from the Forest Stewardship Council (FSC); Programme for Endorsement of Forest Certification (PEFC) and the Sustainable Forest Initiative (FSI).

Cover design by Ethos, from a painting - 'Abandonment' by Cristophe Souques.

Artwork and photographs by the Author unless otherwise indicated.

My thought is
that we are afraid
afraid of the wild heart
that we will not look into the fire directly

We live our job-protected lives
behind the ramparts of a life insured
and keep the wildwood at bay.

Curious how our devil
sports horns, goat's feet and dragon's tail
red his favourite colour,
whilst our hero is St George.
My thought is
he's science,
scepticism his sword,
hypothesis the lance that pins the dragon's head.

Legend has it, when she of the three-fold way was lost to us,
the Merlin held the magic,
but then was lost to lechery,
therein losing himself.

No form now breaks the surface of the lake
where Nimuë sleeps.
Would that we could throw her not just sword,
but lance and armour too,
and walk this magic land,
naked to the wild wild wood.

Introduction to  the British Association of Nature Conservationists'
Wilderness Conference,
Open University, 1995.

# Preface

I am prompted to collate my recent writing on rewilding following the edited volume from Ethos in 2011 (*Rewilding: ECOS writing on wildland and conservation values*). That book updated *Beyond Conservation* written in 2005 and added the work of 60 other authors on this issue. Some of the material I present here has featured in ECOS (Journal of the British Association of Nature Conservationists) but for the most part these stand-alone articles are drawn from background papers presented at recent international conferences.

In the last few years, rewilding has become popularised and gained a welcome broader audience. Perhaps as a result, some conservation organisations once inimical to the concept have come to embrace it and a Rewilding Britain group has been set up. I am concerned to put a marker down on two issues: the first is that rewilding in Britain has been happening for some time – for at least three decades, resulting in more than a dozen large-scale projects on the ground (detailed in the two books above) and this does not often feature in popular discourse with a focus, for example, on large scale future change in the uplands; and second, as a network of grassroots initiatives, all of which communicate with each other, rewilding is a social movement and as such is inclusive, with no set definitions though a broad agreement on principles. The people involved on the ground have invested many years in outreach to farming, forestry, water companies and local economies and recent popularisation runs great risk of polarising opinion.

Further, the dominant conservation paradigm within the political and economic arena is scientific, whereas much of the value of rewilding lies in the interaction between nature and the human psyche. In this compilation, the content extends beyond the normal bounds of conservation science and even most rewilding practices. These stand-alone essays, whilst having a foundation in the ecological science in which I trained, represent my efforts to push that boundary. Our science has proven inadequate to stem the tide of losses, particularly on a global level and I believe we must extend and deepen our methods of engagement if we are to solve the crisis of ecological degradation.

There is now a growing acknowledgement that the world's remaining indigenous peoples hold knowledge as well as wisdom that is relevant to a global dilemma. I believe it is time that all ecologists were trained in shamanic inner modes of perception common to indigenous communities in order to balance the masculinised mentality of science. In a future work, I intend to detail that training, whereas here I can provide only signposts to that path.

Peter Taylor, September, 2016

# Acknowledgements

Much of the work compiled here has arisen from invitations either to speak at conferences or contribute to the BANC journal ECOS. My foremost debt of gratitude is to BANC, not just as a forum in which to share my ideas, but also as colleagues in the endeavour to bring 'rewilding' into focus. I am particularly indebted to Rick Minter as editor of ECOS, and to council members Alison Parfitt and Gavin Saunders, both of whom have been inspirational in their tireless organisational and leadership roles.

During the years in which the Wildland Network was active (2005-2008) Rick and Alison were joined by Steve Carver at the Geography Department in Leeds University, whose constant commitment to wildland analysis and activism made a huge contribution to the establishment of the concepts in academic circles and within the global movement for the protection of wilderness. Within that network, Simon Ayres – founder of the Welsh Wild Land Foundation, has been a constant support. Steve, Simon, Alison and Rick have helped by reading and commenting on the manuscript and encouraging its publication. My long-term colleagues in environmental science – Professor Jackson Davis in the USA and Roger Kayes in the UK, also read and commented on the drafts.

I especially thank Ian Rotherham and his team at Sheffield Hallam University for invitations to address the conservation science community in 2014 and 2015. I much appreciated the spirit of open dialogue.

During my travels on the continent, Anton Robl and Pavlina Misikova invited my contribution to Pilsen's landscape conference in 2015 and we are further collaborating on shamanic and scientific themes at the Institute of Life-based Architecture, in Furth-am-Wald. Jaromir Blaha of Hnuti Duha (Czech Friends of the Earth) invited presentations on Rewilding and greatly facilitated my understanding of the issues affecting Sumava National Park. In France, my friend, the artist Chrisophe Souques, was a stalwart of the shamanic work there and I am grateful for his artwork on the cover. I am particularly grateful to Bridget Lytton of Quillan in Aude, France, for the space at Lavaldieu; for support during a month-long retreat at her yoga centre in Quillan to complete the manuscript; and for financial aid during the writing stages. I thank also Frank Duffy for help in the final production process.

For inspiration, teachings and guidance I thank Leonard Orr and Don MacFarland for their pioneering therapies; and Martin Prechtel, Ivan McBeth, and Vimal Darpan for their ceremonial magic. Finally I thank my companion for much of these years – Monika Michaelova, for her insight and understanding of the human predicament and its healing.

# CONTENTS

# PART 2

# PART 3

# Introduction

Much as it may sometimes appear we are holding the line, the losses continue – biodiversity of farmland, wetlands, undeveloped mountain scenery and wild rivers. We are especially losing the *wild*. In our endeavours to keep people connected to nature, our reserves gain access paths, hides and information boards; and in some cases birds and animals are artificially fed to make up for losses of space to move or simply enough food to sustain the population. This loss of the wild is what has motivated my involvement in rewilding – where we have, as a collective movement, made some gains. We have worked on the edge of conservation paradigms toward a more creative edge of engagement with nature – extending reserves and moving toward landscape scale management. However, the community of rewilders still suffers from a conservationist mentality bounded by science and systems thinking and which fails to reach out to the majority of modern youth.

Conservation thinking is inextricably bound to development issues, with its concepts of progress, sustainability – including economic, and all the values and the vested interests that follow as an inherent part of broader environmental concerns. Whether energy production and use, raw materials extraction, economic development policies, forestry, agricultural and water management, recreation and human habitat design – 'conservation' is simply tagged on to a particular mind-set. Conservationists are part of the development paradigm – one that is clearly failing on so many levels but most fundamentally in terms of global ecology - a failure hardly yet admitted within the economists' realm, but obvious to all scientific academies in their reports on the state of global ecosystems.

Conservation values are inextricably linked to scientific methodology and the institutions of science. These values are seldom reflected upon despite a modern sociology of science that demonstrates the pervasive influence of 'interests' in the growth of knowledge, for example in relation to political regimes and cultural psychology, religion, and gender. No science is value free. These largely hidden values affect the way an hypothesis is formulated and the resources devoted to 'proving' it. The great majority of science is funded by industrial or governmental interests and this also obviously determines what does *not* get funded.

And within science, there are boundary effects driven by the compartmentalisation of knowledge into fields and the scarcity of cross-disciplinary studies – specialisms lead to a narrow research focus, a major problem when it comes to the assessment of complex environmental systems with their ecological webs, energy flows and feedbacks. Science has developed a certain hubris in its assumed capacity to predict. I have written elsewhere on the failures of predictive environmental science, especially with regard to computer models and control of pollution. There has been an ongoing tendency to build complex fancy models of environmental reality based on some flimsy data sets and then retain belief in the model rather than new data that might contradict that model. The same errors in predictive environmental modelling that bedevilled the 1980s, with acid rain, organochlorine pollutants, and ozone depletion, were repeated in the modelling of carbon dioxide emissions (see *Chill: a reassessment of global warming theory*).

In this regard, there exists a strong 'boundary effect' in relation to scientific disciplines – the crossing of which can entail rejection by the scientific community. I have always been careful when, as a critic, it has been necessary to cross that boundary, to do so with great caution – in this case, with regard to the ecological and social science of rewilding. I do so now only after having worked together with conservationists for many years to further that cause. This joint work is described in *Beyond Conservation* (2005) and *Rewilding* (2011),

For the most part, my past work has been *within* the paradigms of science, including adjacent legal systems and institutional structures. At different times I have been a fully accredited member of institutes – including time on the editorial board of a specialist journal. Throughout the 1980s and 1990s, I advised several governments, the EU and the UN on environmental pollution issues and ran my own small independent research group in Oxford. I can readily say that although my team gave several governments, including my own, and a few industrial conglomerates a very hard time of it, we were well respected at a scientific level. I reflect now that in those decades, critical scientific review was valued by governmental and non-governmental organisations alike, whereas in the 21$^{st}$ century, the critical faculty seems to have gone to sleep and we live in a world of propaganda wars and dodgy dossiers. This is particular the case with regard to the science and policy response related to climate change, an issue that now pervades every aspect of environmental concern as well as conservation.

With respect to climate change, critics of alarmist responses are branded deniers and subjected to ad hominem attacks – instead of embracing dissent and doubts about mechanisms seen as potentially undermining a policy response. Without exception, conservation bodies have sided with the 'consensus' view of the UN special committee, and without exception, failed to investigate how such consensus is created and maintained. Lessons of past failures at the UN, which NGOs did much to correct during the evolution of the Precautionary Principle, have not been learned and a false consensus now rules. What has been left out of the models are natural *cycles* of climate change.

The issue is of fundamental importance to conservation and rewilding in particular. Natural cycles cannot to mitigated. If, as I would argue, currently observed warming is mainly driven by forces other than carbon dioxide, then vastly expensive mitigation programmes will have minimal impact upon how future climate evolves. Some argue that this does not matter, since humanity needs to wean itself off fossil fuels for other reasons, not least of which is there limited supply. What is not commonly understood is that 'renewable' energy sources are dispersed across the natural environment – mountains for wind and hydro, forests for biofuels, estuaries for tidal regimes. If we try to power *the same industrial system* from dispersed power sources, we will have to invade every last natural space with advanced technology. Much of what remains of truly wild land, especially rainforest, is home to indigenous peoples who live in harmony with their environment – their communities are threated. Some species will disappear: eagles, vultures, cranes, and storks are threatened by turbines and power lines; bears and lynx by the roads for hydro-schemes; orang utang by biofuel plantations – but above all, the *wild* will disappear.

Energy policy is thus a *rewilding* issue. The only valid option with regard to lowering the environmental cost of energy is *to use less.* This would require restructuring of industrial society and a complete rewriting of the current development ethos where economic criteria over-rule the ecological. To achieve this, it is the *human* that must be rewilded – to get back in touch with the cycles of nature, the risks as well as the sense of awe and the joy of reconnection.


**A wildland network**

My involvement with 'rewilding' in Britain goes back nearly thirty years. It is first and foremost a grass-roots involvement with people and organisations at a local as well as national level, networking initiatives through what was The Wildland Network and the agency of the British Association of Nature Conservationists, of which I was a council member. I would say that the foundation of the rewilding movement in Britain was laid by BANC in its series of regional seminars and publication of initiatives in its journal *ECOS* during the last two decades.

This network has certainly included scientists trained in ecology and conservation, but also professional foresters with a broader remit related to landscape, community and recreation as well as economic production; water companies; land managers with tenant farmers as well as a few independent farmers; game conservationists and fishermen; and a large number of local community groups. Our regional seminars drew government agencies and the larger conservation and wildlife NGOs, but the main initiatives in Britain have been from small grass-roots community groups. In this movement, science is respected, but it is not the only perspective – there is a growing appreciation of older indigenous relationships to the environment and the shifts in perception that are required.

This is where the boundary I talk of should ideally not be an issue – after all, science has boundaries with art, poetry, ethics, religion and moral values. However, the strongest boundary exists between the separated worlds of physics and the world of the psyche. The inner realms are hardly respected by science – despite a century of humanistic psychology. These worlds are the realm of the shaman, sorcerer, 'witch' and 'magician', and not amenable to the observer – unless of course, the observer as anthropologist studies these archetypal characters.

But what does this have to do with rewilding as practised in Britain, Europe and North America? There are no sociological studies as yet, so I write here from my own direct experience and largely unquantified observations. In some respects, I write as an anthropologist – a field in which I have some training and as a current member of the Royal Anthropological Institution.

In one crucial respect, I have crossed the boundary of observer to become *participant.* I have trained in several aspects of shamanic practice and I am also a yogi in the Himalayan tradition – I teach meditation, bodywork, movement and healing arts, and there are distinct shamanic elements in its tradition.

In the latter field, I have three decades of experience as a therapist working with small groups on a path of 'spiritual' awakening. I work with breathing techniques that alter conscious perception; as well as bodywork and movement therapy that release trauma and subsequent blockages to extra-sensory modes of perception. In the shamanic realms I have undergone some of the traditional trainings, mostly in the North and Central American lineages of 'medicine men', but at an early stage, working with the recovery of ancient British and European shamanic knowledge - working for some years with teams of teachers on the integration of yogic healing techniques with other lineages, including Sufi and Judaeo-Christian, Buddhist and Wiccan (Old English) and helping to create a 'modern' Druidry – for example, in the Oak Dragon Project and with the modern Order of Bards, Ovates and Druids (OBOD).

Much of the ancient lore of working with nature, especially in th healing arts, was lost to Europeans (or more accurately, forcibly eradicated). The growing initiatives I have witnessed over the past thirty years have been aided by North and South American teachers coming to Europe, or students travelling to the Americas. However, in the last few years I have worked closely with the Czech medicine woman, Monika Michaelova, and her circle of women healers and herbalists (as well as their male partners). There exists an unbroken lineage of herbalism in parts of Europe, but the wider recovery of early European shamanic knowledge is not an easy road for either men or women. This is the issue upon which most of my recent work has been focussed.

However, very few of the British or European practitioners of rewilding, have much truck with these realms! But some do – whether it be the spirituality of the Scottish group of Trees for Life at Findhorn, or the more privately held realms of individuals working as land managers or in community outreach within the Forestry Commission or the National Trust. And at several points when I have dipped a toe to test the waters, I have been surprised at the enthusiasm among young people when their horizon has been temporarily extended – for example, when addressing students at agricultural colleges or University, or even in secondary schools. Following publication of *Beyond Conservation* in 2005, a steady trickle of mostly young professionals – such as National Park ecologists or rangers, have approached me expressing gratitude for that boundary having been pressed just a little.

And recently, the more traditional conservation community who were initially very sceptical of rewilding, have invited lengthy discourse and debate – in particular, under the auspices of Ian Rotherham at Sheffield Hallam University (see *Call of the Wild*, ECOS 35 (1), Spring 2014). Ian invited my presentation on Rewilding in Britain (page 166) at their May 2014 UK conference on this theme, and further to a more international audience in September 2015. In that second presentation, I pushed a little further across that boundary – taking the conference title of cultural severance further back in time than implied by the severance of land and community we experience in Britain today.

The articles and essays contain some repetition – they were written largely as stand-alone pieces and for varying audiences. I have excised and edited a little, but I think the issues in question bear a little repetition and an approach from different angles.

### Rewilding and the role of definitions

So often we are asked 'how can one define rewilding'? I could say – please don't! There are several well-known answers – some say by scale and dominance of natural processes where the land becomes 'self-willed', whereas others would say even small patches of land or rivers or coastline can be 'rewilded' and much can be achieved by interventions. Academics in particular like to have a definition (and a few theories). Those definitions that exist are usually based on 'ecosystems' thinking: for example, the restoration of large-scale processes and re-introduction of 'keystone' species, i.e. those animals (mostly) that by their presence, alter the system itself and may create more diversity or opportunity (and sometimes perhaps less) for other species. Beaver and wolf are good examples of such species often absent from many former habitats.

I have never liked the process of definition. For me, it is an unwild thing! In the UK context, The Widlland Network created a broad church for networking all scales and modes of rewilding under the principle that all could learn from each other. We encouraged communication across traditional boundaries – for example, with game conservancies and farmer's unions, fisheries and forestry, recreation, water use, coastal defences and the greening of city environments. If something would evolve into a wilder condition than before – then it was 'rewilding'. Nevertheless, in an Epilogue I provide a note on 'how to rewild' and include a definition developed by Rewilding Britain.

Most often, professionals as well as grass-roots activists talk about 'healthy' ecosystems and a requirement for large scale relatively hands-off management to allow natural processes to dominate the system. A healthy system is held to be diverse, more stable and resilient, especially to climate change. But the concept is tautological - if a system is large and 'complete' with its guild of herbivores and their predators, it is then assumed to be healthy and hence more stable. There is not a lot of evidence to support this concept of health and stability. Theoretically, a simplified 'system' denuded of key components – such as the American prairie grassland, may also be stable (and mimicked to produce food, as in cattle ranching). As Tim Flannery argued in *The Eternal Frontier*, those grasslands were substantially the product of early Native Americans using fire and selective hunting to remove mega-herbivores. In the not-so-distant past, natural cycles of climate change have radically transformed systems of grassland, forest and desert.

We may add to this issue of definitions and management or non-management options the confounding problematic of massively increased human dominance and use of space, such that all natural reserves are small and so disconnected that even those complete guilds of herbivores and their predators still present in parts of Africa and India are in the longer term unlikely to be genetically sustainable. Furthermore, climate change, whether natural or human induced, requires corridors and connectivity to enable adaptation. Less often perceived is the fact that human dominated systems rely upon species largely alien to their immediate environments (grasses and trees, as well as crops) and that global trade not only spreads invasive species, but pathogens as well. This latter issue is particular relevant to policies of hands-off management where invasive species would then dominate.

We are left with a conundrum – that no land can be termed entirely *natural* unless, of course, we include humans as natural! This does not prevent us using the term natural – clearly there is a spectrum from minimal to full spectrum dominance, but it should limit use of the terms pristine and wilderness, or schemes for the recreation of past assemblages such as a Pleistocene Park replete with reconstituted mammoths!

Some ecologists now regard *all* ecosystems as irreversibly altered by human action – whether from direct exploitation or as a result of pollution, in particular the recent global warming due to carbon dioxide, hence the term for a new geological era – The Anthropocene. Such wide-ranging is really not so recent, with the aforementioned extinction of the herbivores beginning several tens of thousands of years before present, followed by the previous century's commercial exploitation of the great whales which significantly altered ocean system dynamics. Coupled now with elevated carbon dioxide levels, sulphate aerosol and nitrate pollution, there is not an ecosystem in the world that is unaffected by human action.

**Indigenous culture**

This issue matters because concepts of 'pristine' ecosystems and natural health are still current, yet the last of the world's 'wild' places are far from devoid of indigenous human occupation. Moreover, their conservation or protection depends upon a cooperation between indigenous (shamanic) systems of perception and value, and the forces that may impinge on their boundaries – not all of which are exploitative or extractive in motivation. Governmental programmes, for example, may be concerned to civilise peoples once remote from participation in national affairs, or to provide health, education, electrical power and communication facilities as an apparent human right. Conservation thinking, as articulated at Salamanca, now enlists indigenous peoples in programmes that reflect global and scientific concerns, for example for rare and threatened habitats and species.

There is a further conundrum related to the psychology of any kind of systems thinking – if the observer is not wild, how can a wild 'system' be adequately perceived or conceived? And if human perception is the key, what is it to be a wild human being? And does it matter if an unwild modern civilised mentality necessarily projects itself upon the natural world? After all, that mentality is now the ruling mentality for at least that half of humanity living in cities, as well as most of the rural communities that now exploit the 'natural resources' of soil, water and forests, leaving but a small percentage of wild land.

These issues surface in my commentary on the 10th World Wilderness Congress in Salamanca, Spain, in the summer of 2013 {In Part 1: The Road to Salamanca}. This was the first time that significant delegations of indigenous peoples had been brought together to present their own success stories as well as their concerns to a wider conservation community. It was remarkable how even remote communities had educated themselves in science and legal principles and worked to develop regional strategies of conservation. However, their participation reflected what is largely a one-way process of education – there being but little evidence of the civilised world of conservation seeking to learn from the indigenous mind.

It ought to be obvious why this matters. The civil world is currently on a knife-edge: the global population has burgeoned such that food production only just manages to keep up; energy supplies are limited; the whole system is vulnerable to climate change and epidemic disease; there are internal problems of mental health and growing social disorder with almost constant warfare now focussed upon resource issues, particularly fossil fuel supplies; furthermore, soil loss and growing water scarcity are largely unrecognised global issues yet have huge implications for the future of humanity.

Perhaps the most potent threat to stability is hardly mentioned and was not fully recognised until a US Academy of Science report in 2008 which dealt with the consequences of a 'solar tsunami' - the global electrical system is vulnerable to what are quite regular huge electro-magnetic pulses that would disable the power grids and lead to widespread breakdown of civil order. For those who would trumpet the benefits of science, technology and a civilised life, there needs to be a salutary reflection that this system could be humbled by a common natural event and one that science has known about since 1859 (the last such event which occurred before civilisation became dependent upon electricity). In US congressional hearing on this issue, it was admitted that 95% of the US population could not be fed in the aftermath of a solar tsunami. As I report in my anthropological essay on a modern European 'Ghost Dance' – a project that I led for seven years to the year 2012, in line with a shamanic prophecy from Mayan elders, NASA released papers in 2013 showing that in July 2012 a huge such tsunami had missed the Earth by just nine days of solar rotation.

If this would prove the most dislocatory of natural events, a human failure in global finance and distribution could have equally severe repercussions. And in the aftermath of any such widespread breakdown of order, given the current level of population and resource use, enormous local pressure of ecosystems would ensue – for water, food and fuel in particular. Human society would certainly become much wilder, living closer to death and disease, reverting to tribal lore, though hopefully reliving an earlier history of cooperative endeavour rather than the tribal warlords now evident where much of the modern civilised order decays.

To be wild, the human mind needs to have less fear of death, less desire for creature comforts, less control and dominance over natural cycles of scarcity as well as abundance – in short, more acceptance of nature itself. Some would see that as a backward step, the antithesis of evolution, whereas the indigenous mind would argue that true wisdom comes when the human mind identifies not with its corporeal nature and hence limited physical life, but with its spiritual and hence 'eternal' core – a place where death has no dominion.

In modern society we paradoxically extol the virtues of a long lifespan, comfort and security, yet celebrate artists, poets, musicians and singers whose creative lives may often be turbulent and short. We pursue life-threatening sports. And more sadly, we will die for causes where our freedom is threatened (if we don't strike first!). Yet, when talk emerges of bringing back wolves or bears, or wild cattle even, the comfort lovers and protectors of economic margins so often gain sway! It was Health & Safety bureaucrats and Animal Welfare activists that curtailed the pioneering Dutch 'nature' reserves that brought back wild cattle with their fighting bulls, or herds of horses that might starve under cyclic conditions of scarcity (see coverage in *Rewilding*).

## The awe of abundance

I include here a short piece from my field diary on a visit to my old teacher's ashram in the Himalayan foothills at the turn of the century. It was a reminder of how easily we get used to the modern landscape and its loss of 'abundance' such that most people now have no real idea of what has been lost – the species are still there, though 'red-listed', but the *awe* of abundance is what has really been lost.

The little piece is about the Ramganga in India and I place it here because it is the only occasion since much younger days and an exciting but relatively insensitive crossing of the Sahara, when I have touched real wilderness, and the first time in an environment of abundance rather than the barren reaches of desert, high mountains or ice-fields. I saw here how truly incompatible even the most simple settled village life can be for so many species, and more deeply, the sheer abundance of each life-form when not exploited or limited by human use. I saw then the rationale for limiting human exploitation of enough places from which we can learn – but the learning not of ecosystem interactions, webs, energy flows, recycling, nor even the 'right' of other species to exist – rather it is to touch the wonder of abundance, the true 'mother' that indigenous peoples recognise as much by feeling as any kind of analysis of that which supports them. Only at this level, can the love that permeates all of nature, as of a mother's love, be felt to exist.

- The cliff overlooks the Ramganga river now some 100 km from its source in the Himalaya. Immediately below is a deep rock pool of green water, paling to turquoise at its edges, surrounded by huge round boulders, buff, almost white, then white sand and grassy banks before the dense jungle, crisped and browned by months of dry season. We have stopped on the offchance of tiger drinking at the pool. The scene is very still but for the bubbling rapids rushing between the rocks. There are shapes in the water, at first not discernable, not recognisable - where the pool shallows before the white water there are echelons of long black almost geometric forms, immobile, looking for all the world like black sharks lazing on the bottom, maybe forty, about four

18

feet long and a foot wide at the head, black catfish with huge wide mouths and triangular pectoral fins hugging the bottom in maybe two feet of water. Then the myriad of dark streaks in the shallows to the head of the pool, reveal themselves as fish, each about two feet long, several hundred so that the river bed is obscured in their patterned dance of light and shadow. What look like pieces of driftwood, is an eight foot gharial, and two smaller, and a mugger, or regular crocodile with a blunt mouth, the fish-eating gharial having long thin snouts - their bodies dried almost white in the sun. Everything so still. A troupe of Langur monkeys sits grooming among the boulders. The silence is momentarily pierced by the gull-like mew of a fish-eating eagle, of which there are three species inhabiting the narrow river. At another pool, we had watched two large otters sand-bathing. Suddenly this pool reveals a moving form, surreal in its glide from the deeper blue depths, turning in the turquoise water, catching the sun, a river turtle as big as a sea turtle, incongruously large for the pool.

What is it, this feeling? The quiet? The stillness? Everything at rest. Only turtle moving and so languorously. As if they all know the river will feed them. No need to strive. And so many. So abundant. The fish so large, all so large. I have just spent four weeks on a another river, another tributary of the Ganga, similarly shallow and interspersed with pools, but the forest long degraded, and remote though the valley, dotted with settlements, and watching each day as the net-man walked the freezing waters barefoot flinging his stone weighted trap for a handful of 6 inch fry-ups. I marveled then at the giant kingfishers and huge fishing owls, sustained by such small prey. Maybe there had been a few bigger fish I hadn't seen, but no turtles, no crocodiles, no chance of tiger or elephant that had been there fifty years ago.

That river was an intimate part of daily life at the ashram of Herakhan Baba, the legendary 'Babaji'. The ritual of 4.00 a.m. bath under the stars sustained us in our programme for the day. Which for me, this time, had been the unexpected privilege of looking after the Maha Shakti Dhuni, the sacred fire pit - mouth of the Divine Mother. Her eight-petalled sides are washed and renewed with wet clay and adorned with yellow sandalwood paste and brilliant flowers, everyday before dawn, when she is greeted with singing and ceremonies of gratitude. It demands much focus - the cleaning and cleansing require order and mantra, the ceremony also. Normally, this is performed by experienced initiates, but they had gone off to the Khumbu Mela. The ashram was quiet for a month, and I had understood then why I had been called by that inner voice – 'come for the renewal and regeneration you need'. I had taken my two young children, with some trepidation, but they had loved the life by the river.

There had been a moment, when bathing 'the Mother' with the wet clay water, when I had felt so deeply that the firepit had a living essence. My heart had moved with caring for her, poignant for me then because I had left my own mother, dying slowly of cancer, to be cared for by my sister and brothers, who would bathe her daily. Everything had clicked into place - each step of the

19

ceremony and mantra in my inexperienced devotion had finally come together, and the Dhuni began to vibrate with primordial energy - like a sound-wave emanating in the silence beyond our perception, bathing us, feeding us.

This river below us had something of that emanation. Here now in the rock pool was displayed for us the great mystery and lessons of human existence. This river had not been taken from by man. Its abundance was fabulous, almost beyond reason. How could these clear shallow waters of one small narrow river sustain such lifeforms, such profusion? And they just waiting in stillness. A complete aura of trust, and peace and harmony. At the inflow of that river's great breath, they were fed, a million tiny morsels transformed into that dark shoal, and above and below and to every side, waited turtle beak, crocodile teeth, and eagles talons, death at every turn. With which they were at peace.

The Ramganga flows into the Jim Corbett Wilderness, a National Park since 1936 and the flagship of Project Tiger. In the heart of the reserve there is a small tourist complex, and, sadly, a huge man-made lake formed in 1976 by a hydro development on the edge of the park. This wilderness is not untouched by man. It earns its living, supports an economy, with a network of jeep tracks and hut encampments for 50,000 tourists (90% Indian) a year. Tiger tracks are everywhere. We had been lucky. One stalked our jeep when parked up in silence near a well-trodden route. It was an open top. The tiger no more than 15 metres away and content to lope off after a good look at the inmates. Here, humans are in the cages, locked away at night, or perched ten feet up on the park's elephants. It is not allowed to walk in the park. Here, tiger is king.

A few years ago, in the other valley of the Ganga, an old tiger had wandered from the park, and in the few months it took to track and shoot the wiley old beast, it had killed and eaten 20 people, mostly women and young girls taken while gathering wood or fodder. These are not now simple tribespeople remote from political influence. Satellite TV adorns many a roof near the ashram. My children got to know the valley children - as individual and valued and loved as anywhere - contrary to thoughts I had had twenty years ago, life is not held cheap here. The risks of the tiger are tolerated, and for some, the more modern, it may be out of international duty to biodiversity or eco-tourism, but to the valley dwellers whose children are on the edge of the forest, the tiger is both feared and revered. She is the shamanic 'familiar' of the fierce and protective mother Goddess, Durga, whose eight-armed form is depicted riding on the tiger's back.

I have noticed, since my last sojourn in India, some sixteen years ago, and now alerted to shamanic realities, the depth of contact here with the wild animal energies. Shiva has a bull by his side, cobras round his neck and the elephant headed Ganesh as a son. Ram has the heroic monkey-headed Hanuman as his champion. The animal forms and powers are entwined with the Gods. In present day India, it will not be by attitude that the tiger loses its ground, but by sheer pressure of the human population, loss of forest corridors and isolation of the reserves.

Attitude......when I left, the tabloids be-wailed the beast of Monmouth, a black cat large enough to be one of our naturalised panthers, for it had 'mauled' (three small scratches) the child that had grabbed its tail. Helicopters and police marksmen had been dispatched to the scene. And in my native Snowdonia, where are the animal icons? The Celtic wolf, and bear and boar long gone to be replaced by the holy lamb and the good shepherd's JCB. Cry, the beloved country! It is not a conservation ethic we need, but a spiritual revolution! Then we could have our wilderness zones with the bear and wolf and lynx and boar, and this awe of abundance, and that skipped beat in the human heart at the sounds in a forest where man is not dominant.

**Future prospects**

In the natural world itself, forest and biodiversity loss has slowed but not been halted, despite many pledges to do so at inter-governmental level. Agricultural systems continue to intensify and reduce habitats in those areas closest to human habitation – the fields and meadows, ponds and waterways, where children first begin to connect with nature. Even in well-regulated and protected Europe, the loss of farmland species continues apace and energy technologies now make major inroads into any wild but relatively unprotected space. There is an endless series of warnings in reports to the UN from the scientific community on issues of biodiversity (I make some comments more specifically on the threat of climate change in Part 3).

In short – from the perspective of both natural and social sciences, the system is broken. There then follow calls to 'fix' it, but most of these come from the science community and involve new technologies coupled to old systems thinking.

For that half of humanity most at risk of environmental degradation, which is that half in 'poverty' and hence not able to buy their way out of difficulty, the solutions are relatively simple and the technology already proven. Yet techniques of ecological agriculture and agro-forestry, soil and water conservation, basic sanitation and some modern technical aids to dwellings, such as solar panels, still go without major funding programmes. Between 85-90% of international development aid is spent on programmes designed to improve 'the economy' by moving large numbers of people off the land and into cities, industrialising agriculture and selling scarce resources on a global market. One example is Egypt, a country dependent upon UN food-aid, yet its premium exports of organic potatoes can be found in many global supermarkets. The old mentality of making money first and foremost, and then spending some of it to repair the damage – both social and environmental, is still the dominant development paradigm.

**Indigenous modes of thought (and feeling)**

It was Albert Einstein who said it made no sense to try to solve a problem by the same kind of thinking that had created it! This is my guide for introducing the indigenous modes of thought (and feeling) as a shamanic dimension to rewilding, and perhaps eventually into ecological training itself. The indigenous mind has a different relation to nature: it does not perceive itself as separate and strives to live in harmony with respect for all other denizens of the planet. There are deeper dimensions which I will argue have the power to heal not just our own rift with nature, but divisions within the very 'self' of the civilised mind.

It was the work of 20th century psychology to identify the 'psychosis' of the modern mind – its alienation from life itself, from community and above all, from the sexual dimension. The indigenous mind does not separate energies as 'sexual', rather they are all the pulse of 'life' energy. Sexual energy as we know it, and hence, life energy as they know it, is a mysterious power with much of its nature not measurable and hence not explorable by scientific method. I will explore this issue in greater depth, for I would argue that the *suppression* of this life force, accompanied by fear of its liberation and demonising of its source, has badly deranged and imbalanced the civil mind and made it such a self-destructive force.

In this respect, concepts of a Mother and Father Nature are not just a projection of protective, nurturing and wise counsel, but also essentially *sexual* powers – and ones that indigenous people recognise as *inherent* to the natural world of which they are a part. The civilised mind, having amputated most aspects of the 'mother' as a sexual being, has resorted to a widespread male-mind godhead of Father-worship or else, a mechanistic perception that leaves no room for a divinity within the natural world and separates the human from Nature. Furthermore, the mental faculty (or male aspect of consciousness) has been allowed to dominate the world of feeling and hence the humanitarian 'heart' – and it is in the heart, I would argue, rather than the mind, that essential unity is more readily perceived.

The shamanic practices I allude to have never separated the human from nature, nor heart from head, nor physic from psychic. The indigenous look to nature as teacher in a process of human unfolding *within* nature and they perceive their own love of nature as reciprocated. The value system of the original indigenous human is not distorted by concepts of progress as measured by control of the environment or of disease. Indigenous methods of low-level control may be far less effective, but the consequences are more accepted. The indigenous lives much closer to death and disease, which are themselves seen more as teachers than enemies.

In these realms of shamanic practice and yoga tantra, my recent work has involved the development of ceremonial dance, culminating in 2006 with a seven-year commitment to a European form of the Ghost Dance (drawn from the North American tradition). Since the end of that programme in 2012, I have spent much time in France, Spain, Germany and Czech Republic engaged in programmes of recovery of our own shamanic traditions, now long under repression first by religious fanatics, then by the scientific institutions of medicine and psychology. There is a groundswell of new expression in the realms of music, dance, vision quest and healing. The Native American shaman, Martin Prechtel has called this *a movement to recover the 'indigenous soul'*. This book opens with an essay I wrote on the nature of this recovery programme whilst on my European travels in 2012 {Part 1: Travels on the Continent}

In shamanic culture, death is integral to life in ways that are shunned in western Judaic-Christian and eastern Islamic religious iconography. Only in India, in Vedic symbology do we find Death as a Goddess - the dark destroyer of worlds, yet also the generating creatrix of life. Living closer to death is the ultimate *wildness* and paradoxically it appears to lead to a greater acceptance of change and joy and trust in life itself.

This is directly relevant where indigenous communities are faced by the 'threat' of climate change. Our current obsession with control is predicated on models that purport to show mitigation is possible, when in perhaps equal likelihood or in my view more than likely, the future course will be dominated by unalterable natural forces. Even were this not the case, climate models actually predict unavoidable change because emission controls would take decades to have effect. In this case it is a valid policy option to direct at least half expenditures on programmes of resilience that focus upon communities remaining on the land, and safeguarding their soil and water resources, forests and biodiversity.

For such a switch of resources there would needs be an acceptance of the power of nature – even that some of that power is amplified by human activity, and an accommodation with it. However, any sociological analysis would readily show that the apparently objective scientific view of predictive potential and control is also allied to systems of technical *products* (turbines, generators, solar panels, Genetically Modified Organisms etc), expertise, consultancies and profits for global corporations – very little of which would be satiated by a resilience-based approach.

It is not a big step to see that the male-mind world of science and industrialised production (whether capitalist or communist) becomes a gender issue. The direction of science, knowledge and policy are inherently biased in favour of largely male-dominated interest groups. I will argue that the indigenous mind is more balanced between masculine and feminine modes and hence may teach the world new ways of saving itself from itself.

## Dances of life and death

There remains one other reason why I would argue for a more shamanic ecology – it relates to modern youth. In my experience as a dance teacher and having met thousands of young people at music festivals, a great many young people of today are strongly alienated from the civilised world they inherit. They turn to other cultures – in particular African drumming and rhythms, Indian ecstatic dance, Native American sweat-lodge and vision quest, as well as a more infamous predilection for designer drugs. To *this* growing community, nature as a shamanic experience is not an alien concept and schools of western shamanism are growing rapidly. In my observation, very few of these young people actually know much about the ecology of the animals they admire – whether whale, or dolphin, wolf, bear, tiger or black panther. Even most Druid neophytes would be hard-pressed to distinguish raven from crow in full flight.

It is an often-heard lament among educationalists in conservation that most young people emerge from a primary schooling with a well-developed fascination for nature, but lose that connection during their teenage years. Sex, drugs and rock 'n roll take over – or for the studious, the academy of science with its grip upon methodology. In recent years, educationalists further lament that even the realm of primary education has now been subverted by virtual realities of screen and keypad and that many children simply do not get out into the natural world.

I would argue that in any recovery process – for the natural soul of young people especially, we must tackle the systemic damage to community, base-level security, sexuality, personal authority, the primacy of heart and love, the freedom to speak the truth and above all, the faculties of inner-sight and senses, all of which remain intact in the indigenous world (I deal with these aspects of recovery in Part 4). It is only when the senses have fully recovered from centuries of damage and repression that the wild-type human can be resurrected and then see with wild eyes the nature of the wild itself.

## Of shamanic and tantric dimensions

I am wary of the use of terms such as shamanic or tantric – for the majority perhaps, their meaning is obscure. Real understanding in these realms can only come from direct experience. What is it to be a *shaman*? What are *tantric* realms of experience or training? There are many schools available for the uninitiated and many pitfalls. I will make no specific recommendations, rather set out to provide a guide as to what to look for and what not.

I have a simple test as to whether a shaman is real, or not – and there are many in the Western world who are not, and who are heisters and hustlers on the make in an expanding market. Some of these are former indigenous tribal teachers and one has to be especially wary of such. For me, a true 'shaman' is defined by the community to which he or she belongs. They seldom call themselves shaman – an anthropological term foreign to the majority of indigenous cultures. The shaman is a natural *position* in the community and goes by many names – usually one of healer, 'medicine' man' or woman, and ceremonialist. Almost anyone can have shamanic abilities and I will go into that in more detail, but the real legitimacy is conferred by the position.

If the shamanic teacher is not recognised by a valid community wherein he or she lives and has an acknowledged active role, then beware! This is especially problematic in this modern age when communities are dispersed – however, there *is* an international shamanic dance community with acknowledged leaders and teachers, many of whom I know and can recommend; there is also a growing European movement of ceremony, music and dance centred on drinking the South American 'medicine' tea from the vine *Ayahuasca,* which in Brazil has become a national institution.

The shaman is necessarily engaged upon healing work. In my essay, *The Healing Forest* (first published ten years ago in *Beyond Conservation),* I attempt to explain the difference between curing a disease and healing a sickness. Certain cancers, for example, may not be curable, but great healing may occur as the result of the experience – such healing being often within families and close communities as well as within the suffering individual.
The original 'witch doctor' as the charlatan portrayed by early western anthropology has eventually come to be respected as 'shaman' and potentially a more advanced practitioner in the healing of psycho-somatic disorders. The switch of perceptions involved a necessary widening of viewpoint to encompass psychology as well as medicine at a time when most western-educated doctors were not trained in any form of psychology. In certain circumstances, healing involves 'trickery' – the mind has to be tricked out of certain beliefs or patterns of negative thought. Almost all real shamans are tricksters, some much more than others.

The iconic Kogi, for example, made famous in the 1990s by the work of the BBC journalist, Alan Ereira, are an apparently isolated indigenous tribe of north Colombia, confined to the massif of Sierra Nevada de Santa Mata. They famously eschewed all contact with the civilised world. And then they called in the BBC! They had a message for their 'little brothers' – us, the *civilisandros* who were destabilising the planetary ecosystem, including their own. They had a water problem. To my uninitiated mind at that time, their massage was galvanic. Of course, as ecologists, we knew they were right, and here now was the authoritative indigenously wise voice of Nature telling us to wise-up before it was too late.

This message was reprised in 2015 by a second visit of Ereira to Kogiland, as well as one of their elders visiting Britain. But now I looked with more shamanic street-wised eyes and also those of a more experienced forest ecologist. The Kogi are unusual in that the tribe has a network of male shamans who work together – the *Mamas*. The women are hidden, but I am informed that the men always look to them for guidance. My informants, by the way, are fellow dancers who have made the trek to find indigenous teachers in the Amazon and eventually have been led to the Kogi. The tribe are also unusual in that shamanic initiation involves nine years of immersion in the darkness of a cave – usually starting as young as the end-of-weaning. The Kogi shaman is thus most adept in the inner realms of sight, as all shamans must to some extent.

The mountain tribe is surrounded by jungle. To the North and East and perhaps also the West, the jungles are full of both military men and the Colombian mafia. Ostensibly the military wage war on the drug barons, paid for by an accumulated $10 billion from the United States. As is often the case in the War on Drugs, exports have boomed and the price fallen. Corruption and violence is rife. Whilst to the South lie forests once infested with the last Communist insurgency in South America, or indeed, worldwide – the FARC. We can add to this a rapidly growing problem of migration and dislocation as peasants are evicted from subsistence living – often in the name of biofuels for climate salvation. Colombia has the biggest migrant crisis outside of Syria, with an estimated 1.5 million dislocated peoples. The Kogi are surrounded by trouble. Small wonder then that they bring in their ally, the BBC and with it the environmental concerns and undoubted guilt of the Western world which might provide them a protective mantle.

So far, not so tricky. But to the ecologist's eye, the Kogi uplands are degraded – the natural forest cover is not as it should be for an indigenous community living sustainably. Yet in the BBC films there are no livestock. The mystery for me was solved last year by an appeal from a pair of ornithological surveyors in the Sierra's National Park – they had rediscovered a rare and spectacular humming bird that had been assumed extinct. Its habitat was the 'sub-alpine' zone of grassland above the tree-line, an area normally in pristine condition, a special habitat of amazing flowering plants and of a biotypic zone often regarded as 'sacred' territory by indigenous people around the world. I have explored such zones in Africa and they are very fragile ecosystems. The ornithologists complained that the endemic species was threatened by Kogi cattle ranching and burning to maintain the grassland. Not only are cattle not indigenous to South America, the Kogi are not indigenous to the mountains – they fled there during the Spanish genocidal conquests.

26

Without an indigenous culture adapted to high-mountain terrain, the Kogi are destroying their own habitat. Burning increases pasture over scrub, but leads to soil loss. Loss of soil affects water availability – creating rapid run-off and floods (the second of Ereira's films shows dramatic flooding in the adjacent downriver regions). One might be inclined to forgive the trickery – after all, the survival of the tribe is at stake. But as with all tricks – and shamans mostly know this, they can backfire upon the trickster. There is now a movement to link the plight of the Kogi to the War on Climate. Professional green media propagandists are already at work. The problem is, of course, that there are propagandists on the other side of the climate debate only too ready to exploit the real story as a stick to beat not just 'climate alarmists' but the whole environmental movement and its science-base.

This is a good example of where a two-way flow of knowledge would be invaluable. The Kogi are not a simple primitive culture – they do have deep wisdom, born of a separate reality to that of the western mind. They are also very willing to cooperate. And in a two way flow, they can learn from the ecologists!

**Indigenous Europe**

The traditional world of the shaman extends to old Europe in the form of herbalists and their knowledge of the healing power of plants. And in myth, at least, to the realm of the magician – the seer, the *Merlin* and the ceremonialist that sat in a powerful position next to the King or Queen. We think of it little more than that – influenced as we are by stories of Arthurian knights or Harry Potter, but there is a factor very easily overlooked. Millions of women and a good few men were terrorised and burned at the stake for working with the magic of herbs or potions.

The shaman territory is also that of the psychic adept. And here then is the rub – the western world, from the time of the early Greeks city-states, separated *physic* from *psychic* realities. Gradually, the latter became the world of dream-states or hallucinations, Gypsy fortune-tellers and Victorian-era séance, with science according value and validity only to physical realities that could be observed, replicated and predicted. Only in the 20th century, long after the scientific method had established its hegemony, particularly in medicine, did psycho-somatic realms become accepted and the collective as well individual unconscious realm become subject to analytical techniques.

The psychic *realm* should be seen as 'real' as any physical realm. Everything we see around us in the modern technological world, had first to be 'dreamt' – that is to say, envisioned internally. Even in the history of science, great breakthroughs owe much to the dreaming habits of their instigators. Dreaming, is of course, a psychic mode. And it can be trained.

Dreams can be active musing or passive reception, either in wakeful meditative states, or during sleep, later to be recalled. Dream states can also be induced – by trance-dance, fasting, certain forms of meditation or as more widely known and often feared by civilisandros – by dream-inducing 'medicine' plants or fungi.

And this brings us to an essential part of the indigenous and shamanic world and its widespread repression by the civil order – what the shaman would call the world of *allies,* the western world calls *drugs.* And there is a huge hypocrisy involved. The world of cities sucks in billions of dollars of mafia production, most of it from Colombia – the cocaine capital of world supply. Yet in indigenous Colombia the coca plant is a revered medicine spirit, and is respected and honoured by ceremony where only the entire leaf is taken.

The fermented South America brew of *Ayahuasca* is likewise related to as a spirit – in fact, as the *highest* 'Queen' of the forest, served by both jaguar and serpent powers. I will later delve a little more deeply into what this really means by translation into western symbolism and understanding of energies. Yet, some of my ayahuascero friends have been subjected to great harassment by European and Antipodean police forces ignorant of its revered status in Brazil and who operate within societies where the lethal effects drugs such as alcohol and tobacco are quite legal and where young people are poorly supervised and highly vulnerable.

We could make a list of many such 'substances' (and their abuse by western pharmacology and market mentality) – from marihuana (sacred to the Himalayan schools of yoga), *datura* (likewise, and also in Europe), psilocybin mushrooms and *Amanita muscaria* (Europe), Mescalin and Peyote (Mexico), and the opium poppy (Afghanistan). These plants have been termed *entheogens* by ethnobotanists – essentially, they have the capacity to turn the senses inwards, induce dream states and enhance a connection to the 'divine'.

One could hardly say there was a single country that has a balanced and tolerant attitude and working practical policy that deals with legitimate shamanic use compared with the damage that comes from substance abuse. As most people are well aware, there is a War on Drugs that perpetually increases supply, vast profits are made and channelled by various mafia into the banking system, and the toll of casualties continues to rise, as does the number of prison inmates in those countries that have refused to legalise production and distribution. There are at least several states that have recently decriminalised personal use and a few that have legalised some production – for example, Colorado State in the USA, for marijuana. So the tide may be changing.

Anyone setting out on a path to enhance their shamanic awareness will be faced with the choice of *plant allies.* They are integral to the shamanic path. An education on entheogens needs to make a solid distinction between *narcotics* that stupefy, and *hallucinogens* which amplify dream and connect to psychic states associated with divinity. I would argue that trance dance states, the use of plant allies, and the risks of fasting, austerities and vision quest, are as important and far less risky than many of the outdoor pursuits currently licensed to invade wild places. Spending several days alone and without food in the forest or on the mountain is a lot wilder than a Gore-tex protected hike and return to a warm bed and a hot meal!

**Sex and divinity**

Finally, the issues of sex and divinity are rather obviously and intimately linked and would be seen perhaps as inseparable if patriarchal societies had taken a different cultural route. The serpent as mythic temptress and woman as culpable ally, is basic to 'western' mythology – as much to early Greece as early Judaism. That supposed temptation was not primarily a 'sexual' motivation, more to do with the nature of *knowledge* and forbidden fruits. The patriarchal mind-set was focussing on the psychic nature of the serpent-power – the source of *inner* knowledge through developed intuition, but as we learn from tantra, it is precisely this inner knowledge that can be activated by a more conscious sexual union.

Women, even in the civilised world of early Greece or the Judaic kingdoms, had this faculty of inner knowledge in more natural abundance than men. In indigenous community, the psychic power is more evenly balanced – but even here, it has to be *developed* in shamanic trainings and women are usually trained separately from men. In those early days of civilisation, the male shaman was known as a *magus* (from the Greek)– one who had developed psychic awareness and apparent powers of prediction. In Christian tradition, the three 'wise men' or *magii* at the birth of the messiah come from further East. A shamanic aside has it that messiah means not just the anointed one, but one anointed with crocodile fat – a sacred rite of Egyptian shamanic practice.

In early Greek tradition, the serpent is further evident as symbol of prophecy (The Python Oracle at Delphi) and as the twin coiled serpents of the Caduceus, representing medicine and the power of healing. Serpents abound in the pictographs of all Egyptian dynasties. They are depicted strongly also in the Goddess cults of Minoan Crete and appear on metalware depicting shamanic ritual in late Celtic culture.

Why would the serpent be associated so strongly with healing, sexuality, women and prophecy? The answer comes more readily from further East – in the Vedic realms of yogic knowledge, where the serpent is a key symbol for the rising energy in the spine associated with yogic meditations and the attainment of union. This has been called in the West, erroneously in my opinion –

29

'enlightenment'. Yogic practice is the reverse – more an endarkenment through the summoning of an earthen power, the kundalini, depicted as coiled and asleep at the base of the spine. I would cast this as a 'dark' energy rather than a light. The path of union – an aspect of tantric practice, raises the serpent power upward through channels and vortices in the body, to the crown, where it meets the downcurrent of 'light' from above. In my own tradition, the union of light and dark energies takes place in the heart.

What this has to do with healing relates to two aspects of the kundalini or serpent power – it is both a cellular energetic force capable of dissolving blockages that lead to tissue disease (a matter well understood by Chinese practitioners of acupuncture, who call this energy Chi or Qui); and it is a *psychic* force that works upon the various psychic centres of the body – a concept not so readily understood because physic and psychic forces have been separated in our understanding of what is, in nature, an interpenetrating reality.

I would say that the psychic and physical realms are dimensions of *one* reality – both capable of in-depth exploration, the one using the inner world senses, the other the outer. In the West we have traditionally called these inner world senses the 'sixth' sense – a combination of gut-feeling, intuition, hunch, insight, clairvoyance and clair-audience, which interestingly, yogic practices associate with the 6$^{th}$ wheel of consciousness (or chakra) located in the brow.

In the Celtic tradition and in neo-Druid lore, the poet-magician Taliesin is initiated by the dark goddess Ceridwen (White Sow) – and his name in old Welsh means Bright Brow. The consequence of raising the Chi or Qui or what I would prefer to call Ki, is to open and power-up the brow-centre of sixth senses, which in most individuals unless specifically schooled, lies dormant. I say 'consequence' because this resultant power or *siddhi* is not the goal in yogic practice – that goal is union with the cosmos.

In women more usually than in men, this centre in the brow may be naturally open at birth and remain open throughout childhood, unless suppressed. It may also open during the surges of Ki experienced during sexual initiation or in childbirth. In the eastern Tantric tradition, sexual initiation for men could be gained through female adepts. In the Tibetan folklore, such adepts were reclusive wild *dakinis* living in caves. I have met some such women with extra-ordinary powers of perception, telepathy, telepathic empathy and prescience. Several have been borderline psychotic and barely able to handle the civil order. Such women are disabled by modern society on many levels, with a history, of course, both psychic and intellectual, of violent torture and ritual death in those centuries prior to the rise of science and the industrialisation of the world. This places into sharper context the witch-hunts that possessed

European patriarchy for almost five centuries – most of the women were shamanic herbalists and the few men who ran foul of the Inquisition were practising magii.

This is the unacknowledged wild side – particularly of wild women. The psychic realm extends further than individual consciousness, further even than human collective consciousness. And it extends back in what science assumes is a Universe where time is a constant and linear. The latter is a naïve assumption yet to catch up with the latest in quantum physics. If we take time out of the equation, then all of the past exists in the present moment, and the future is there too! In deep meditation and dream states, the yogi or shaman learns to explore realms where time appears to stand still. Past moments and what appear to be past-lives flash by and sometimes futures are seen that ultimately come to pass. Psychic experiences are challenging to both individuals and society.

It is for these reasons that so few in the modern world with its scientific education and values will engage with psychic realities – there is a fear of ridicule, but also of what might be revealed. Yet if we are to rebalance the mind that now threatens to destroy itself, there must be a healing of the psyche and an end to its separation as a denigrated realm. The alchemical marriage so revered before the advancement of science was no less than the marriage of these worlds – and I believe that only a spiritual renaissance on this level will prevent the ecological holocaust that is rapidly approaching.

I would like to provide a manual for this recovery – and I am working on such a project across Europe. I will however, finish this introduction with more of a warning than a guide – with two short essays written more than twenty years ago at the outset of my own shamanic training in North Wales. The first relates to the issue of male initiation – a key element in all healthy indigenous culture. I recount a little of our efforts to create a meaningful home-grown ritual in the chapter on Coed Eryri, drawn from *Beyond Conservation,* and this essay explores the darker side of what we men usually get instead. This is followed by a short polemic on *the shadow and the shaman* – it deals with the pitfalls on the path of awakening to the realms of power associated with western shamanism.

These pieces presage the final chapter – which introduces a path to recovery through the arts and science of bio-energetics. It is not enough to think differently. In many cases we already know what needs to be done. We have to *feel* differently – to trust the heart, to cooperate rather than compete, and above all to take real risks if we are to turn around the project we call humanity.

**The shadow and the shaman** *North Wales, July 1995*

This was written sometime around 1992, for those few questing students when I had embarked upon western shamanic trainings but had also a strong background in eastern yoga practice. After 24 years of experiencing the dance between these two polarities of east and west and male and female, these points are still prescient.

> - So much talk of empowerment, and it appears so necessary. So many people feeling dis-empowered, by parents, the state, the global economy. Walk on hot coals. Yes! Elation and triumph over fear, and you grow stronger. Sweat lodge, earth grave, power animal journeys, dancing into ecstasy. Slowly the self -image improves. Hands-on healing, clearing the chakras. Slowly the energy rises. Empowerment begins.

And all along, the shadow waits contented. It has not been threatened. Its lair is hardly recognised. It feeds on power and a good meal is coming.

So many times – the heart is expanded and the person on the path feels immense love, declares it, promises it for ever. And so many times, comes betrayal, revenge, cruelty, coldness, and all this seldom owned – rather, dismissed as the whingeing of the weak who could not live with the newly empowered.

The shadow has also been empowered, for it lives a commensal existence in the heart.

The heart it is - the seat of resentment and revenge, the holder of grievance, repository of the ungrieved unreleased pain of the past. And hidden, always - for who has the courage and tenacity to journey into their own heart? In mirrors it is found, this shadow, not in form, but in reflection. And those people that the newly empowered draw to them are almost always carrying a victim within and one thus vulnerable to revenge.

And here is the rub – everything is shamanic. Reiki, shiatsu, acupuncture, hands-on anything, cranio-sacral energy balancing this or that – for all begin to clear the energy body and allow it to generate more power. This power feeds the heart and at first, elation is there. Then the shadow takes its turn – it loves the time after elation, when there is so much more power to play with.

The 'shamanic' *is* the web of life, the intricate play of energy between all beings. The recently empowered would-be shaman enters this web largely unconscious of his or her every move.

In true shamanic initiation, the shaman is not empowered. He or she is *humbled*. This is vital. The true shaman must emerge with no room for the shadow. We say, with 'no ego', but this tells us little. What is the ego, but that sense of separateness, of individual boundary, of me and mine.....my territory, my clan, my home, my spouse, my mind, my history, and all that is mine is therefore defended. How many ever let go of that consciousness?

Not so important if the person has been truly loved and cared for and fostered in their total self-expression, always validated, never betrayed, served but not coddled, safe but not too safe. But when that person has been left with a sense of disempowerment, unparented, not loved for who they were, a whole childhood betrayed from the moment of birth......there lies a potently *vengeful* shadow.

And it resides in the unconscious. In the disempowered who stay disempowered, it may lie dormant for a lifetime. But the moment they meet love, it will out. And the moment they gain power, it will exact its revenge.

Love received from another feeds the shadow, almost always. Love frees the heart and the heart in sudden freedom gains in power. Self image improves. The one who loves has made themselves vulnerable, for sure that is also the nature of love – but they too have a shadow behind their love that commonly seeks not revenge but punishments appropriate to a culture of sexual guilt and shame. And so the lovers dance.

The one who is loved must begin to embrace that part of themselves that they have not loved, for love demands it. And they will not, for the shadow that feeds on love from another, cannot feed on love of itself, and resists. The lover from outside seldom sees the shadow until it is too late. Some will be strong enough to love anyway and suffer the pain they have brought to themselves. Others will respond with judgement and distance, the pointing finger of betrayal.

How often have you seen it – the person on the path of empowerment, and the first thing they do with their new power is to enter into a new relationship, often discarding the old. And how often the dance of oppressor and victim is danced.

Here in the West, there is no true shamanic initiation. We are not brave enough to allow it. For it to work, there must be a real risk of death or madness. In the West, it is not a simple ego that has to be rattled free of the cage, it is a shadow that must be unmasked and robbed of its power. The West is the place of shadows. The East the place of enlightenment, the dissolution of ego. The methods of the East do not work so well in the West. So, the shadow must be faced alone, and curiously, by the *conscious* ego. This is the work of the West. It is long and arduous. Socrates gave the first rule – 'know thyself' (and his society executed him!). Examine the heart. Know from whence you came – family, childhood, birth and all your relationships. Lay bare the stored heart - every resentment, every desire.

**Male Initiation**

This short piece was also written over 20 years ago – following work with Eric Maddern in the development of initiatory rites for male teachers of initiatory rites!

- Male initiation....some say we don't have it. But we do. Superman and Green Lantern, 11-plus, GCE, CCF....first exam, first love, first sex, first job, first child. It happens to us, conscious or not. We are put through it by others. Preparing the psyche is relegated to comic strip writers and the social lore of the playground; and the testing comes via anonymous boards of examination to a performer alone at a desk and a pen. It is not for us but for *them*, that amorphous order of the unwild. It is conspiracy by neglect. Be sure, you have been initiated by shadows into their shadow world.

Remember your fear? Unsure of the ground, of your performance, of how you would measure up, of what the rules were, of their expectations, and of the unknown? Remember any help with that? Real help on a feeling level? What was your strategy? Compliance, doing the minimum to get by? Competence, doing well, coming top? Rebellion...were you one of the few who maintained the rebellion through all its consequences....expulsion from the order of school, disapproval of parents, jobless, homeless. - consciously, or driven by the madness of it?

Fear is essential for initiation and is cultivated by the initiator. So how did you do? Were you one of the majority...the failures? Or were you a winner? Either way you were initiated into competition. You were above or below. To get higher you had to compete. The job you got meant someone else did not get. Top of the class meant someone you beat into second place. Do you remember the bottom of that class, can you remember the face? Doubtful unless you were close to bottom yourself.

Yes, in some schools this has changed, and there is a glimmer of light....but still at that tender age of awakening, the playground rules. No teacher will take that territory on. Parents are asleep, television operatic takes over the preparatory process....in a world of the desk and the filing cabinet there is no mystery. For girls romance gets pumped in like a drip feed.

And the tender boy is pulled. Yet not by romance....what boy wants that then. His body awakens to the magnet, but it is of the loins and the lips. The breast of woman, or the penis of man, haunts his dreams and he knows not why. Urgent secretions follow. The fever between his thighs demands a rub and so much better with the other. He doesn't know of woman, or for what she waits. He pretends love, but this is the love of incessant disco song. Alas, she is easily fooled, taking long to wake up to the reality that he is a puppy. She had no other schooling.

Did you fail there too? First ejaculation. No feeling. No meeting. Strange cooling. Do you still know her? Or did the Gods smile upon you? And were they there too at your first interview, first job, first introduction to hierarchy, order, orders, pay and boredom? If it went smoothly, they were not. By thirty you have no time, it belongs to the order. You belong to the order. Your initiation is complete. This is an order with no magic, no mystery, no belly, no heart, no loins. It has a mouth and an asshole, and a very big shadow. It has consumed you and the Earth, and now sits in the shite.

This vacant body has many rooms. Which did you occupy? Teacher, soldier, salesman, clerk.... banker, baker, businessman....or did the Gods smile on you there, keep you under the sun, close to the soil, time with your children, did the woman reach under the performers mask, tease away the armour, did pain and loss kindly crack the hardening shell, tears transform the mime? Oh, lucky few!

So, the rest of you, you have been initiated into the uninitiated. The body is empty. It offers no resistance. You have colluded with the destruction of the Earth. And more, of Mystery and of true Love. Only your shadow, there on the pale Earth, tells of solidity, of real flesh, and that you can be reclaimed. And what you are now offered is not classical initiation. That is for the uninitiated into the initiated, and you are not that. What has been done must be undone.

You are no longer innocent. You have not the divine wonder of the fourteenth year to protect you. It is no good looking for the father you never had, nor the absent mentor. If they came now you could not trust...well, for no longer than the workshop lasts. What you have to do now is work. Unceasing, vigilant, committed. Your whole life must be committed, as a warrior, to spirit. Nothing less will do.

And the first step is to dance with the shadow. This is your mentor now. There is everything you never had with your father, in grief and tears and rage, there is your mother, your escape from the apron of her possessing desires, there the breast denied, the haunting nipple of your need for woman, the destruction of your love and your manhood, there the competing brother, desirable sister, the first humiliations, the collusions,.... violence, rape, incest, real or imagined. Your shadow has it all on tape, in dreamtime ....waiting.

Afraid to dance? Of course. Who is not? That is the beginning of our real initiation. Fear is good. It is preparing the body for work. Taste it. Breathe it. Get the body ready. This is no competition. The dance is for you. Big and small, fat and thin, athlete or cripple, clods and flatfoots....there is no one for whom there is no music. First ally. Find it. That source, that contact with the divine, the rhythms of nature....the reclaiming begins here. Drum or whistle, flute or mandolin, keyboard or tapedeck.....listen and begin to move and to breathe more freely.

Second ally....the Earth herself. She birthed you. All of her is here for you. That is the deepest ecology. You are not insignificant. That was guilt speaking. She knows your glory. She knows why you are here, from whence you came and where you are going. Be content with the mystery and let her work on you. You just have to ask. All her creatures are there for you, waiting for that request. They will come to you. First in dreams, then in your wakeful awareness. They will bring teachings, the medicine of soul. Water, wind, rocks, wood, sunlight and moonlight....the elements will strengthen you. This is preparing the ground of your being.

And when you are ready, Initiation will come. There will be no ritual. You will not know its time. It is not that you will reclaim the divine, it is the divine that will reclaim you. It is a Grace.

Then you will be yourself. Then you will be a man. Then you will love.

For many of the adults we see around us in Britain - I am not aware of how it is in other western countries - there was a crucial Rite of Passage, an initiation, at the age of eleven. In my time it was called the 11+. It marked the transition from 'primary' school to 'secondary' education. It was the finals of childhood, once-and-for-all and determined where you went next in some senses that were much deeper than the name of the next school.

For those of other cultures, who may not know how it was then, and as things did change when that system was abolished here, for those who did not experience it, we may usefully take a closer look. The exam was taken by all of the pupils at the primary school in their last year. In most cases, up until that point they had not been graded or separated - they were a *community*, and for many of those children, this was their only community, the only place they came together, worked together and played together.

Now the exam would separate them into two groups. Those that performed well and 'passed' would go to a 'grammar' school, and those that did not, would go to a 'secondary' school. These were different buildings, different places, perhaps miles apart. For many of the parents, there would be a desire for their children to 'do well', pass and go to the 'better' school. Thus, the exam was a social process of separation. The results would be witnessed by the wider community. First point of initiation - the reality of the social world and its expectations. This would create one of the prime elements of a Rite of Passage or Initiation, the possibility of failure in the sight of others, of social stigma.

There are other less obvious elements. What will be examined is the mind's abilities within a very narrow range of competences -rote learning, solving of intellectual puzzles, remembering what you have been told, and loosely called intelligence. These are the academic qualities of the masculine part of the mind. The Rite signals therefore that it is these that henceforth society will value. And performance. You will be measured now, and many times to come.


The feminine qualities of mind are not valued. Your intuition, personal and individual creativity, play, art, bodily integration, sport, song, poetry, music.....these society does not at this stage value and will not even try to assess. A dedicated singer or athlete may break out for the sake of their art, but this is always exceptional. Who you are is not relevant. It is how you perform that will be rewarded.

This must be energetically ingrained. Hence initiation. It takes the form of an initiation into silence. It is a silence not just of the voice, but of bodily movement. You sit still and think and write. And the sitting is a ritual subservience. Your superior, as likely as not, will walk around imperiously as you bend to the task and sweat against the clock.

And then we come to the most crucial element, so easy to miss. All of this ritual has an ancient origin and purpose: the conversion of women into men. A woman cannot be a woman unless her womb speaks. To speak it has to be free. Here it will first be chained. At eleven it may only have begun its first gentle murmur and the real caging will come at the next examination when its blood-voice has broken. How to bring this to silence!

First, the girl child is shown no discrimination. She is treated the same, which is to say, as a boy. She is initiated into performance bound by fixed dates, not respectful of bodily cycles. She is initiated into the non-body mind. Society tells her, your woman voice is not valued. Not your intuition, not your feeling, not your love. Later, it will be more forceful. If she bleeds on the day, this will not be respected. She will fear the bleeding, the time seated, the blood-spattered skirt and mocking eyes. To pass, she must silence the womb.

That is how we make women become men, and they have become proud of the transformation. Even where the dice are still loaded, they struggle on with fierce pride, the pride that demands and fights for equality. It is not that this is not right! Just that what it has forgotten is still to be reclaimed. The womb is still silent.

What is so shocking is that for most women, they have to be shown how to give the womb its voice. But then, their teachers were systematically exterminated. Some estimates put at 9 million the number of 'wise women' killed by the Inquisition over 500 years of systematic suppression. It is not enough to gain this knowledge as an understanding. The womb voice has to be awakened and nurtured. In its fullness it is a social voice, a reality of a whole and healthy community.

We are aware of so many of the feminine qualities: intuitive knowledge, graceful movement, artistic expression, poetic truth. Robert Graves honoured them as the White Goddess. In his time true men aspired to serve Her. In this age, some aspire to embody Her in their own feminine. In the age to come, men and women alike must discover that deeper element, the Black Goddess which was to Graves but a signal on the horizon of his tomorrows. She is the womb voice.

This is what initiation into womenhood would look like. Women would be separated and prepared for the time that their womb would find its voice. Silence and stillness would be valued, but not for activities of the mind and the pen, nor as ritual initiation into subservience to a social hierarchy, but as connection to the divine darkness, the earth, the void of internal space, the ultimate creatrix of life. Here is deep listening and deep knowledge, but more - for we can readily appreciate that which is spoken from a deeper place, but that which cannot be spoken, that which is channelled not *from* the darkness, but *to* it...yes, *to* it! The uncaged womb is a deep channel of energy, like a black hole that draws energy toward itself, a drawing down that cleanses and connects. It is physical and it is psychic. An integrated society knows this, honours woman with space and time for her bleeding, time to sing, to be with the earth, to stay open, to connect and to *give back.*

Only from this connection is love made whole. Only from this connection does love grow without condition. Sever this, and madness ensues. Have we not seen it in the young women of this age. For so long they had to stay repressed, and then, during my own teenage years, the stopper was taken off, and all around there were explosions of hysteria, thousands upon thousands of girls shrieking at male idols, performers and stars - and precisely those men, or women, that had junked the academic system! Those that had liberated their poetic powers, or rent the bars of the body's cage. But for those millions of girls, there was no such freedom, the energies came too fast, untuned, untrained, untutored.

I have a feeling, no more than intuition, that all of the madness of war, territory, religion, sex abuse, pornography and the rampant destruction of nature, is linked to this caging of the womb. Were we to give Her her due, this Black Goddess, Her time and space, sanity would grow again in this world.

There is a question now difficult to answer. Woman can develop like a man, perform with the best in the mindgames, so long as she denies the voice of her womb. But what of the man? Is there a wombspace for him? Is it like Graves' relationship to the Muse, for us to honour in our woman as partner, or is it, as we have discovered with the White Goddess, time for us to enter the energy stream itself.

On this, I have little wisdom. My apprenticeship with the White Goddess is not over. There has been too much of Graves within me, too much of the man needing to disown the crazed maleness of the past. It has been good to honour Her, to touch the Grail in this process of transformation. But there is a rebuilding to be done in the celebration of separate maleness. And yet, I pause....maybe this too cannot be whole until something else has been touched. Not the Grail itself, but the blood within the Grail. And for it to touch deep and internal, as in the drinking. This blood is not that of the divine avatar who broke the bread, but the menstrual blood of his lady, the Magdalen, Birth Song of the Universe.

# PART 1

*These four essays represent my focus of the past five years since publication of Rewilding – firstly, my Travels on the Continent, whilst engaged in the recovery of indigenous knowledge both of nature and the place of humans within nature.*

*I also report on the seminal meeting of indigenous tribal peoples from all over the world in 2013 at the 10ᵗʰ World Wilderness Congress in The Road to Salamanca: a clash of empires (a longer version of an article that appeared in ECOS 34(3/4)2013 pp21-27).*

*And in 2015, I was invited to make a presentation on Landscape and Memory – which I termed Bridging the Divide – as part of a cross-border initiative between German and Czech landscape architects and a part of Pilsen's year as 'European City of Culture'.*

*Later in 2015, I was invited to the second international conference at Sheffield Hallam University on the issues of rewilding – with a focus upon the nature of cultural severance. I chose this opportunity to embrace shamanic and tantric dimensions inherent in the human relation to nature and within the context of ecological and evolutionary sciences.*

# Travels on the Continent: A shamanic perspective on rewilding

**At Lavaldieu, Aude, Languedoc France. February 2012.**

There are vultures overhead as I write. They seem to be very much a theme of the past four months of continental travel, which began in Czech Republic with a visit to the vulture specialists at Prague Zoo. That visit was at the behest of my companion in shamanic work, Monika Michaelova, who always gets VIP treatment at both the zoo and the botanical gardens. At the zoo she heads for the vulture enclosures. The back-room staff collect feathers for her, and at the botanical gardens she shares a passion for medicinal herbs with the director.

The gardens have regularly hosted concerts for our mutual friend and teacher, the shaman Vimal Darpan, an *ayahuascero* – who for several years now, has held ceremony in Czech Republic. For many people, especially professionals, drinking the Amerindian 'tea' with Darpan is their first introduction to the inner worlds of the shaman. I marvel at the way this Slavic society seems closer to embracing shamanic forms of perception.

Darpan is of Dutch extraction, Australian in nationality, trained in India in tantric traditions of yoga, followed by time in the Amazon where he studied under Amerindian guides. He is a shaman of this translocated age where the community that would normally mark the role of the ceremonialist and healer is dispersed throughout many countries and cultures.

My first ceremony was in 2004, when few had heard of the 'medicine' that is Ayahuasca – a mixture of one specific vine and a leaf from another plant, brewed for several days under the guidance of the local shaman. There is constant singing. The subsequent tea-ceremony is highly ritualised: the fermented brew is a powerful emetic and contains the natural brain-hormone di-methyl tryptamine (on its own, this component would be denatured in the stomach, but the specific mixture contains an inhibitory enzyme.

Ceremony is the only way to describe how Darpan works with the medicine plant – every moment is a ritual, with song fundamental to the gathering. The brew can also be taken alone for intensive personal 'journey', but in a gathering, its function shifts toward liberation of the voice and prayer. This is not the prayer of supplication, rather songs of gratitude and requests for guidance.

If there is a 'deity' it is the plant itself – Queen of the Forest, though in Brazil there is a fusion of Christian and Amerindian dance and 'worship', with more of a leaning to the Mary of Magdala, than the Mother of Christ. In Amerindian culture, the Mother is the Earth itself.

One anthropologist, at least, found his way to partaking in Ayahuasca ceremony. Jeremy Narby had been engaged in aiding Amazonian tribes to stake their land-claims in the face of encroachment. His experiences are related in *The Cosmic Serpent* where on inner journeys, he comes to 'see' the deeper nature of serpentine structures both at cellular level and in the greater cosmos.. There is even an urban myth that Francis Crick first 'saw' the structure of DNA during an 'acid' trip (LSD). In fact, the 'serpent' spiral is a fundamental building block of Universal matter – it exists not just in DNA, but in the very centre of atoms, in the transmission of cosmic rays to the solar system, within the Sun itself, and as I will relate in later sections of this book, within the human spine.

I recall, on the rare occasion when I watched a television programme (I have an aversion to virtual reality!) wherein a redoubtable English vicar visits various tribal peoples. In the Amazon he partakes of the special brew only to stagger around in a state of inebriated confusion. Normally, one would sit in meditation for hours! But that would make for a very boring TV programme! The shaman follows him around pleading for him to *sing* the songs he has taught him. Eventually, the white-guy relents. Suddenly he stands still – 'Oh my God, they are coming! The animal spirits are coming!' They talk with him. He listens with a humble sense of awe.

That is the secret of the shamanic way. Songs are fundamental to ceremony and are a *request*. They are made to spirit – whether the spirit of the Earth, the Forest, the Queen of the Plant Realm, a specific animal or plant....names matter less than the intention and the 'power' that is invoked. They are made in a personal spirit of humility.

We in the 'West' – though I would rather use the Spanish term *civilisandros*, have to *practice* humility in the face of Nature – it does not come naturally or rather culturally. And of course, we have been taught that mind-altering 'drugs' are dangerous. They are mostly also illegal, and Darpan has faced-off the authorities on several occasions. Fortunately, Ayahuasca ceremony is regarded as a native religious freedom in Brazil and there are many influential emigres in the West.

Plant-spirit-medicines are the fundament of shamanic healing and there is no philoshopy of separation between the chemical matter and spirit of the plant. Of course, not all are 'hallucinogenic' – a scary term invented by professionals that means simply 'dream-generating'. There is, of course, a mass repression of such substances in the West that many see as irrational, considering the widespread use and abuse of pharmaceuticals with a long history of serious error and its consequences to health, or for that matter, the legal drugs of alcohol and nicotine both with considerable health implications.

However, my companion is here engaged upon the recovery of our own western indigenous knowledge of herbs. She teaches mostly women. And she loves birds. Like certain plants, certain birds have a place in the early shamanic history of humanity – and not just in tribal cultures, but at the very outset of civilisation.

It is a great wonder for me a long-time birdman used only to male company in this shamanic realm. And it is curious to find someone with such an unlikely bond to vultures, though they have been revered since the first Kingdom in Egypt where they are depicted in almost every ritual. Obviously, they are a symbol of death, but as we sat with the birds – a breeding pair of very rare black vultures *Aegypius monachus*, - they are less obviously also love-birds! The two were settled close to each other on the ground and constantly 'necking' affectionately. They mate for life.

*Black vultures – breeding pair at Prague Zoo, 2012 (Monika Michaelova)*

The black vulture is also a potent symbol of European rewilding. The zoo has a successful breeding programme and release to the wild – with some releases taking place in southern France and the Pyrenees, where small isolated populations hang by a thread.

These are very large birds and a real symbol of wild land where there is an abundance of large herbivores. In southern Europe, there are no really large natural areas and wild herds, so all European vultures rely upon domestic animals – cattle, horses, donkeys, goats and sheep. However, following recent sanitation laws requiring all livestock carcasses be removed even in remote pastures, these large vultures are threatened. In Spain, however, they have been holding their own and slightly increasing.

Other captive breeding programmes are aimed at restoring the magnificent Lammergeyer *Gypaetus barbatus* – the 'bone-eater' or bearded vulture, to its former haunts. This huge bird, weighing up to 7 kg and with a 2.8 metre wingspan, is built more like an eagle than a vulture, and is always the last to the carcass, carrying away the bones, which it swallows and digests for the marrow.

I have seen them in the High Atlas and Himalayas, but not yet in Europe, where there are about 250 pairs. The French and Spanish Pyrenees hold half the European population with the rest in Greece and the Balkans. They were at one time relatively abundant in the Alps, but disappeared at the end of the 19th century. Now they are returning to these mountains thanks to a prolonged programme of releases, and six pairs were present in the Alps during the last decade.

**Vultures as a key indicator of wild land**

There are two other vulture species – the Griffon *Gyps fulvus*, another huge bird with a 2.7m wingspan, and the smaller Egyptian *Neophron percnopterus,* a whitish bird that migrates to Africa for the winter. The family represents an essential presence in wild ecosystems, even though they have a reputation for closeness to human settlement. They are the last part of the cycle of life and death - the scavenger, the cleaner and the recycler. In the wild they require a sizeable population of large grazing animals and clearly, large populations of wild ungulates are now rare or completely absent over the former range of these birds. Their current stronghold is Spain, where large areas of land have been subject to cattle grazing regimes of a semi-wild nature and where some of the mountains still have extensive populations of wild goat such as Ibex and Chamois. Interestingly, when the Dutch experiment at Oostwaadersplassen first established its herds of wild horses and wild cattle and allowed carcasses to remain on the ground, a wandering black vulture took up residence on the reserve!*

The Dutch experiment ran foul of European agricultural and veterinary safety regulations, as well as animal welfare activism, and the carcasses are now cleared away and the vulture long gone. These sanitary regulations afflict all vulture populations, as domestic stock are now micro-chipped to ensure compliance.

Ironically, it was not changes to these wilder grazing regimes that so seriously afflicted the most common of the vultures – the Griffon (600 pairs in France and 20,000 in Spain), but the curtailment of dumping fatalities from Catalonia's intensive pig production units. The 60 or so Griffons now circling overhead have moved from the Spanish side of the nearby Pyrenees searching more widely for food. Local members of France's bird-protection league have established a feeding station close to where I am temporarily based, in the department known as Aude, near the legendary mountain of Bugarach, in the heart of Cathar country.

*Pair of breeding Lammergeier, Prague Zoo, 2012*

This is a region of extensive forest and dissected limestone plateau with immense spectacular gorges – in comparison to Britain, an area 20 times that of the Mendips, with two or maybe three times the scale of Cheddar gorge – ideal for vulture nests on the crags, but not for natural food supplies. The forests are intensely hunted-over, largely for wild boar, but there are no herds of deer, chamois or mountain goat in the foothills, and domestic stock is usually high-grade pedigree beef or mountain dairy. I was amazed to encounter some pure-bred 'white cattle' in the forest, looking for all- the-world like England's wild Chillinghams, but with tinkling bells and a much gentler disposition.

### Steps toward a shamanic ecology

There are other surprises. My network of friends here largely revolves around the shamanic community of dancers, and this is my main work for the year 2012. This region is a magnet for young people re-discovering a spiritual connection to the land and to their ancient pre-Roman heritage. That heritage was, of course, very shamanic – concerned not with the scientific attributes of species, nor with how they evolved to occupy whatever niche, but with the teachings that certain iconic species could bring to the aware and enquiring human.

In shamanic traditions, animals hold a 'power' - hence the term 'power animal' used for the particular animals with which the shaman has a close relationship. A particular power constitutes the essence of the species – the bear for example, is revered less for its predilection for honey, as for its propensity to retreat to a cave and spend the winter dreaming. Thus, bear 'medicine' is the power to hold the dream when conditions in the outer world are not conducive to its manifestation. A shaman would ritualise the connection to bear – often in a dance-form, and *invoke* that power, such that it could be embodied on a psychic level.

The Egyptians termed such animal powers *neter*s (they had no term such as 'gods', which is how neter has been translated by western archeology) and they, along with their tribal antecedents, sought to *embody* these powers. By an act of *extended awareness* practiced shamans could so effectively unite with the animal as to be able to feel and sense its power as their own.

Owl medicine, for example, would enhance the shamans' ability to see beneath the surface reality of things and was particular good for detecting acts of deception. By the time of the Greeks, such powers had been civilized and humanized as Gods or Goddesses, though the Goddess Athene always had a little owl (*Athene noctua*) perched on her shoulder. Scholars note that the early Greeks were educated in Egypt and there was a gradual transition from shamanic culture to civilised God worship. The act of worship then essentially externalises the power – with people then becoming subject to the whim of the

Gods. This results in a consciousness of supplication rather than invocation, and generates the role of priesthood as mediator.

I am constructing the outline of a thesis – a *shamanic ecology* that would chart this relationship throughout the latter parts of human evolution. To get a sense of its significance one would have to imagine the early hominids still embodying the stance, postures and overall self-image of our anthropoid cousins, the chimps, as they wandered out onto the savannah and began to admire the lions that lorded it from African grasslands to the cold tundras of Alaska.

At the end of the last Ice Age, *Panthera leo,* particularly its Asiatic sub-species, ranged across both the old and new world as king not only of the savanna (never the jungle!) but the steppes, marshes and open country of Europe from Greece to the Mendips, across to China and over the Bering Straits into North America.

There is a serious rewilding movement in the USA intent on bringing back the American lion! A small remnant of about 200 Asian animals hangs on in a protected area of the Ran of Kutt on the border of India and Pakistan and there are recent moves in India to re-introduce this lion to other regions. It is a big issue for a crowded country with Western aspirations, one that still experiences significant casualties from big cats

It may appear at first far-fetched to suggest that the lordly creature that emerged from a line of shuffling apes drew its inspiration and evolving self-image from the lion, but in my own encounters with remote tribal peoples in Africa, I was vividly impressed by their regality, particular the warriors. At some stage there must have been a transition from the skulking prey-animal with its well-honed extra-sensory perceptions, to the top predator that humans became.

There is some evidence to support the supposition – one of the first human works of art, much earlier than the Venus of Willendorf, was a half-human, half-lion ivory figurine that predated the female figurine at about 40,000 BP. It is similar in its 'essence' to the magnificent diorite sculptures of Sekhmet, the Egyptian lioness-headed 'Goddess' of four thousand years ago. It is my contention that none of these half-animal 'gods' can be fully understood unless the archeologist has widened a scientific training to include the shamanic practice of invocation and power animal journey..

There is a difference between metaphor – such as the human 'lionheart', and the *experience,* however 'imaginary', of *being* half human and half lion. It is my contention that once experienced, individual human nature would have been transformed. There would be an ongoing cultural inheritance of posture and attitude. In the modern therapeutic realm of 'body work', posture is central to healing and brings both physical and mental changes.

46

What we have regarded as 'gods' in Egypt, for example, and hence subject to 'worship', are coloured by our own separation from nature or even from 'God' in whatever form. We then project our own mindset onto the archeological material. Instead, we might look at Egyptian sculpture and painting as bound with the ritual invocation of animal powers – an act of union from which something could be learned and incorporated into the psyche.

### Caduceus: The healing serpent

If the lion is the first sculpted artefact, one of the most pervasive later images is that of the serpent. In Egypt, it appears in almost all paintings and depictions of ritual, especially initiations. In India, likewise, the tantric yoga traditions of the Himalayas would understand this completely…the *kundalini* power, an energy that rises from the base of the spine, is depicted as a cobra, and 'union' of this 'dark' power with the 'light' of consciousness is an initiation on the mountain-yogi's path.

Our western training in science and logic is profoundly ethnocentric. From a cultural perspective it coincides with patriarchal dominance and sexual repression, including several hundred years of vicious suppression of women teachers and healers branded as 'witches'. There are now few remaining strands of teaching relating to tantric knowledge that was also current in Egypt and passed to Greek culture in the secret mystery traditions later to be termed Hermetic and Alchemical.

Tantric knowledge, however it was coded, must have been known to the very mystical Egyptian culture, who ritualized every aspect of life and saw 'magic' (*ket*) permeating all material things. They envisioned the magical union of man and woman using the symbolism of entwined snakes, and by the time this knowledge was passed to the Greeks it gained the human symbolism of the psychopomp male-god Hermes, who's winged feet enabled him to travel between the physical and psychic worlds.

In these traditions, the snake very much symbolizes the elements of earth and water, which can be regarded as 'dark' compared to the 'light' elements of fire and air. The task of the initiate it to effect a union of the dark earth and water powers – the feminine, with the masculine realms of light and fire – and this by conscious raising of the serpentine power in the erect spine.

Modern western Yoga has sanitized the serpent power and learned to project itself within the language of science. Hence the kundalini current is described in almost electrical terms. In western tantra trainings, the power is categorized as an ecstatic pleasure, as if an orgasmic plateau was some kind of goal or end in itself – rather than a gateway or an initiation. In the indigenous Himalayan traditions, the dark serpent powers of earth and water, are not merely physical, but also psychic realities. Only in western science has physic and psychic become separated. In reality, the two worlds interpenetrate and more importantly, evolve together.

We could see the 'dark' realm as also containing of the 'dream-world' – not just of individual dream states but the collective consciousness (and unconsciousness), with its rhythm and cycles of life (and death). Western and Islamic traditions have not just repressed feminine modes of knowledge – along with the suppression of women, they have amputated the dark hemisphere and banished the dark gods. It is not hard to see this reflected in the modern ethos of conservation in the suppression of natural cycles and processes and the paranoia over extinctions, rather than an embrace of unbridled natural forces.

Many other cultures associate the serpent-power with medicine and healing, and the double coiled serpent with sexual union. In Amerindian culture, where Monika Michaelova was initiated, 'sexual' energy is not seen as differentiated from the life force itself and there are many parallels with yogic practices.

Whilst every man or woman recognizes the ebb and flow of sexual energy, science has yet to find instruments subtle enough to measure this life force. Only the much derided Wilhelm Reich – both therapist and scientist in the times of Freud and Jung, attempted studies of the subtle flows of orgasmic energy.

However, Chinese acupuncture has mapped how this basic life energy moves and is channeled, stored and distributed. Its practitioners train for several years to develop sufficient sensitivities of touch to be able to describe and diagnose variations in the flow of such currents and their channels or meridians. Mainstream western Science, though acknowledging the medical successes of acupuncture, still fails to recognize this energy form.

As noted, sexual union as potentially the highest form of knowledge or state of consciousness, was not confined to the Eastern traditions –the Hermetic and Alchemical practices that flowered in Europe in medieval times were part of a *secret* mystery tradition within the developing and increasingly repressive patriarchal culture. The secrecy was no doubt essential to protect initiates from the potentially fatal attention of the Roman Church. The reasons for oppression may simply be restricted to whatever fears underlay the sexual repression, but elevated states of consciousness in yogic practice are associated with special powers or *siddhis* such as inner sight and psychic abilities. Thus empowered, practitioners of conscious sexual union would not perhaps have been so readily deceived by the covert operations of Emperors and their burgeoning and largely secret society of administration, political control, and the amassing of extreme wealth.


Curiously, the original Egyptian teachings were attributed (by them) to an animal-headed deity....Thoth, who had the head of an ibis. Thoth taught the

Egyptians all they knew of mathematics, geometry and engineering, language and medicine. He was the fountainhead of their whole society as far as any depth of knowledge was concerned. I have been asking myself - why this bird?

As a bird-man myself – my favourites are the falcon, and at times, the crow and owl….and now it seems, the vulture, but I *can* relate to the choice of ibis. I first saw the western European species – the glossy ibis *Plegadis falcinellus*, in southern Spain for the first time two years ago. As it landed among 'ordinary' wading species, it stood out from all other birds. Its delicate presence commanded attention. It was a royal bird, something very special…not seen at first in the plumage of this species, which at a distance looks dark brown, but then you see the glossy purple sheen as the sun strikes the feathers, and 'wow!' you know you are watching a very regal bird.

Later that same year, I watched three such ibis among other waders on the Avalon marshes! A sign of the changing climate, these birds now visit every year, when during my boyhood they were an extreme and exotic rarity. And this year, in addition to breeding great white egrets – the first recorded of this southerly species, four white storks frequented the Somerset meadows! But I will write of the very deceptive elements of climate change in another chapter – for white storks nested on Edinburgh cathedral in 1200 AD and natural cycles are at work.

**The White Lady**

Here in New Age France, it is said that the Greeks learnt all of their esoteric knowledge in mystery schools taught by the Egyptians, and that even Jesus spent time in a short hop across the border, before his mission began. I have been working in a region of Languedoc that welcomed his mythic wife Mary Magdalene and their daughter. And just over another border, his brother James completed his own mission, with the bones now venerated at the end of a long path, the Camino de Compostella that officially 'begins' a few miles from here in the foothills of the Pyrenees, but in fact has a huge web of pathways stretching all the way to central Europe.

When I first arrived, I took time to visit a statue that some locals would call The White Lady….she is a life-sized modern sculpture above a chapel to Mary Magdalene and standing close to the old Cathar 'Castle of the Troubadours' at the edge of the small sleepy town of Puivert.

In distinction to the usual Mary as Mother, she has no child in her arms, which are folded over her heart. She is in white marble and it is easy to miss, but her left foot rests gently upon a serpent's powerful body. The serpent is lightly painted with brown spots and is at peace. She is not stamping on it, certainly not fighting it – in stark contrast to our English patron saint with his lance sticking the serpentine dragon!

Clearly, the serpent is a *power animal* and her 'familiar' – to use that old British witchy language. I surmise that the symbolism is of mastery. Legend has it that

49

the Magdalene, far from being a 'reformed prostitute' was a tantric priestess of royal descent and educated in the Egyptian mystery tradition of sacred union. Jesus, in loving her 'as no other' – to the consternation of the disciples, was, in the understanding still extant in these parts, party to an alchemical marriage. *Al chem* according to some sources, meaning 'out-of-Egypt' – and where Chem has several layers of meaning related to black soil, the homeland and the fertility of the Earth upon which all human life depends.

This was the knowledge the Catholic church tried to suppress – not so much I would wager because of contradictions in dogma, or even the outrageous possibility of Jesus having descendants alive today, but because such depths of sexual experience liberate the serpent power – for them, a patriarchal apoplexy.

There are plenty of historical facts that would support such a supposition – by 1220, this whole region gave itself over to a 'religion' that many here consider derived from the earliest Christianity, when man and woman were, as Jesus and Maria, equal in their religious and ceremonial roles – *both* were healers, ascetics and worked as a couple. They loved nature and simplicity – indeed, the natural world of woods and fields was the only church they needed. The Cathar couples (as healers and teachers) eschewed both the building of churches and the system of tythes that went with it. They also practiced the equality of men as brothers and thus held no allegiance to fiefdoms or feudal lords.

These 'beliefs' were clearly a growing political threat to the church and the feudal system with which it colluded. In 1250 a vicious crusade was launched by the Pope in Rome. The Cathar teachers....which the Church labeled "perfects", both men and women, were rounded up and burned alive – unless they recanted, but none did. As for the common people under their influence – they were also given the option of recanting – or the sword. Whole towns and villages refused and thousands of men, women and children were slaughtered.

Oddly, the term Cathar was not used by the people it described. Some locals say it was a term of abuse by German clerics, meaning 'cats-arse-lickers' and referring to what they thought were the adepts' disgustingly close relationship to cats. Clearly, in Europe at the time of the inquisitions any shamanic relations were going to get people into deep trouble.

The Cathars called themselves 'good men and good women', lived simply and despised the Church of Rome, its wealth and finery, together with its concept of marriage and subjugation of women. The centre of the culture was at Albi, east of Toulouse, and the crusade was launched against the Albigensians – which could be translated loosely as the original 'white people' .


This is ironic for me, since one of the more famous forms of shamanic dance ceremony – the Native American Ghost Dance, so poignantly last performed at Wounded Knee, led to a similar wholesale massacre by the invading and controlling 'white man'. That dance was truly a 'peace dance' in that the

50

dancers sought to reconcile the spirit of the white man with that of the red....or as they would have seen it, the lost 'white brother' with the true human being.

Had the Cathar 'heresy' prevailed (the word heresy being derived from the Greek meaning 'freedom to choose'!) perhaps the Red Man's white brothers would not have been so 'lost'.

One excuse given by the Church for its genocide, was that 'Cathars' held that the Universe was moved by two equal forces of good and evil or dark and light. It is not that easy to access the doctrines – since the deeper Cathar initiations were not written down, and modern words such as 'evil' are unlikely to touch the concept they actually worked with. Considering that the church then regarded both snakes and women as fundamentally evil, it is not a long stretch of the imagination to suppose some subliminal fear of the dark serpent power of which women tend to have a far greater command. Thus, the charge that Cathars held the dark and the light forces as 'equal' was readily upheld by the Inquisition that followed the massacres.

On the deepest level of tantric teaching, this power is the dark magnetic force itself, and is the ultimate creatrix – a force that permeates all matter, is fertile and pregnant, embracing the conceiving power of the male with which it unites to create the amazing diversity and beauty of evolutionary life. Not so far from the conceptions of modern physics and evolutionary biology, really!

### Les Corbières

Such is the mystery of this land! One remote area of its forested hills is called 'Les Corbières'.....and the word is close to that for crow and raven. It is little visited, with no spectacular peaks or lakes or gorges to draw the dreaded throngs of tourists and nobody knows much of what it holds. I spoke with an elderly English recluse who related how last year he and his neighbours witnessed a circle of domestic cats all sat around the seated peaceful form of a lynx! The cats were simply watching from a safe(ish) distance, perhaps not knowing that lynx will have pussycats for breakfast.

The lynx has been re-introduced to the Jura and Vosges, but is not supposed to be here in western France. Further to the west, in the Haut Vallée de 'Aude, a bear was reported last year and wolves are sometimes seen in the forest. The bear is either a long forgotten indigenous remnant, or a wandering Slovenian introduction from the Pyrenees; the wolf, likely a wanderer from Alpine France more than 200 km to the east.

It can therefore be said, that in modern France, the tide has turned for some wild species....wolves, lynx and bears are increasing, with a little help from a few newly reformed white men and women. Unfortunately, there are still too many old white-men in places of power – French men lost to their own feminine, and certainly, I would wager, lost to their kundalini serpent power. They strut about on the world stage as owners of 'neutron' bombs and purveyors of the latest plutonium-fueled nuclear power stations. Their future is

51

one of genetically modified plants and animals. They over-engineer the roads and clutter the landscape with ugly bare metallic pylons. The telecoms companies now replace the old wooden poles with unpainted galvanized steel – thus supporting their factories and steelworkers and depriving the local forest workers of much needed sustainable incomes.

These echelons also have plans for arrays of giant wind turbines over the whole of the region, irrespective of the immensely significant ancient landscape – or the surviving population of vultures. Last year, in nearby Spain, a country that has massively invested in rural energy grids with their turbines and power lines festooning the hills, over one thousand vultures were killed by turbines alone – fully 5% of the population.

This whole landscape around Bugarach and Rennes le Chateau in the Aude, one of the windiest corners of Europe next to Scotland, is under threat. The fact that it is held sacred may count for little among the Parisienne engineering cults, but it is also a major tourist honeypot, with its Cathar castles and mysteries of the Knights Templar – warrior monks that reputedly carried on the traditions of the Cathar in their honouring of the divine feminine.

The Templars flourished but didn't last long, their leader eventually being 'outed' and slowly spit-roasted for his beliefs. But long enough to found international banking and money orders. It was *here* that our local ruined fortress hosted the nine noble Knights who led the main crusade, taking Jerusalem and bringing back from their excavations of the crypt of Solomon's temple various treasures of which the legendary holy grail was supposedly one.

Who knows what *that* relic may have been – here the legend is that it was not a material object but secret coded knowledge of the alchemical marriage – the union of 'good' and 'evil', male and female, light and dark, order and chaos…..and through the powers not of logic, but of surrender of the conscious mind to the unconscious….like a death. Or, put more simply, that Jesus and Maria were lovers.

We are also embarked on a little archeology – of an old Templar crypt. And we are wonderfully accompanied by dozens of vultures overhead. In Egypt, the 'funerary rights' so beloved of archeologists, have long been questioned – as in most cases, no actual bones were found. The evidence points to the 'funerary' practice of such rituals well before death! And this, we may suppose, was also the case here. My companion made us wands from feathers scavenged at the feeding grounds, to be used in ritual cleansing with sage-smoke before our ceremonies of dance and vision quest.

As I paid homage at the feet of the White Lady and her serpentine power, in the corner of my eye, I caught a flash of white undersides from a distant circling eagle….the snake eagle! I eyed the bird and the sculpted snake's eye in the same visual field – a nice little synchronicity that told me, 'you are on track'!

We see what the German's call *Schlangenadler* – and which to the taxonomically obsessed English is the 'short-toed' eagle, *Circaetus gallicus*, almost daily overhead – and one is calling right now as I write from a little table outside my forest cabin! This magnificent eagle is a proficient specialist predator of snakes. Curiously, I still have a drawing of one I made from a bird I flushed from hawthorn hedges at Flamborough Head in 1962. It would have been the first English 'record'…if anyone could have believed a fourteen year old. Perhaps also as a sign of climate change, in recent years one was seen quartering the heaths of Dorset.

Eagles are, to the shamanic world, transcendentalists. They are always associated with the journey of the spirit, especially the warrior spirit, to higher realms of consciousness. So, here we have funerary vultures, serpents and snake eagles as companions, as we examine an old ruin dedicated to the death rites of a mystic Christian warrior sect that founded modern banking. They had in all probability lost much of the totemic associations…so far, there is no sign of any, other than that the Lady they so revered, had close relations with a snake.

The other day, my lady companion called the car to halt, shouting 'snake on the road'. I leapt out and grabbed what turned out to be the Aescalupean *Elaphe longissima*, the original species that inspired the healing symbol in Greek culture. It was about a metre long, with a muscular body, unmarked pale olive-green above and white-almost-lemon-yellow below. After we had a good close look, I let it go, but it darted under the car and our efforts to cajole it out were confounded as it spiraled up into the engine compartment!

We still had three kilometres to travel and it was late – so reluctantly, given the nature of hot engine exhausts, off we drove. I assumed it would depart as soon as we left the car parked on a small meadow – and only some sixth sense caused me to lift the bonnet at around midday the next day. There it was coiled comfortably atop the shocker well – recoiling slightly to strike if molested! In a land of snake-eating eagles, perhaps the engine compartment of a Peugeot 406 was a useful and warm place to hide, but it felt a bit special all the same.

So there it is – my French shamanic ecology! The modern shaman's world began in Egypt, but curiously, the Hermetic traditions, eventually called Alchemy, which hung on not just with the Cathars and Templars, but also with the later Rosicrucians and Freemasons, are not embraced by the modern developing shamanic world in Europe. Modern shamanism has tended to draw upon Native American lore, Mexican dance traditions, Amazonian plant-spirit medicines and some Siberian practices….and ignores both the Egyptian and Himalayan dimensions of shamanic perception and their role in the evolution of the human psyche.

## Apocalypse postponed

My work in France began not with rewilding conservation, but in the task of developing a European 'Ghost Dance' tradition. The mission was to reconcile the past, through times of terrible wars, crusades, torture and massacres, but especially also the massive disjunction between the male and female psyche that is the legacy of the Roman church. Finally, also there is the disjunction of inner and outer worlds that separates the human from nature and accounts perhaps for the arrogant sense of dominion that is leading us inexorably on to our ecological demise. The Ghost Dancer enters the realms of psyche – the collective mind and its emotional shadows, and within the physical body, in the heart-rhythm of the dance, makes the prayer of healing.

A few months ago we stopped by a small-holding at the foot of Bugarach. A woman friend in our party was friends with the wife and tea was made, whilst the husband was engrossed in some high-tech enterprise in the barn. In the courtyard was parked the very latest Range Rover in gleaming black livery. Glancing in the barn, I could see an array of computers.

My French companion mentioned my interest in solar flares, and the husband suddenly gained interest. He worked as a consultant for government. He knew all about the current threat of a massive solar flare, as did many of his government agents. They were prepared, with water and food stores, protective clothing, radios and guns. They well knew that a simple and regular natural event, the last of which was as recent as 1859, could take humanity back to the Stone Age – in an instant.

This region would be more resilient than others. The population could feed itself. There is plenty of wood and running water. Above all, people know each other and there is a cooperative spirit. It is this recent revelation of science that has given meaning to the Mayan prophecies and to the year of 2012. But the event was clearly not in line with their timing, the sun is relatively quiet at the moment, but the odds are it will come soon – NASA thinks 2013 is the danger year at the peak of the solar cycle.

I will add here, that in that year of writing – early 2012, despite the culmination of the cycle not occurring until 2013, there *was* a massive solar flare. It was just out of alignment around the edge of the solar disc and hence did not hit Earth. It missed by nine days of solar rotation! I will discuss this later.

Meanwhile, ecological activists, caught as ever in the separate and rather deceptive world of modern science, know only the mantras of global warming and carbon emission reduction, and I feel a long way from home in their company! This week the Meteorological Office has announced that aggregate temperatures have not increased since 1997…over 15 years of what they assure us is a 'pause' in global warming. That no such pause was predicted by their sophisticated computer models is not shared with the press, nor the fact that those models took no account of natural cycles.

Again – an addition, this 'pause' held until 2014/2015, when a very large El Nino – a natural cyclic event, close on the heels of a previous big one in 2010, brought global temperatures above the zero-trend line. This made media headlines, of course, but journalists do not remark that higher 'temperature' in the atmosphere marks the movement of *heat* from the oceans (the only heat store that can generate natural cycles). That heat is actually *leaving* the planet.

As I argued in my book *Chill*, a pause was to be expected as a natural warm cycle peaked and turned downward – and that not only was it now counter-acting the carbon effect, but the upswing of the cycle had fooled the computerized world of modern science – which did not understand cycles, into thinking the whole of the rise was carbon driven. In that book, extrapolating from science that the UN's special commission chose to ignore, I could predict that the Sun's magnetic field would all-but collapse. This affects the disposition of the Jetstream which would soon be seen as the main driver of weather shifts and perhaps also longer term cycles. All this now is now percolating slowly through more recent scientific literature.

The cycle may turn up again, or go down – and I suspect the latter if the magnetic sun stays down too. In which case, ironically, we face a repeat of the Elizabethan 'Little Ice Age' where northern hemisphere temperatures deliver freezing winters and cloudy wet summers.. Equally ironic is the thought that carbon dioxide would potentially ameliorate the slide - but don't tell that to the 'Climate Coalition'. Not that being right where the Met-Office flounders, counts for much. The Greens refuse to read the book or engage in rational discussion. I am still labeled *heretic* and one local Friend of the Earth wrote a 'we know where you live' note to the Central Somerset Gazette! It gave me my own chill feeling that I would not like such people ever to have the gauleiter status they crave in order to further a green agenda.

In the Mendips stands a solitary testament to that agenda…a mega-turbine that was refused planning by the elected district council and board of the Area of Outstanding Natural Beauty, only to be appealed by the developer Ecotricity (funded also by the ethical and sustainable Triodos Bank). Local democracy was over-ruled by central government in the interests of its world-saving carbon policy. I thought that Rio 1992 had been about joining up sustainable resource use, with such qualities of life as beauty and democracy – but alas, ideologies now dictate a 'war' on climate to join the wars on cancer, agricultural pests, terrorists, drugs and poverty.

As in all wars, truth suffers first, then the taxpayer! The soldiers of these modern wars – a new model green army advocated in a recent speech by Caroline Lucas, the UK Greens' lone parliamentary voice, they do alright – there are jobs aplenty with the crusade. As do Siemens, GEC and AMEC, nuclear builders of old, now anxious to frog-march the government into massive subsidies for more turbines, barrages, wave machines and…guarantees for nuclear electricity, with the bill for non-carbon Hinckley Point now approaching 14 billion pounds! {as of 2012 – the latest estimate is £24 billion and the French financiers are baulking. Even their massive state-monopoly, EDF, would not have enough without capital from that distinctly marginal democratic source - China}.

It is a world upside down….and not one I would have predicted for the second decade of the 21$^{st}$ century. It is marked by subterfuge and deception, widespread financial corruption and nest-feathering among the representatives of the people, self-denial of anti-democratic tendencies, and ridicule of any dissenters from the ideological constructs of the crusade itself.

Somewhere in all this, our fifteen years of creative 'conservation' now heads for obscurity! The rewilding word that was on the lips of a former Labour Secretary of State now reverts to the network of practitioners who, thankfully, walked the talk from the beginning, and set up real initiatives – now documented in the BANC/ETHOS book – *Rewilding*. We have a long way to go to rewild the human part of the equation.

Thankfully, also, on my travels I have seen many signs that all is not lost on the ground in Europe – I watched a family of golden eagles in the Sierra Nevada of Spain, where we could climb to within feet of the nest site (after the young had flown) that looked down on the small tourist village we stayed in. The vultures are still here! There is renewed hope for the bear, and the wolf is once more a growing 'problem' animal.

But other signs are not so good. It hits me more strongly in Europe to see the growth of US-style malls with all the global market players – and here they erect massive metal 'flags' to advertise their presence, as they encircle beautiful old cities such as Prague, or ancient market towns like Limoux and Carcassonne. The first ring-road of malls is followed by a neural network of 'distribution centres' and new motorways. Nothing has been learned in the last 20 years – all this funded by development banks and the EU.

The old town centres are now populated only by restaurants, banks, hairdressers, estate agents and escape agents. Prices rise, net incomes fall, unemployment increases and the people seem oblivious to the structural nature of a global business machine that sucks them dry and reinvests their money in replicating itself in India, China, Brazil, Indonesia and Russia….wherever ''growth" delivers their percentage return and high profits. It used to be that 'green' meant a critique of 'growth'….and on paper it still does, but is this now just lip-service?


Is the Green movement too much a part of the structure, too corporate, too mindful of its professional status, advisory role and pension funds? What can we do? In times not conducive to progress, the I Ching counsels retreat. But there is also creative retreat. First disengage from the policy world. The likes of WWF, FOE, RSPB and the Wildlife Trusts were never any match for the

Mandarins. They have tried collusion and it has failed. Witness the recent dismantling of the environmental dispensation in the EU agricultural policy.

Instead, bury corporate egos and pool resources - £20 million a year is not unreachable as a joint rewilding fund – and *buy* land. We need something iconic – and lynx, wolf and bear may be a step too far beyond cranes, bustards and red kites, so I would like to see a string of *natural sanctuaries* with the value of wild nature espoused *above* some scientific paradigm of biodiversity.*

On my travels in Czech Republic (a small enclave of a State that nevertheless has bears, wolves and lynx within 100 miles of the capital), I had the salutary experience of looking for old-growth forest in the 30% forested landscape. Eventually we were led to the 200ha reserve of Boubin in the south-west. We walked for several hours in search of the fabled stand of mixed forest among the working plantations. At last, there it was behind a three metre wooden-slat fence. The beech and spruce towered into the heavens, close by each other, and at their feet, fallen giants, and between them, standing dead trees riddled with woodpecker homes. The light was fading, but we sat for hours in their silent presence. How long would it take to recreate such stands of old trees in our own forests? Maybe two hundred years just to get the first feel. But let's start! And make it clear that this is an exercise in beauty and presence, in honouring of natural processes – those processes contained in the very word *natura* - that which gave us birth! Do this and the flowers, birds and butterflies will follow, as also perhaps, will a rewilding of the jaded human psyche.

I will add here also that as I later got to know Prague, there is another white statue to the Lady. Again, she has her hands clasped in prayer, and her foot rests gently upon a large snake. She stands near the old Monastery that looks down on orchards near Prague castle – the seat of government. In the castle square there is a statue of a distinctly androgynous St George pinning the dragons head and if one looks closely, other dragons are emerging from the rocks beneath his horse. It is a modern statue and I suspect the artist had an informed sense of humour.

# The Road to Salamanca

*A shorter version of this essay appears in ECOS 34(3/4) pp21-27. 2013*

The rewilding issue was prominent on the agenda for the 10th World Wilderness Congress or WILD 10, in Salamanca, but what drew me and my companion, Monika Michaelova, was the extended invitation to engage with indigenous peoples and their perception of conservation. Indigenous conservation specialists had been invited from all corners of the globe.

We are all by now aware of the deeper shamanic dimension in which tribal, 'native', or First Nations people relate to their environment and I wondered how far this affected their incorporation into the western conservation paradigm of science and econometrics

## Indigenous communities and conservation

Although some indigenous peoples have reshaped their environment on a large scale, including with mass extinctions – for example, the first wave of aboriginal Australians between 40,000-60,000 BP, and native Americans around 13,000 BP, we would readily concede that it is industrial society that has radically reshaped habitats on a global scale. Where tribal or indigenous culture is still intact, it is largely in harmony with the natural world. The problem now for these remaining indigenous cultures is that they occupy the margins – the non-productive wildland of remnant rain-forests, the Arctic tundra, the deserts and more remote mountains, and it is in these margins, that a ravenous resource-hungry globalised economy is hunting for its last-gasp of oil, gas and essential minerals.

These threatened cultures have now combined as activists under the banner of ICCA (Indigenous and Community Conserved Areas) and the first two days of Salamanca were taken up by their meeting with those representatives from government more naturally disposed to help them – the agencies concerned with conservation and wilderness protection. Almost all of the world's remaining wild places contain indigenous people and those models of 'protection' based upon species conservation or zero-impact concepts of wilderness are generally not adequate to accommodate them. They came therefore seeking alliances: from East Asia there were representatives from remote islands off the coast of China; communities from remote mountains in the Philippines and Nepal; from Australia came a large delegation from the Kimberley Range in the west; from South America there were representatives from Brazil, Bolivia, Ecuador and Guatemala; from North America came many representatives from the Salish reservation in Montana, and along the north west coast from Mexico to Alaska, where tribal peoples have been reclaiming fishing rights and negotiating protection zones; Africa brought Toureg from the Aire Massif; tribal peoples from the Congo forests; Senegalese fishermen; where Madagascar and Mozambique provided high level government representatives responsible for indigenous affairs.

Ordinarily, the agenda for the two-day intergovernmental meeting would have been driven largely by officials from the US government – but at the last minute they were ordered to remain on home territory as their government 'shut down'. It was a shame to lose some of the most informed and experienced agents dealing with indigenous affairs – especially from the forest service and National Parks, but this hitch had an upside in that the representatives from far-afield had more of a role in heading the meetings.

## The scale of devastation

I usually regard myself as well-informed on environmental issues – I read the daily press and a few specialist journals, but the sheer scale of the invasion faced by indigenous peoples, especially the acceleration in the past five years, was deeply shocking. Even where their homeland has acquired the status of World Heritage Site – there was little protection. In some cases, protestors against bulldozers had been murdered, including a pregnant woman and her two teenage daughters.

In all cases, the protests were about loss of 'home' and way of life, rather than issues of health or safety (for example in mining), where oddly, their rights might have had more protection. There was little documentation of the health risks of mining uranium, iron ore, copper, gold and coltan, or of the pollution from gas and oil – simply because these peoples were fighting not against pollution, although that was a common threat, but for the survival of a *way of life*. Universally, they did not want the developed world's model of development – which all too clearly meant loss of community, loss of young people to cities of crime, prostitution and disease. Inevitably, mining and logging roads brought unmanageable contact, with un-supporting governments that for the most part wanted an end to indigenous cultures and turned a blind-eye to illegal activities.

It was clear also that a new threat was driven by the hunger for renewable energy sources in the form of hydro-schemes, biofuel plantations and vast arrays of wind turbines and their associated infrastructure – the latter now a major intrusion in the wilderness of the Sami people in Lapland. All of these energy developments bring roads and settlements of non-indigenous 'workers'.

## A two way paradigm shift?

On the podium listening to these presentations over the two days in advance of the main conference (it was largely an old-fashioned conference set-up), were sympathetic conservationists from the secretariat. The aim was to build an alliance. Here there was an interesting dynamic. For the most part, representatives of the indigenous cultures were highly articulate, educated and well-able to take on the conservation paradigm with its focus on biodiversity and ecosystem services – there were several presentations showing how this had succeeded and could act as a model for other regions.

But the indigenous peoples also had a message for the *civilisandros* that had created 'conservation' as a major concern, and this, despite the work of ICCA, did not appear to be registering among the concerned conservationists in the Wild10 secretariat. Indeed, as the representative of two million nomadic Iranians pointed out to the rapporteur, his comments on what was needed to turn the whole thing around had not got past the typist. The Iranian had said that nothing short of a revolution in consciousness (in the West) could salvage the global situation! The response from the typist, who was an experienced member of the conference secretariat, was that she 'did not feel comfortable with his phrase'. And so it was left out!

I tried to say something similar about the need for a revolution in approach in 2005 in *Beyond Conservation* – with a chapter titled 'The Healing Forest' (which I have incorporated into this volume). I sought to bridge the divide between scientific and shamanic perceptions of nature and argued that we needed a shift in our own consciousness.

Since then the eerie conviction has grown that 'conservationists' are party to the destruction. We do not speak strongly enough from our hearts and too easily collude with the corporatist world-view. There is also a massive hypocrisy afoot, where environmentalists have created a climate alarmism and then aligned themselves beneficially to the solution – without a single detailed analysis of the environmental consequences of the mitigation programmes they have unleashed.

Thus primed, alarmist writers from the environmentalist fold, such as George Monbiot in *Heat*, Alistair MacIntosh in *Hell and High Water* and Mark Lynas in *Six Degrees,* have pleaded for carbon neutral power sources, without any thought as to the consequences of the technology for both indigenous community and wildlife. Perversely, having created the renewables monster, environmental campaign groups now seek funds to reign in the more destructive technologies they helped to unleash!

Unfortunately, the scale of the destruction is beyond control – especially the loss of primary forest to palm oil in SE Asia, parts of Africa and South America. The Sami look with horror upon the blighted horizons of northern Spain with its thousands of giant aerospace turbines and distribution pylons because that is what the Swedish government is proposing for their territory. Green advocates of a carbon-free nuclear renaissance, such as the recently retired ex-director of Greenpeace UK and including a recidivist Monbiot, should visit the uranium mines in Australia or Niger and enquire about the health, safety and social impact of workers as well as the management of toxic wastes (if they could get permission).

In all of this gloom, there were some bright spots – like the coalition of indigenous peoples along the Pacific coast of Central and North America brokering a marine protected areas system through Mexico to northern California (led by the Sinkyone Wilderness Alliance). The brightest element being the combination of cultural values with a scientific framework expertly articulated by this coalition, *and* the receptive ear of the US and Mexican governments. In some of the more developed democracies *things have changed.* But perhaps not in the UK as it now turns to uranium fuel with help from Chinese state-owned corporations that elsewhere are accelerating the invasion of protected areas.

**Indigenous Nature**

Indigenous peoples are now central to the management of the remaining wild places of the world – that much is clear. And their values are gradually being respected and honoured in management agreements. But what characterises the indigenous, their perceptions and attitudes toward nature?

Whereas the first use of the word Nature in English was actually with regard to *human* nature, not 'the environment', most tribal peoples don't have a word for environment in the sense of something separate from human – for them, nature is simply 'home' or 'mother' . The Latin *natura* actually means 'birth mother' - so somewhere at the back of our minds we do know the Earth as Mother! Something suppresses our indigenous nature. It is clear we do share something very deep and very human with indigenous peoples, but it was also clear at the WILD 10 conference that we 'white' people (of varying shades), constantly repress the deeper side of ourselves.

And in conservation we do so because it is politic to do so. I can personally attest to what happens professionally and publically if you do not! It is part of the scientific-econometric paradigm to which the conservation sector has attached its colours. It is fine to talk of indigenous cultures as separate from our own scientifically advanced societies, but to suggest that in consciousness terms they may be *more* advanced, is mostly met by blank incomprehension.

I would add, that in the four years since this report on WILD 10 was written, the embarrassment factor of 'mother' Earth and the incomprehension or resistance to shamanic dimensions has significantly diminished. It may not yet translate into practises and policy – but the paradigm *is* shifting.

We can become very passionate about the beauty of wildlife – our award winning television documentaries attest to that. It is not that the heart cannot be engaged in conservation. But it is the inner nature of the heart, the realm of an enquiring and perceptive faculty of inner vision that is suppressed in our culture. And I would argue, deliberately so. It is too scary on many counts, not least of which relates to the nature of the *creative power* – which indigenous people know how to meet within themselves and acknowledge as real, loving, present and parental. This inner knowledge is relegated by conservation biology to the realm of the subjective, the personal and private category of religion – which many, if not most scientists believe is a delusion.

The scientific paradigm is the dominant *political* reality. Religions are acceptable within that reality only as long as they are separated – and not just from the state, but from the sciences as valid bodies of knowledge. Religions co-exist with science but as 'belief' systems. These politically acceptable 'religions' are themselves almost entirely patriarchal and long-divorced from an equally active earthen *mother*. But the divorce is much deeper – the feminine aspect of mind itself is denied as an intuitive modality and source of valid knowledge of the world. Thus meditative and entheogenic mediated modalities of a *direct* and personal knowledge of nature are diminished or absent in the education of young people and certainly, most professional ecologists.

I would add a sociological note that science as a social movement has a distinct advantage over religious movements – the latter tending toward fragmentation and cultural diversity, whereas science is a commonality with similar institutions across all cultures.

The indigenous nature, which in Britain we would have shared in pre-Roman times at least, and perhaps as late as the $7^{th}$ or $8^{th}$ century Celts, did not separate the creative power from the realms of nature and the realm of human.

This is not a subject for discussion at the Wildlife Trusts, Greenpeace headquarters, the IUCN or modern crop of wildlife writers and environmental polemicists. On asking the nature-writer Peter Marren why in his review of *Beyond* Conservation for the Independent Newspaper, he omitted all reference to the Healing Forest chapter, he said – because it made him feel uncomfortable.

Why the discomfort? On a political and hence also rather challenging religious level, perhaps because there is a *consequence* of going *inside* and meeting the creative power itself…and realising as most indigenous peoples do that humans and this creative power *are not separate*. In actuality, even 'western' masters have said the same thing. 'Ye are Gods' said the founder of Christianity, two thousand years ago – but there were few ears listening then, and perhaps fewer now. Love and science we can handle, separately, but being at one with the creative power – not yet!

Then there is the real consequence, and I submit, the real reason for the suppression of all roads to inner knowledge that lies within our education system – and that is as independent creative beings, we are all actually *equal*. Indigenous knowledge is not about being equal 'in the sight of God' and then being legitimately exploitable by men, it is about being equal *in community*. In that state of consciousness it is simply not possible to exploit your fellow human. Tribal peoples who maintain their roots on the land and in community generally do not exploit each other.

**The legacy of empires**

In this latter respect, the venue of Salamanca was apposite. Here toward the end of the 16th century, Queen Isabella of Spain legitimised the conquest of the American native peoples. She was chided then by Francisco de Vittoria at Salamanca University, a man now seen as the founding father of international law, to respect indigenous people as equal in law and humanity. That equality, he added with a nod to the imperial power, nevertheless brought with it a responsibility on the part of the natives to engage in trade!

And the most important tradable commodity for the Empire was land. From that deal evolved the modern development model – first come land-rights, but *individual* land rights against which the individual can raise money or sell land on the market and above all then accumulate property. Various tythes and taxes militate against poor landowners and gradually wealth and power accumulate in the hands of a few. The less smart lose out on the trading floor, become landless labourers or head for the city. Actually, vast millions occupy not the cities but the periphery of cities, excluded from the centres of power and wealth, suffering real poverty (which is not the absence of money, but the absence of a sustaining environment). People are cut from their roots, their land, their culture and language – what ICCA calls 'legacy disruption'.

Everywhere we could look today, the global economic development model has not changed and this exodus from the land to the cities continues. We, in the UK, of course, are long-distanced from our own personal legacy disruption.

**Enter, stage right – Rewilding Europe**

I was not looking forward to the special day on Rewilding Europe. Not since reading expensive glossy brochures extolling the opportunity now presented by 'abandoned land' on the margins – in western Spain, Croatia, Romania and Slovakia. Here could now roam wild cattle, wild horses, bison, boar, many species of deer, and more predators like bear, wolf and lynx. What's not to like? Is it not a conservationists' dream? There on the podium were WWF, Birdlife, The Dutch rewilders with their surplus wild-grazing stock, and the Zoological Society of London – announcing a European rewilder's network.

I sat through, thinking - 'This is all smoke and mirrors'. Indeed, none of the podium speakers was a practitioner – apart perhaps from connections to eco-tourism, safari lodges and large herbivore breeding programmes. Britain's contribution was a dot on the map – Alladale in Scotland.* I have to admit to being ill-disposed. No one active in building the UK Wildland Network was represented or had been consulted on the lessons learned from 20 years of rewilding practice. No one referenced any of our work.

I contributed reluctantly from the floor, not wishing to dent the exuberance: first that I felt alienated by the top-down approach – we in the UK (led by

BANC) had many years of experience networking best-practice on the ground, had conducted four regional seminars, three 'issues' seminars, founded a University institute (Wildland Research Institute at Leeds), and published two books, the last entitled *Rewilding* with over sixty contributing authors, almost all being practitioners! If they had no idea or simply overlooked the work in the UK, despite their multifarious connections, then what did that say for other countries like Spain and Romania?

It got worse. The new European 'network' - for which they had received liberal funding (Dutch and Swedish Lottery), had 'criteria' of membership that makes uncomfortable reading. They were looking for local partners who can see a business opportunity in a large scale enterprise bringing in the charismatic herbivores. It would appear that if you are a nascent Alladale, then apply. If not, they are not interested. I have to work hard to avoid cynicism when the Zoo people get involved – they can do good work in some rewilding schemes (like re-introduction of Bearded Vulture), but are prone to hunt for 'spectacle' as well as species conservation.

How might this all play on the abandoned hills of western Spain - where there are thousands of sad 'ghost-villages', hardly populated – and then only by old people from another paradigm? Who cares, as long as we get the conservation benefits? Wolves are returning. Vultures can thrive again. Natural processes can re-assert themselves.

It is an opportunity lost. Old-thinking conservationists are now jumping on the rewilding bandwagon as a way of re-invigorating the *sector*. They at least could have asked us here in Britain what we thought – even what we meant when we said we also have to rewild the human heart. In their new-found enthusiasm there is a great danger of misreading the political mood and being seen as opportunists exploiting a situation where others are desperately trying to restore broken communities.

How to do it differently? Well - like we did in Britain! There is a spectrum of rewilding and everyone can learn from all ends of the spectrum. If we are to achieve significant core-areas, as exist in other parts of the world, we need cooperation for buffer zones and corridors – we need a political profile that is *inclusive*. Not one that appeals only to high-end ecotourism (or the bear hunters).

Enter stage left, *Guardian* journalist George Monbiot, giving a star-turn as keynote speaker at the larger conference gathering. He spoke eloquently of our long-lost European megafauna – the elephant and rhino, bison, lion and hyena, and their inimitable grazing and browsing pressure - "Which no-one in the conservation movement had given a thought to". Yet the chapter on herbivores in *Beyond Conservation,* commissioned by BANC almost ten years ago, addressed this head-on and in detail. He later in the press conference acknowledged he had been influenced by the book. I then reminded him that northern elephants would have needed to migrate over hundreds of miles and in

*Beyond Conservation* we had concluded it was rather impractical. But the phenomenon is aptly illustrated – in the European market that is now conservation funding and book sales, it does not do to mention a history that might obscure any 'unique selling point' in a breaking market opportunity.

## The future road

The prospects for wildlife and wildland in Europe are mixed. There *is* a wildlife 'come-back', well documented by a Wilder Europe publication * (a separate but linked initiative for the conference). Wolf, bear and lynx are recovering, as are most eagles, vultures (three out of four), bison, deer in some places – and the areas under protection are also increasing.

Some of this change is due to abandonment of land in marginal areas and some to more active legal protection and to successful re-introductions (like the Bearded Vulture, Sea Eagle and Red Kite). And although much of this needs to be seen within the context of past depredation and depletion, there *is* a good prospect. But to make headway in a world of economic priorities, unemployment, energy scarcity and proposed infrastructural development at the margins - on that wider stage, how does Rewilding play?

One of the indigenous conservationists commented – 'we can handle our own ecosystems, it's your *egosystems* that cause us the problems'.

On the road to Salamanca, I thought long about the legacy of empires, including the scientific and the economic. What is now left of the natural world, the wild, in both landscape and community, is rare and threatened. The tragedy at Salamanca is that conservationists still fail to see that they are part of the old empire, the old way of seeing and exploiting. They are the modernist's egosystem. When they seek to repair the world, they also seek to place their ego within it.

Who amongst us can say we are free of this shadow? But the indigenous people I sat next to had something that emanated in the conference hall – even that they were dressed in normal western garb (except the Brazilian Yawanara chief, who unselfconsciously wore his feathered headdress and his business suit, wherever he went!) – they had a certain joy and a peaceful way that continually reached somewhere behind my eyes and welled tears whenever they spoke. They were not part of the egosystem. Their legacy was not yet disrupted. And they were looking for help to maintain the life they knew.

Meanwhile, at close of debate, the secretariat introduced them to the well-known dangers of climate change and alien species invasion. Most of them had not thought too much about these things. But secretariats are tactical – with an eye on the funding streams for the next event and the boxes to tick along the way.

That's not the road.

## Rewilding the human

The wild does not have to be an abandoned land, safari-lodged and ring-fenced. In Romania, shepherding communities co-exist with healthy populations of large carnivores. Certainly, there is a place for core areas with no domestic stock – but in the corridors and buffer zones, there can also be revitalised wildlife-friendly communities. And some of those corridors can come right into the cities. In this latter respect, Europe could learn a lot from the Chicago Wilderness project, quietly presented at the conference by Cathy Geraghty and reminding me that years ago, twelve community forests were initiated around cities in Britain.

I remain convinced by the argument made in the 'Healing Forest' chapter – the road ahead needs to be one of revelation, a Damascene conversion to the values of the heart and human community. Just as we lost the wolf and the bear, we lost a part of our soul, our direction and our dream. We in Britain led the industrial revolution and too easily forget it was built on land clearances, migration to cities, economic exploitation and abject slavery, often coupled with outright genocide in the colonies. To now truly go beyond the conservation paradigm is to realise its way of thinking is rooted in an imperial economic and scientific mind-set. The remedy is not out of reach – it lies in the humble grass-roots initiatives such as we experienced in the Wildland Network through the Neroche Project where people are reconnecting in practical ways to the forest, children learn around campfires, and an old wisdom indigenous to our own land is rekindled in stories and craftwork.

As conservation professionals we need to *listen* to the voice of the indigenous peoples – *both* within the fragmented communities on abandoned land in Europe, *and* those further afield still with their legacy intact. There needs to be a two-way flow. The future of European wildlife is not just about species and spectacle – it is about *us* as humans in a wilder world. If we are to make the landscape wilder, then we need to become wilder to live in harmony with it – and for that we need teachers. We need to go back to school and *unlearn*. The rise of the scientific paradigm has separates us from Nature, whereas direct experience, guided by the practices of indigenous knowledge, *connects* us to our legacy. The civilised world of Salamanca in the 16th century legitimised the domination and exploitation of nature and natural peoples, and only in the 21st century have the official apologies to those peoples begun. How does it look to apologise to Nature itself? To say - 'Thank you'? To say - 'Sorry'? To say, 'I love you' – as we would our own birth-mother? The indigenous mind does that every day.

## References

MacIntosh, A. (2008) *Hell and High Water* Birlinn, London

Monbiot G. (2007) *Heat* Penguin, London

Lynas, M. (2008) *Six Degrees* Harper, London.

Taylor P. (2005) *Beyond Conservation* Earthscan, London.

*Wild10 publications:*

A Vision for a Wilder Europe (2013) 30 page booklet, www.wild10.org

Rewilding Europe, 2013 (36 page brochure) www.rewildingeurope.com

**Other links:**

Chicago Wilderness Project, www.chicagowilderness.org

Wildland Research Institute: www.wildlandresearch.org

Wildland Network: www.wildland-network.org

Neroche woodlanders www.youngwood.org.uk and see Saunders, G. (2015) *Community conservation at Neroche – surviving adolescence.* ECOS 36(1), 26-35

# BRIDGING THE DIVIDE
## Memory and the Healing Powers of Landscape

*This essay formed a background paper to a visual presentation in a lecture to the Pilsen conference on Landscape and Meaning, as part of Pilsen 'European Capital of Culture' year in 2015.*

In all contemporary cultures, there are shadowlands to the collective psyche, places within the mind where people prefer not to go; likewise with the landscape there are places of reluctant memories and emotional pain. The border region of Czech Republic with Germany is a landscape that prompts such memory. Here there are few recent settlements and the ghostly remains of former villages that were evacuated and razed to the ground in the vengeful aftermath of the Second World War.

Following these forced evacuations, the resultant Cold War left a borderland of under-used or abandoned land – ironically, rich in wilder species of birds and mammals, but poorer in its human cultural heritage. Recently, there have been calls to create a European 'green corridor' along the old route of the Iron Curtain – a project that would require a lot more cooperation between German and Czech forestry than is currently the case. And in many other areas of Europe, where population changes are now forced by economics and migration of young people, regions that are 'borderline' for economic land-use are experiencing a return of wildlife and drawing the attention of 'rewilding' conservationists [1].

Here I will draw from a few examples to show that new forms of settlement may be possible that can both enhance the wildlife 'come-back' and provide for a revitalisation of communal life – and further, may help to heal ancient wounds that stretch back in time to indigenous European culture and its separation from the land. I will argue that the physical separation driven by the industrial revolution and both capitalist and collectivist social policies, is accompanied by a separation of the psyche itself from its roots – leading to a culture of insecurity, alienation and a longing for a deeper relation to Nature; and further, that cooperative cross-border landscape projects have the power to heal these deep divisions within the European psyche.

However, the opportunities presented by demographic change in wilder and remote regions are threatened by infra-structural developments such as wind turbines, biofuel crops and hydro-power schemes which target marginal land, particular in mountain regions. A utilitarian electro-technical landscape is emerging that competes with prospects for co-existence with wild nature in new forms of economy.

## Ghost Villages

These issues are not restricted to borderlands and previous histories of invasion and expulsion. The Czech part of the border region shares many characteristics with other abandoned land and 'ghost villages' created not necessarily by former conflict, but by modern economics. There is a tendency throughout the European Union for young people to migrate to cities in search of an economically sustainable lifestyle, leaving the more distant periphery depleted of its youth, with further abandonment of traditional farming practices. Ghost villages proliferate, with a few elderly inhabitants remaining, and then begin to take on another ghostly form, whereby the more economically successful city-dwellers purchase properties for renovation as weekend homes or summer holiday residences. A market for the best such properties then discriminates against economically disadvantaged local people who are priced out of that market, and a vicious spiral concludes with similar mid-week and winter 'ghost villages' with little in the way of cultural activity.

This growing disconnection is the culmination of a long process of separation from the land and a cutting of the roots of community. This process generates a pervasive insecurity at the most basic level. In a modern market economy, large numbers of people fear for their jobs, payment of rents or mortgages and in the poorest sections of society can no longer afford good food or fuel to stay warm through the winters.

This collective insecurity erodes the natural protective feelings society has toward nature and beauty – and thus, despite an avowed love of nature, animals, countryside and wilderness, sacrifices of all these values are made in the name of economic and energy security.

Fear of climate change also drives the massive intrusion into wild lands of industrial scale renewable energy production in an effort to reduce emissions and mitigate what is often expressed in apocalyptic terms.

Despite these pervasive societal fears and the policies they generate, there is a more holistic potential for these borderline regions, that could offer new forms of settlements, new relationships to the land and the safeguarding of beauty amid a regenerating natural environment. Building on wide-ranging observation of cultural shifts, we at the Institute of Life-based Architecture (IlbA), situated in these borderlands, propose a new model for development where ecologically sustainable community is fostered in borderline regions, primary through the purchase of old properties and appropriate new-build, then rented at low rates to migrants from the city – particularly people who do not *have* to pursue land-based activities as a primary livelihood. Instead, there is an opportunity to develop sustainable local organic food production as well as regional exports aimed at the specialist organic market.

69

I will present some examples specific to the border region of Czech Republic and Germany; and also extend the conceptual framework to other border regions, some of which may have similarly problematic emotional histories.

## Abandoned agriculture and the rewilding movement

All regions remote from centres of population are, by virtue of modern economic forces, likely to suffer from lack of employment for young people, lack of investment by government, 'ghost village' dynamics and abandonment of traditional farming. The resultant weaker communities are likely to offer less resistance to forms of outside development that 'extract' resources – whether recreational, or in recent times particularly, energy from wind and rivers.

Mountain zones often characterise border regions, and they are particularly targeted for wind turbines, biofuel developments and new hydro-schemes; additionally, tourist development brings ski-lifts and winter tourists, but little in the way of a positive contribution to cultural life. These latter infrastructure developments also compromise the natural integrity of the landscape and its returning species, especially large herbivores and their predators such as lynx, bear and wolf.

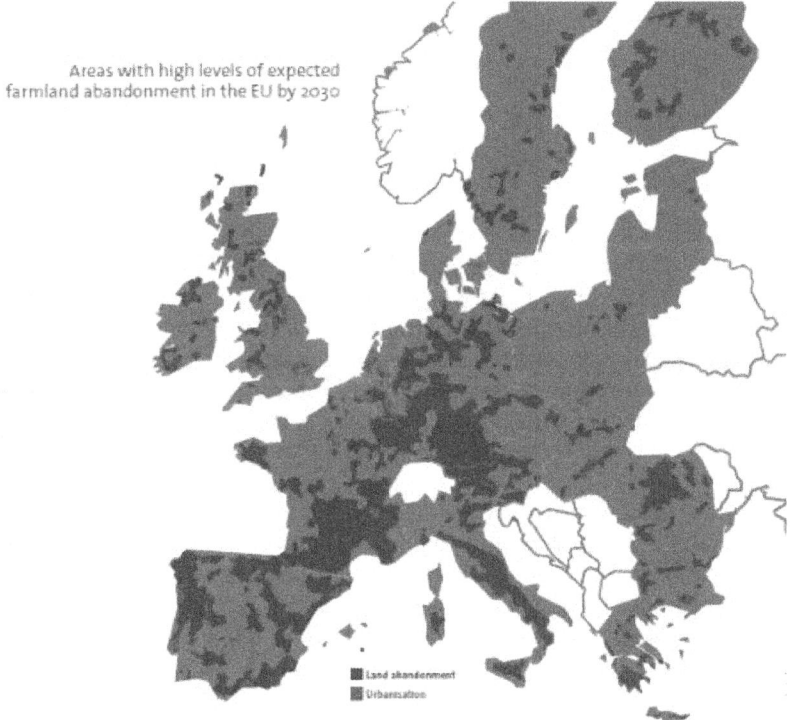

*Areas with high levels of expected farmland abandonment according to research for Rewilding Europe, 2012.*

Whether the high levels of 'abandoned' land do manifest depends very much upon definitions of abandonment and the range of other pressures for development and land-use. However, there are large numbers of people, both young and old, who would gladly return to the land and community. They would delight in living more closely to nature, without the need to engage in those traditional practices, such as extensive grazing, that have limited the regeneration of natural forest cover and the recovery of wildlife. Many of these people would be economically viable in crafts, arts and home-based work, if property costs and required capital investments were not a barrier.

The question arises as to how a reverse migration might be enabled, but also, what barriers might also exist to integration of young people into older and perhaps still traditional communities. Much experience must already exist throughout Europe – and we would like to see this material collected and evaluated.

In whatever future unfolds, decisions about landscape impact, the economy and cultural integrity reflect competing political interests- and in the modern era, econometric values clash with the less easily measured qualities of landscape and wildlife. Further, the historical path of economic development has militated against community, with modern values embedded instead in individual livelihood and economic survival or prosperity. This background leaves fertile territory for those advocating sacrifice of wildness, beauty and community in the name of climate change and survival of the economic system.

**The soul of the land**

In this world of competing interests and ideologies, there is an aspect of landscape that seldom has a voice – that is the *love* that develops between people and place. It is borne of familiarity but also of perceptions of beauty – something always in the eye of the beholder and not amenable to measurement. It is that aspect of human nature that enfolds the land, that cherishes, cares and protects that which is loved but which holds an awareness that love and the landscape is a two-way process. Land nurtures the human psyche.

Nature is acknowledged the world-over as a healing power. We speak of the soul of the land. Buildings can have soul. Old trees and rivers that run wild and free, exude qualities we associate with soul. Yet, we seldom acknowledge a need to *feed* our soul, to nurture that aspect of our heart that needs its homeland and those places it can come to know and love.

In this respect, marginal communities when faced with a choice of economic survival or loss, more readily acquiesce to the loss of soul in their landscape. In order to counter this negative trend, it is essential that we rejuvenate human community and connection to and love for the land. New forms of community have the potential to welcome the return of wilder nature as well as to embrace a more ecologically sound agriculture. New villages offer opportunities for off-grid technologies of energy and communications in conjunction with appropriate modern low-energy architecture.

With respect to a returning wilder nature, I have argued within conservation circles, that to fully appreciate the qualities of nature, especially wild places where human domination is not absolute, we need to *rewild* the human. Only a wild heart can truly appreciate a Nature that is free to be wild. But Nature is not all sweetness and light, not all plenty and pleasures – it has a dark side of cycles, death, decay, parasites, predators and their prey; and when not controlled, it can be chaotic and unpredictable. The history of human agriculture, forestry, water catchment management, and energy supply, is fundamentally about *control* of natural tendencies in order to provide security for human settlements. Of course this level of control is necessary for any form of agriculture, forestry or water management, even also for wildlife management, but it can become excessive, even obsessive.

It would be trite to say that excessive control is a consequence of patriarchal modes of education, but nevertheless there is some truth related to the growth of science, logic, economic assessment and risk-benefit analysis, and the demise of feminine qualities of love, beauty, acceptance and a deeper wisdom related to death and disease. In this respect, some elements of apparent scientific progress have proven illusory: from acid rain devastating forests; invasive species; crop diseases; water pollution; financial instability; climate change and ultimately, the insecurities of modern warfare and its formidable existential threat to community. A more balanced appreciation of life can only emerge from embracing more internal values of community and creativity, even they bring less in terms of material security.

This imbalance should not of course be under-estimated It is so pervasive and resistant to change. At the top of the economic pyramid, decision-makers are well aware that basic insecurities forged from a disconnection to the land and existential concerns about economics, lead to a more malleable workforce and an apparently more competitive economy.

This dynamic of fear is also clearly present in concerns over climate change, where the occurrence of natural cycles of warming and cooling is down-played in favour of alarming projections of future increases in global temperature. In the face of this apocalypse, communities are cajoled into embracing massive technical intrusions into the landscape.

It is curious that aspects of the science of climate change and the responses in terms of technological solutions and mitigation show psychological components that affect both the direction of research, the presentation of the threat and the apparent solutions. There is a culturally ingrained gender imbalance evident in the science that also runs through all aspects of landscape value and assessment of future development options. It is worthwhile to explore this imbalance as a preface to seeking landscape-based solutions.

Neuroscientists have differentiated the left and right side of the human brain according to the kind of processing that takes place: the left hemisphere is associated with logical construction, a 'masculine' mode; and the right with intuitive modes characterised as 'feminine'. Of course, every person has both modes available regardless of their sex, but Western institutional education favours the masculine development and has done so over many centuries - with serious implications for a healthy and balanced psychology.

The following set of dichotomies (the terms structural and generative were suggested by my artist friend, Sue Quatermass) illustrates the territory of imbalance:

| STRUCTURAL | GENERATIVE |
|---|---|
| Mind (thought) | Body (feeling) |
| Logical | Intuitive |
| Linear | Cyclic |
| Fixed | Evolutionary |
| Repeating | Spiralling |
| Constant | Changing & Irregular |
| Ordering | Chaotic |
| Protective | Embracing |
| Light | Dark |
| Imaging | Dreaming |
| Building | Birthing |

Curiously, the current highly charged debate around climate modelling and its projections, centres upon the modellers' failure to incorporate natural cycles into their simulations. Such cycles have irregular periods and chaotic elements that do not lend themselves to mathematical modelling. Some fundamental natural shifts in climate are poorly understood, with some mechanisms unknown and some thought to be generated by changes in solar output. Where once the Sun was seen as a constant source of light, it is now seen as beset by invisible magnetic moods that vary its energy output. Controversy surrounds the effects of these dark and changing magnetic fields compared to the more constant visible light and linear projections of change are being questioned as the effects of cycles and natural variability become apparent.

73

Thus, a dominant physics of light with poorly understood cycles of darker magnetic realities struggles to cope with irregular periods and chaotic elements. The same mentality then generates engineering *solutions* to the perceived threat. In this, the psychological alternatives of acceptance and communal responses of adaptation become marginalised.

These solutions are presented largely in technological terms of replacement energy supplies rather than an acceptance of limitation. Community and landscape values which are largely internal and intuitive are over-ridden by logical and linear thought, measurement and calculation of risk, the construction of defences, and of course, the generation of new business, tax structures and global bureaucracy.

Thus, the unbalanced, overly masculinised mind perceives a structural threat, developed from linear models and constructs technological solutions – which then benefit globalised industries and the banking and brokering community, rather than real community on the land. Outside of the EU, such policies accelerate the movement of people from rural areas to cities and pose serious threats to indigenous peoples and biodiversity hotspots (from dams and biofuels in particular).

There is a need for a new model of development, not only for remoter rural regions of Europe, but also in the developing world where an uncritical embrace of these masculinised values threatens widespread ecological and communal damage to indigenous peoples.

**Healing the wounds of the past**

As landscape ecologists we have a responsibility to offer solutions that are sustainable and take reasonable account of future risks. The term 'resilience' is now used to describe programmes which create robustness to change, whether of political, economic or physical climates. Here we look at some features of programmes aimed at developing a better relationship with nature, the economy and the healing of past divisions.

The border region of Czech Republic and Germany, and also with Austria and Poland, is characterised by natural beauty and sparse habitations. The original populations of German-speaking people were forcefully evacuated – regardless of how much they had integrated into Czech life. Such policy has left deep scars, particularly for older people. They now live in villages marred by decaying but once grand houses, slowly subject to purchase by wealthy people seeking a second home. Here we explore the potential to reverse that trend – to bring young people into these villages, people with broader attitudes and less scarring from the past, and with no pressing need to work the land in ways that conflict with nature.

74

### Sumava as the Wild Heart of Europe.

The *Sumava National Park* in Czech Republic is part of a trans-border forest – on the German side of the border, it is *National Park Bayerische Wald* (Bavarian Forest). Most of the forest is on high ground up to 1260 metres (about 4000 feet) and consists of native spruce *Picea abies.* The area of the Sumava Park itself is 68,000 ha, with a buffer zone of protected landscape of 100,000 ha. The National Park is 80% forest, with 10% meadow land and numerous small glacial lakes and peat bogs. It is the largest piece of contiguous forest in Central Europe. It receives about 2 million visitors each year, and the non-forest land is under rapid development for its tourist accommodation, second homes and recreational activities such as biking and skiing. The Czech forest is protected as a UNESCO biosphere reserve.

On the German side, 24,000 ha of similar forest forms the National Park, of which 55% is zoned as already 'non-intervention' and 22% in development of forest stands *toward* non-intervention, with the rest zoned as recreational use – essentially, the forest is being returned to as near-natural as feasible with minimal intervention. Altogether, this contiguous trans-boundary forest is the largest protected forest stand between the Atlantic and the Urals.

On the Czech side, management is now rather problematic. It has a long history of state commercial forest operations and these state forests now being sold into the private sector. On the German side, the original state forests were given to the National Park ( a state-entity) and thus remain in public ownership under management for non-extractive uses. Friends of the Earth, Czech Republic (*Hnuti DUHA)* has mobilised to prevent logging in the Czech forest, but in recent times, it is policy surrounding bark-beetle damage that has engaged them most.

At the higher altitudes in Sumava there were vast areas of dead trees. It was not a question of 'damage', but total wipe-out of the forest for miles in all directions. It was a salutary experience to stand among millions of tall leafless spruce, ashen grey in colour, in a silent landscape. Once dead, the trees are easily snapped by storms and I was reminded of those pictures of a World War 1 battle ground. The Czech government has decided that the dead timber should be cut and harvested over accessible areas, or cut and left to rot.

On a visit in the summer of 2014 with a group from *Hnuti DUHA*, we were met by the chief forester on the German side. He showed us their non-intervention policy with regard to bark beetle – some of which stretched back to the first outbreaks in the 1990s – so almost twenty years ago. The difference was truly remarkable – but had to be *heard* to be appreciated. The birdsong was deafening in its intensity – mostly warblers, finches and pipits.

My Czech companion, Monika Michaelova, who is active teaching modern women the old ways of healing with medicinal plants, bid everyone to close their eyes and *feel* the difference also! It was tangible – a vibrant almost radiant energy of the life-force itself, where only a few hundred metres away in the Czech landscape, there was silence and the feel of a deathly stillness.

*Dead timber is cut for removal in the Czech National Park*

*Once cut logs are removed, grazing deer prevent regeneration. Wooden cages protect a planting programme using nursery grown broad-leaves such as Mountain Ash.*

*On the left, Czech Republic; on the right, Germany: showing the difference in approach to dead trees*

*Dead stands when left to fall naturally, showing tangled undergrowth, preventing grazing by deer and fostering rapid regeneration.*

77

The German forest manager was asked about the level of cooperation and exchange of knowledge and ideas…and he sighed. His side was willing, but the Czech side was closed to dialogue.

There were key ecological factors at work – where the dead trees had been allowed to stand and fall with the winds, the tangle of trunks and dead-branches was avoided by deer, and protected by both remaining standing trees and fallen branches. The resultant the micro-climate supported a luxuriant undergrowth of ferns, mosses and flowering plants. Protected from deer, there was a surge of seedling trees, mostly mountain ash and regenerating spruce.

In contrast, where the dead trees had been felled and removed, deer had ready access and the ground flora was mostly grass with little in the way of regrowth. One international charity had a plaque sticking out of the bare ground advertising its financial support for the planting and protecting of seedlings! We saw paid workers carrying pots with nursery-grown mountain ash. In contrast, on the German territory, the mountain ash were 15-20 feet high without any human intervention.

I asked the head forester about wolves. There were already lynx in the forest – subject of a re-introduction project of twenty years ago, and now numbering 70-100 animals, but wolves only occasionally passed through. He admitted to being relieved that they did not stop to raise young, explaining that when the wolves were there, red deer stayed much lower down and were a problem for farmers outside the Park. Bears would be even more problematic, since the only bear to appear in Germany since medieval times – wandering over from a failing re-introduction project in Austria, had been shot under license because of the damage it caused.

As we left the German side, crossed the high ridge of forest, back into the Czech zone of forest and meadow lands, we were shown an 'abandoned' village. The Czech environment group was very interested in land-abandonment and potential rewilding projects. Only this was not an 'abandoned 'village – it had been German-speaking (as was most of this borderland) before the Second World War, and after the liberation, the Germans were expelled. A decade later, the Czech military bombed the old village church and wrecked the graveyard. Following the fall of the Communist regime that graveyard had now been lovingly restored by the descendants of the villagers – despite that there was now no habitation within miles. A strange 'Ghost Village' of a kind I had not hitherto imagined.

I reflected later that day on the clearly felt desire on the part of the German forester for reconciliation and cooperation *for the sake of nature*. The forest could be a symbol of a new relationship. Perhaps there was also a desire for forgiveness.

However, the collective Czech heart remains unforgiving (as it also does toward Russia). It is understandable because, of course, there *was* immense suffering, but this is a great pity, because Czech people have a lightness of being, a real magic that when fully expressed is truly a jewel at the heart of Europe.

I would make a plea that this lightness should not be shaded out by old resentment. This jewel does shine within *Hnuti DUHA–* and together with a small number of National Park officials, media professionals, politicians and academics, they are keen to cooperate with the Germans. There is a Wild Heart of Europe campaign to unite the forest management and extol the values of wilderness and non-intervention. In this project, we can see a prospect for cooperation in the rewilding of nature conservation as a focus for healing. The wild forest becomes a symbolic heart within which past grievances can be reconciled.

*The Water Mill at Tunechody, near Stribro, Czech Republic.*

### Tunechodski Mlyn, Stribro, Czech Republic.

The Old Mill at Tunechody, near Stribro, was renovated 15 years ago by Dutch entrepreneurs who created a spiritual centre for yoga, dance and shamanic courses. It is now for sale. It was originally built by a German family in 1896 as the first electric-turbine powered flour-mill. The family were forced to evacuate after the Second World War and the confiscated property was eventually sold on, first to a Czech family and then following the liberation from Communist ideology and control, it was bought for extensive renovation by the Dutch couple.

79

Monika Michaelova and I lived and worked there alone for a year, experiencing the closeness to nature, the ancient memories of the site, and all the difficulties of modern living, finance and community in a remote location. Issues of transport and heating costs are paramount. We ran courses in our own shamanic work as well as hosting other workshop leaders. We also developed good relations with the local state forest manager who was initially very suspicious of 'ecologists'!

The property is again on the market, but a Czech buyer who would have completed the renovation, improved access and maintained the traditions of a teaching and healing centre was turned down in favour of a potential better price on the Dutch market.

This property illustrates some key problems. The design of the buildings is not energy efficient and costs are high. Access is poor (via a forest track) and expensive to improve. The elderly owners had no interest themselves in developing a small community - for example, with chalets, yurts or eco-dwellings, with permaculture activities on land they owned adjacent to the main building.

In such situations, old properties can be either a liability or a great asset with regard to generating incomes and acting as an educational resource. All depends upon the availability of capital and funds for renovation.

**An eco-village concept in Portugal.**

*Artwork: Vale das Lobas (VdL)*

This project in the borderlands of Portugal with Spain, was begun by a small group of young British people connected to the International Rainbow festivals. They have bought land, renovated properties and are now seeking to create an international community centred around permaculture, shamanic teachings and experience of wild nature. A number of ruins on the land have been put up for private sale.

*Vale das Lobas: Upland sparse forest and abandoned meadows (VdL)*

What is remarkable about this project is that it has drawn the approval and involvement of the Portuguese authorities, who are keen to see the borderlands resettled and the communities revitalised.

Much of these mountain lands have been ecologically degraded – forests have been cut, exotics species planted, and soil lost as a result of over-grazing. When new communities are formed which do not need to make a living from livestock grazing, the forests can return (with added benefits of soil retention and water conservation) and with them large herbivores and predators.

How far sustainable community can be recreated is a question of further research – and there are many such eco-communities with a variety of ownership models that would repay analysis such that lessons-learned and best practices can be derived.

*Property for purchase and renovation within the Vale das Lobas Project. (VdL)*

It is our intention to study this Portuguese community and look at the lessons for other initiatives in western Europe – for example in Spain and France. We would also like to explore the potential for a Foundation to purchase and renovate property, as well as form a network for sharing cultural experience.

The project here describes  the setting up of future *Biodiversity and Nature Conservation zones:*

*'Ecological regeneration hinges on improving biodiversity, and we are establishing the area comprising Vale das Lobas as a Biodiversity Zone. This newly coined concept gives priority to land management activities that serve to enhance ecological well-being. Reforestation is a key component to land regeneration in general, and the Vale das Lobas Biodiversity Zone will have a strong focus on agro-forestry and forest gardening. We will harvest rainwater in large lake areas, to maintain the water levels and provide security against summer fires. The focus is on improving soil quality. The monitoring of flora and fauna within the biodiversity zone can involve a whole community, particularly young people. School children and college students will monitor and record plants, insects, and animals species.*

> *'The creation of the Biodiversity Zone does not only make ecological good sense, but it will also produce economic rewards for the region and its inhabitants. Once facilities for visitors have been established, Vale das Lobas will become a site of special interest to a wide range of*

82

*visitors, and will help to establish a niche position for Fornos de Algodres in the tourism market.*

The community advertises a Shaman's Retreat: which will be opening in 2016 and 'offers a unique opportunity to truly reconnect with nature in a magical forest setting. The centre is about 10km from the Seminario (the heart of the Vale das Lobas project) and is hidden away in a remote part of the valley known as Alagoas. Despite its seemingly secluded location it is easily accessible by road, rail or bus via the nearby town of Fornos de Algodres.'

The chief instigator, describes his 'vast experience of life "on the wild side" having spent many years amongst tribal people in remote regions of India and the Himalayas. He learned 'the art of weaving magic from nature's beauty' at Rainbow gatherings all over Europe and helped to create the legendary tipi chai shop "PachaMamas", a 'sacred oasis of calm' loved by festival folk in the UK and Eire - while the main woman involved describes a 'journey (that) has been more of an internal one, exploring various healing arts and therapeutic teachings. A respected yoga teacher for many years, 'her passion is to support folk as they release limiting beliefs and destructive patterns and rediscover their joy'. She was closely involved with the Santosa Yoga Camps before moving to Vale das Lobas and lives by the 'profoundly simple' values learned there.

In addition to these ecological and spiritual dimensions, of equal interest for study in such developments are issues of ownership, capital for development, members rights in the community, incomes and individual and shared resources, modes of decision making, leadership and authority. All of which have the potential to undermine dreams of a spiritual idyll.

**People and property in Snowdonia National Park**

*The Rhinog Hills in Snowdonia National Park, North Wales  (SNP)*

In the 1990s, I lived remotely in a cottage in North Wales, surrounded by woodland and scattered farms that pastured sheep and cattle. Despite the

83

remoteness of the location, this region of Welsh hills known as the Rhinogs, is popular for the purchase of second-homes or retirement properties. Houses in open country command high prices and local people on small incomes cannot compete.

The loss of community is a key social issue, made more prescient by the need to preserve the Welsh language and its connection to the landscape. Despite its apparent cultural role, sheep farming is a relatively modern development, as are extensive conifer plantations. Both have become uneconomic and an ageing farming community, propped up by government subsidy, is not being replaced.

The prospects for community development are limited by planning laws, poor communications, high cost of property and general conservatism with regard to incomers and prospects for change.

However, this region has a number of large land-owners – in particular, the National Trust as well as private and State forestry organisations, which have an interest in nature conservation, retaining community life and appropriate economic development. A landscape-scale initiative could be developed by cooperative organisation. A portfolio of properties could be sourced for eventual rental to Welsh-speaking families who do not have to make a living from the land (writers, artists, craft-people etc.) but who have an abiding interest in nature and community. Some farms could be purchased where the buildings were used for eco-tourist or educational resources, and the land reverted to woodland to create connections with other forested land. A gradual process of rewilding forest lands with native herbivores (currently absent), native species and wildlife-friendly forest economies could offer a unique experiment in new forms of settlement.

**Lessons from Case Studies**

The above examples serve to illustrate the issues and offer a direction for much work that could be done on the economic and cultural shifts taking place in more remote areas, and with more intensive examination of pilot projects. But one thing appears to be clear – there is a very large reservoir of young people who would leap at the chance of a new life in the countryside, and moreover, people with skills suitable for a sustainable independent economic livelihood, such as artists, musicians, and writers; permaculturalists and small scale artisan food products; as well as small-scale institutions for education and health, spiritual retreat, and even 'senior' houses for retired people. Such people constitute a growing and vital sector of the population that is known to struggle with the high cost of life in the city. However, because of the factors of young age (and lack of inheritance), as well as low income professions, such people do not have the necessary capital to purchase and renovate property – and especially not in competition with high-income groups.

84

Thus, some form of land and property purchase would be necessary, as well as a programme of advice and help in the transitional period to establish community life. Purchased houses in villages could be offered at low rental to professionals with a proven track record of economic stability and most importantly, an interest in new forms of community. Additionally, farmland could be purchased for the express purpose of small-scale permaculture and local provisioning – with first options given to local people. A mix of local, national and even international young people could be sought, with a balance of suitable skills. Small schools operating outside of the more rigid State system could be grant-aided to support the growing population.

Within this cultural shift, the natural landscape acts as an inspiration and container for the emotional healing that city people need – a healing that is more usually expressed in isolation, either by taking holidays or purchasing weekend and summer retreats in natural landscapes. The current trends of purchase will not cease, but a well-funded complement could compete for properties and rebalance the village culture that is damaged by individually isolated purchases.

An organisation that purchased property and land – both farmland and forest, that renovated houses using local skills and local materials, and which sourced as much food locally and organically, could favourably alter the modern dynamic, and bring a sense of healing and even prosperity to these areas at the periphery of the economy.

**Strategic assessment and Geographical Information Systems**

As a member of the Wildland Research Institute at the University of Leeds, I have been involved in strategic thinking with regard to community and wildlife conservation strategies. GIS projects at the Institute, led by Steve Carver, the director, have mapped several indices for wildland, such as remoteness from roads and settlements and natural vegetation cover. Such mapping is now at an advanced stage in the EU and provides a visual guide to the landscape and displacement of people.

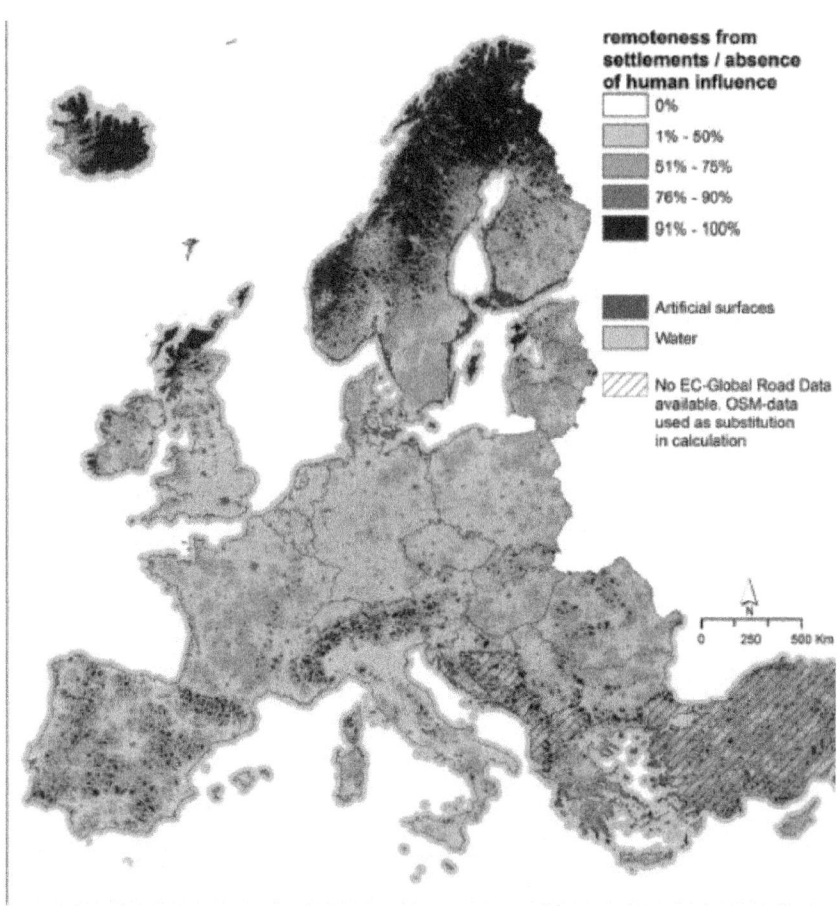

*Wilderness register and indicator for Europe, from Kuiters et al. (2011) Wildland Research Institute.*

These maps show clearly the connection between wilder nature and the problems of human settlement: remoteness tends to coincide with depleted settlement but also more natural land-cover. These are also the areas of maximum forest regeneration on abandoned pasture land and act as corridors for the migration of large herbivores and their predators.

**Communication by visualisation**

Such a major shift in settlement pattern and demography lends itself to new techniques of visualisation – such as computer simulation of landscape use, the presentation of eco-architecture and the web of knock-on effects. Such sustainable development paths can then be contrasted with those that are less sustainable and involve damaging the inherent landscape quality of the regions. In this respect, Ethos has pioneered the integration of renewable energy, agricultural and forestry strategies as represented by computer graphics – and essentially, to act as a *tool* for decision-makers, rather than in the advocacy of any particular path (4). The cross-border cooperation of landscape design professionals could lay the foundation for specific regional studies, and this work could be extended into schools and Universities within the region as a way of cultivating responsibility for landscape decisions. For example, in Fig.12 below, rapid insensitive development that exports energy from the land is contrasted with (in Fig,13) slower, more sustainable development that takes account of scale, community, and the feeling of nature, whilst offering local-based solutions to the energy and climate problems.

*Computer-generated future landscape with insensitive development of large turbines, forest-residue biomass power stations, short-rotation coppice and commercial forestry on the hills.*

87

*Sensitive and sustainable development with smaller scale local resources, rewilding on the hills (native forest regeneration acting as carbon sinks), with a major focus upon biofuels and solar power for local use.*

We would like to see this approach taken into rural communities throughout Europe and adapted to local circumstance. Computer graphics can be made site-specific and involve local educational institutions in the creation of a knowledge base to inform local decision making.

**In Summary**

Two keys to healing the past are offered here: the conservation of natural beauty as a healing power in itself; and the involvement of people in new communities that live closer to the land. It is feasible to evolve strategies that foster vital rural community that is currently suffering neglect at the margins of economic life, as well as to create natural sanctuaries for the return of wilder nature.

*References and further reading*

1.  a) *Rewilding Europe* (2012) Brochure. Nijmegan, Netherlands.
    b)   *Rewilding    Europe*,    Annual    Review,    2013.
    www.rewildingeurope.com
2.  See 'Rewilding the Human' in Taylor ed. *Rewilding: ECOS writings on wildland and conservation values.* Ethos. 2011
3.  See Perspectives from Anthropology in Taylor, *Chill: a reassessment of global warming theory.* Clairview, 2009.
4.  Visualising Renewable Energy in the Countryside of 2050. Ethos & Countryside Agency, UK.

See also:

Peter Taylor, (2009) *Beyond Conservation* Earthscan, London.

Blaha, J. et al (2011) Can Natura 2000 mapping be used to zone the Sumava National Park, European Journal of Environmental Sciences, Vol.3.No.1, 57-64.

And

www.ethos-uk.com for computer visualisations
www.valedaslobas.com  website for the Portuguese project
www.banc.org.uk for writing on conservation issues
www.wildlandresearch.org is the research centre for mapping wildland (download here a copy of *A vision for a wilder Europe).*
www.hnutiduha.cz for forest policies

# Cultural severance, ecological science and rewilding.

*This is a background paper to a presentation at the second Sheffield conference on rewilding themes, in particular: cultural severance and conservation issues, September 2015.*

Rewilding can readily be seen as a reaction to a long-standing cultural severance – from the land, from the wild in wildlife, and perhaps also as a subliminal desire for wholeness. In this, the re-introduction of exterminated species plays an integral part – they are the ghosts in the landscape, provocateurs of an unconscious guilt that we, humanity, killed them off in acts of hubris. Rewilding offers then a kind of redemption.

But there is a problem. What has been lost is the wild in human experience, as well as the animal or plant allies to that experience. Former ecological managers and campaigners now suppose that science and its institutions, or government and its agencies, or voluntary sector activists, can reconstitute what has been lost – but that is the problematic, for none of these institutions is wild.

In my paper to the second Sheffield 'Wild' conference, I argued that such institutions have been created by the same mentality that destroyed wildness in the first place. The modern human is now by nature or training, working with only half a brain – the tame half. Science itself, and hence all ecological science is manipulative of nature, with motive and controlling agenda. And all media, most particular journalistic, and all campaign groups that rely upon media, also seek to control outcomes. The path to wildness is not tame, it carries risks of life and livelihood, disease and starvation, vulnerability to nature's cycles and to other humans – a path away from which has marked the apparent progress of civilisation. I argued that humanity will have no choice but to come full circle and embrace its own wildness, but less of a circle, more of a spiral in time and consciousness such that we do not return to where we started.

## Rewilding in the context of evolution

I want to take a considerable liberty and present what wild and wilderness mean to *me* as an individual. Some of what I present, I know, means a great deal to individuals outside of the world of conservation – which I have argued elsewhere, has become a political ghetto, obsessed by largely irrelevant scientific indices and currently threatened by economic extinction.

In the wider world, animals, plants and wildlife *mean* a great deal. They have enormous cultural significance – and that cultural legacy remains largely ignored or marginalised, most certainly in the standard education of ecologists. In defence of weaving across many disciplines, I refer to my contribution in the previous Sheffield conference on this subject, where I detailed the wide-ranging ecological and cultural projects that represent rewilding in Britain (see Rewilding in Britain in Part 3). In this paper, I seek to broaden the horizons of rewilding and talk about the *primary* cultural severance – from wildness itself, and to offer a pathway for its reconstitution.

It is the size of the human brain that marks out *Homo sapiens* on its evolutionary tree – yet, neuroscience still struggles to find functions for large areas of what appear to be dormant parts of the neural mass. That brain, unchanged in size, has been subject to about 100,000 or 200,000 years of 'natural' selection – that is to say, evolution within an entirely natural environment [1]. Toward the last quarter, the human animal evolved art, dance, rhythm and ritual; tools and pottery; cooking and fire keeping ; hunting and burning; complex language, clothing and habitations, and in doing so, colonised almost every environment on Earth – from the Arctic to the Tropics, including deserts, forests and savannah, swamps and mangroves, islands and continents [2]. In all of this time, the dominant *form* of consciousness was *shamanic* [3]. I will attempt to explore what that term meant for the evolution of consciousness – and in doing so, will stray from the tame realms of the anthropologist in my training, and draw from my own shamanic experience [4].

In parallel to my work as an ecologist and anthropologist, I am a dance shaman. I have worked closely for over 20 years with Native Americans, Guatemalan Maya, Himalayan yogic, Eastern European traditional, Ayahuasceros of several kinds (working with the Amazonian herbal brew Ayahuasca), and the Neo-druids of England – the latter comprising an eclectic bunch of which I am an elder of the Megalithic Order led by Ivan McBeth (noted for not taking itself as seriously as other Orders) and some-time tribal dance choreographer for a number of music festivals [5].

My shamanic experiences are thus 'hands-on' – no theory involved. In my further defence, given the rational nature of this conference, I presented a paper at the World Congress of Anthropology at the British Museum in May of 2012 and remain a member of the Royal Anthropological Institute [6] (as well as the British Ecological Society and council member of the British Association of Nature Conservationists).

I say this, because much of the science of rewilding, ecological realities, cycles and climate change that I will refer to, is subject to intense media scrutiny – I have a media profile on these issues, and have been roundly attacked, even considered 'mad' for some of my apparent 'beliefs'. Much of what I will say here can be readily (and deliberately) misinterpreted – so please excuse some more lengthy explanations of what my position is not. For example, I work hard not to hold on to any 'beliefs' about reality. [7]

## Ecology as redemptive ideology

We take ecology as an academic discipline largely for granted, but in the 1960s, Max Nicholson, one of the leading 'political' and ecological thinker of his time, saw ecologists as potentially a new managerial class that would (and he though *should*) eventually replace out-dated economists [8]. By the 1970s, Ecology had become a political movement – anti-nuclear, pro-organic, activist and philosophical, yet this movement continually failed to change 'economic' paradigms. It eventually developed its own brand of 'green' economics.

By the 21st century, Ecology as a brand name has faded somewhat, but Green has been added to the primary colours of the political world, and the concepts of ecological economics and sustainable development underpin an apparently rational ideology. In this, much of the original ethos of wildlife conservation appears to have taken a back seat. The dominant rhetoric has become rational and survivalist – with humans at the centre of concern. Various threats to human survival are used to justify a new 'green' economic paradigm: these have ranged from chemical pollution, radioactive wastes, loss of soil, loss of forest cover, over-population and resource depletion, species extinction and collapse of ecosystems, with now, finally, an apocalyptic view of climate change [9].

All of these threats and the policy responses they engender, are based upon scientific assessment and prediction – and although 'ecologists' as a class have not taken over the top of the pyramid, they have a seat on the advisory board. That seat is justified not by their inherent love of wildlife and practical conservation – we know that is in the furthest back-seat, but by the scientific identification of threat and potential destabilisation of the established economic order [10]. As several modern commentators point out, that old economic order, or at least the ideology that underpins it, goes back little-changed to Adam Smith and the 17th century, and the Greens are still talking of the necessary transformation based upon ecological precepts. [11]

I have argued that conservation is an out-dated paradigm created in response to that old order and its impact on the environment. [12] Its light is now fading along with its income-streams. Where green economists and experts in renewable energy technology may have a seat at the table, conservationists do not. Somehow, the link between conservation and survival has been broken and I would argue, it has been broken by the Greens as they abandoned the realms of Nature for those of ecosystem modelling.

92

Conservationists are thus playing a catch-up game – re-inventing their agenda as 'ecosystem services' and the conservation of 'natural capital', but thus far, with no obvious effect upon the dominant paradigm. Ecology may be redemptive in the sense that it aims to save humanity from itself – but nowadays, only by tinkering reforms of the old extractive economic system and its structures of capital and power. [12]

Where then does Rewilding fit in? In the UK, the movement began as a network of conservation practitioners – several of whom have been working on the same project for 20-30 years. With the help of my colleagues at BANC, I have documented that movement. Now, in the summer of 2015, Rewilding Britain emerges as a well-funded campaign organisation backed by such 'greens' as Friends of the Earth, scientists from the Royal Zoological Society, and some billionaire land-owning funders, as well as a growing media campaign directed by the left-wing liberal Guardian journalist, George Monbiot. The same kind of alignment of players also comes together in campaigns to 'prevent' climate change by 'decarbonisation' – a government programme now enshrined in law.

This programme entails massive intervention in an otherwise neoliberal market system, as well as, we should note, coming with huge implications for industrial scale intrusions into wild land and the territory of indigenous peoples [13]. It is a curious alliance of thinking considering that large areas that could be candidate wildland in the UK are in private and relatively conservative hands – in the blue corner of the political spectrum and one notably sceptical of man-made climate change, government subsidy and the rigging of markets which they see as a red-corner strategy of eventual global governance.

It will be interesting to see how long it is before right-wing anti-environmentalists in the media begin to bracket rewilding with climate change alarmism and a closet agenda for a Green-Red 'command economy' .[14] And interesting also to see what happens to the deeper elements of the heart that motivated all of those operating in the grass-roots network of conservationists – people rooted in and committed to community and involvement. [15]

Already I detect a shift toward the eco-rational in arguments for the return of lynx and wolf, or the ecosystem services of carbon sequestration and safari-lodge economics in place of destructive subsidies for hill-farming. [16] There is, however, a growing awareness that subsidies are essential for maintaining community in the uplands, and the more extreme positions of rewilding advocates have been softening toward a more collaborative approach – an approach I admit, from personal experience in Wales, will not be easy. The farming community, even in the uplands, still has an essentially industrial (and scientific) business mentality.

I have argued for a deeper ecology – one that embraces the human psyche in our project for rewilding, and that our current projected ecological demise is one of degradation of the human condition as much as that of the ecosystems that support it. In this, I see Science from an anthropological perspective and how it allied itself early on with the destructive forces of industrialisation, and indeed, may well have been a causal driving force of that destruction.[17]

Science has developed its current self-image of humanitarian mission that began with medicine and disease control and has now moved toward the current eco-ideology of 'saving humanity from itself'. Further, the politics of the Green movement is ever more closely bound to the politics of ecological science. In that mission it has, I would argue, become blind to collusions with the destructive power it formerly sought to replace.

However, this is not the place for a political treatise – but to point out that ecological science does not exist outside of any political sphere – its aims and methodology are determined by social and psychological factors. And less obvious, perhaps, it is subject to the broad political and psychological gender bias that currently afflicts humanity. Perhaps if ecologists had to study Jungian psychology in relation to their faculties of perception there would be more understanding.[18]

**The shamanic realms**

In modern society (or even post-modern), the realm of the right brain is supposed the realm of the artist and poet. In educational systems, therefore, a separation in training occurs. Ecologists are very largely scientists – gone are the days of the *naturalist* observer. When I was a teenager in the 1960s, I was advised that if I wanted to work in nature, and to protect it, I would need a degree in a biological science. I chose Zoology. That training completely shut-down my right-brain. Only twenty years later, through yoga, did it start to re-open. The ultimate initiations for the right hemisphere came from expanding conscious awareness with plant and mushroom entheogens. And in broaching that subject, we are entering some tricky political territory – we live in a society that has outlawed and criminalised such use - although times are changing.[19]

In shamanic actuality, *both* hemispheres must operate in balance. Hunting is both a left and right brain activity – demanding skilled observation and action, as well as intuition, instinct and above all, development of the dreaming faculty. Where the human brain is yet to reveal its functions, they are likely related to the last of these realms – for dreaming is fundamental to shamanic awareness. The shaman learns to dream and stay awake, to see with the visual system and the inner eye of the dreamer *at the same time*.

We have been schooled to think that civilisation separated these functions. The logical mind developed geometry, mathematics and engineering, and with it, temples and architectural systems, cities, sanitation, water supplies and the hierarchical structures necessary for complex decision making. But as with many a battle for consciousness – some of which I shall detail, the victors write the history. Ancient Greek consciousness – where city and democracy and the antecedents of science seemed to first appear, was preceded by the Egyptians from whom the Greeks admitted they had learned almost everything they knew.

Egyptian consciousness was as much shamanic as it was architectural and masonic. Its symbols are everywhere readily visible – the serpent is ubiquitous, and with it vulture, crocodile, lion, falcon and dog [20]. Its 'gods' are half-human: in anthropological terms, *theriomorphs.* And if a Greek philosopher had asked of this priesthood and its engineers, wherefrom came their knowledge – of writing, mathematics, geometry and some very sophisticated sculptural techniques, the reply was always the same – from *Thoth,* the Ibis-headed theriomorph.

But the Greeks were well on the way with their own civil journey – and were keen to lose the animal nature. Thoth transformed into Hermes – to all intents a Godly human form, but with winged feet, perhaps the only concession to the bird-shamans of Egypt. [21] It should be noted that the Egyptians had no 'gods' as such – only *powers* (neter) and this is a crucial difference between shamanic realms and the 'religious'. Powers can be invoked and incorporated into the human, whereas Gods remain essentially beyond the human realm and their powers essentially unavailable. [22]

E.R. Dodds, classic scholar at Oxford, writes in *The Greeks and the Irrational*, a series of lectures at Berkeley in the 1940s, that early Greek thought was suffused with the shamanic, albeit somewhat hidden – and drawn from contact with tribal society in neighbouring Thrace. In one lecture he explains how the human mind was seen as potentially possessed by the Gods and driven to irrational action for which the actor could not be held responsible. And Aristophanes, in the first recorded piece of political satire *The Birds,* anticipates the evolution of both religion and perhaps also science as some kind of magician's trick (see Nan Dunbar's student edition and commentary on the play).

Shamans are, of course, required to be tricksters, just as modern magicians are illusionists. In that play, the central character is a shaman shape-shifted as the Hoopoe *(Upapa epops)* - 'king' of the birds, and aid to two corrupt politicians in the creation of a magical intercept between the 'gods' and a gullible humanity. That intercept is a celestial 'cloud cuckoo land'...a phrase still with us 2400 years later, but somewhat debased in meaning. In Aristophanes' drama – the first recorded political satire, it was a walled city in the sky, manned by birds -not an imaginary repository for fanciful politicians or activists (I have myself been metaphorically consigned there by my adversaries!), rather, it was a carefully camouflaged dimensional space with spell-binding powers [23].

Before proceeding further, I will draw briefly from the work of the Oxford anthropologist, Hugh Brody in *Maps and Dreams*. Whilst on his field work with a tribal unit in a North West Canadian wilderness, Brody went out on a tribal hunting expedition. The men drove out to a suitably remote camp in moose territory, lit a fire, and sat amusing themselves for several days. When the anthropologist enquired when the hunt would start, he was pointed to an old man who sat most of the time eyes-closed – 'he is dreaming the hunt', they said. On the third day, the old man awoke, and the party jumped into action and went direct to *the* moose that the old man had identified in the dream – and for which he had permission to take the life, permission given not by 'gods' but *from that particular moose itself*.[24]

There is another anthropologist's story that does not limit the point to animals and human consciousness. Jeremy Narby, a fully doctored scientific and Swiss anthropologist, was intent upon helping Amazonian tribal people to lay effective claim to their native territory. In collecting ethnographic material – as is their wont, the anthropologist in him was continually struck by the complexity of herbal and medical lore, and in particular how to make the psycho-active brew known as Ayahuasca. This foul-tasting herbal tea (some few like it!) is a powerful emetic, but when mastered, brings a great depth of visionary experience. Chemically, a vine used in the brew, contains a harmaloid that acts as the brain chemical DMT – the dream-generator (Greek-using obscurantists call it a 'psychedelic' or 'hallucinogenic' which mean much the same thing, but with some negative connotation regarding hallucinating). This compound, would, however, be rapidly denatured in the stomach. To the brew is added a particular leaf that contains an appropriate digestive enzyme inhibitor. The anthropologist asks from whence came this unlikely knowledge – not only of usable species, but methods of preparation taking several days. The answer was 'Egyptian' in the sense that they had been told what to do by the plant spirits directly. In fact, the vine is revered as the Queen of the Forest. The tribals offer Narby the advice to ask any question of Her, whom they also call 'The Library'.

Narby accepts and participates in the ritual drink. His documented journey is told in *The Cosmic Serpent: DNA and the origins of knowledge* where he 'sees' the internal structure of DNA, and further, fractal realities of the 'serpent' nature of the Universe. This story is easily dismissed, of course, as mere fantasy – but it has an important civil world parallel. In his autobiography, Francis Crick describes how the structure of DNA was revealed to him at first not by X-ray crystallography, but by taking an Acid tab.[25]

In the shamanic realms, plants are primarily healers and expanders of human consciousness. Even in the chemical realm of pharmaceuticals, the most potent chemicals originate from the plant realm – opiates (the poppy) and aspirin (willow bark) as painkillers, cocaine as stimulant (coca), cannabis as relaxant – with potential cancer-healing properties. The plant entheogens of all known tribal cultures work by doctoring the brain and enabling the human spirit to connect to a Great Spirit. Ritual use creates a firm foundation for this experience.

Whilst promising to avoid theorising, I have related earlier my small theory concerning that long shamanic pre-Egyptian period of human evolution. At some point, a shuffling chimpanzee-like character emerged from its jungle origins onto the savannah . Actually, some would say, more likely from the Bonobo lineage – an altogether more sensual animal than the Chimpanzee – a theory argued convincingly by Harvard primatologist Richard Wrangham in *Demonic males: apes and the origins of human violence* . [26]

Climatologists will be aware that human evolution accelerated at a time of global cooling, when extensive tropical forests were reduced to 10% of their interglacial extent and replaced by savannah – a cyclic event we should note, on a 100,000 year beat period, with 10,000 year warm intervals, one of which we are now at the end thereof! Thus, at some point in the climatic and cyclic fragmentation of the Congo forests, our potential ancestors were separated from their more demonic cousins.

One could potentially imagine a new political movement based upon carbon dioxide not as demonic underminer of civilisation, but as a kind of unconsciously Gaian molecule of redemption – as we approach the next descent into an ice-age. There being hardly room now to adapt to such wide-scale climate change. But I will not tempt my critics further! [27]

On the savannah, as I argued earlier - *lion* is king. Not that the emerging human need have concerns on that score – lion is not an habitual predator of apes (that honour falls only to the leopard). And the emerging human form was then prey not predator – as leopard-tooth marks on the earliest fully human skulls amply demonstrate. Those damaged skulls were originally interpreted as signifying a violent culture of early hominids, later revised when the holes exactly matched the canines of a leopard. [28] As also argued earlier, there exists within shamanic training, the act of dreaming oneself *into* another animal, and its reverse, of dreaming that animal form into one's self. In both, there is much humble ritual and request – this is not something to be ordered or summoned. The shamanic experience can be quite awesome – a full-body experience of the animal's state of form and consciousness, whilst at the same time remaining aware on a human level.

Such dreaming is known as a 'power animal journey' and particular shamans have their favourites, their 'familiars' to use a witchy term, whose *powers* they work with. Such journeying is a relatively easy practice (at least the mental part, the full body experience is much rarer)– and a straw poll I undertook before a recent talk on Al Gore and the Inconvenient Truth at a Green Gathering, found a good 50% of about one hundred in the audience had experienced such a shamanic journey with an appropriate teacher.

The animal powers obviously extend far beyond our own unaided power: consider the ability of owl to see in the dark [29]; or the serpent to move using a waveform motion; or the long distance acuity of an eagle's eye, the power and grace of a jaguar, or the dance of a crane. During that long glacial incubation, human consciousness learned to absorb and contain these animal powers – and even at the outset of civil worlds, this trick was still being honed. For example, the first Buddhist monks to arrive in China rapidly evolved what we now call the *martial arts* – and to this day, the basic fighting forms of the Shaolin are derived from animals – the monkey, the snake, the crane, the panther. In early Egypt, the Ibis was the conduit  - but for my theory, it is the lion that takes pride of place.

It is an imaginary theory: one imagines a bent and shuffling ape, a scuttler and dweller on the threshold, a runner, a digger, and essentially, a leopard's dinner. That humanoid learns the skill of conscious absorption and extension when first it *admires* the king of beasts. Somehow the skilled transference of consciousness evolved at that outset and humans began to walk tall – as if *they* are the kings, an evolutionary feat that could take them immediately above prey-consciousness. And as any tribal will testify – it is this sense of fearless confidence that is the greatest security when walking in the savannah. [30]

*New King of the Savannah? Ivory sculpture from 40,000BP*
*in Germany and the first human figurative art.*
*From a photo by Ivonne Muleisova, Stuttgart Museum.*

Once, when on biological expedition in a very wild and lawless part of African semi-desert, our landrover was forced to halt by the imperious hand gesture of a small family party – a warrior, his lady, and their small son. The party was miles from any water or obvious habitation. The adults were decked out with the best of bangles, and with physical form that would have graced any Olympiad. Having stopped and looked at the assorted party of pale faced biologists peering from the metal box, the hand waved us on. That was my first encounter with the real indigenous human. I have seen it several times but it is not common – a sense of dominion and ease, a grace of movement, and a smiling countenance. The original human!

As support for this theory, I claim the first human artefact – a piece of wood sculpture approximately 20,000 years BP, at the depth of the ice-age and from the German plains, a theriomorph, a lion-headed man (or woman). I would then add the serpent as second power – the kundalini serpent of yogic practice, the power of tantra and sexual union as depicted on Ancient Celtic cauldrons, Minoan frescos, Egyptian temple paintings and the earliest sects of healers. The first yogis – from the time of the Vedas, absorbed the powers of the serpent. [31] This power is also known to the Druid (and early Chinese landscape architects) in amplified earthly form as dragon-lines in a geomantic grid. As we know rather well, the dragon energy was later demonised by Christian cultures, the dragon's head now pinned by the lance of St George, Patron Saint of all England![32]

In the shamanic realm, the serpent power, as appreciated by Narby, is not *local*. This waveform *is* the sexual energy itself, the creative power, and is cosmic in extent, as one would logically expect. In my own experience, it is also more naturally accessible by woman than by man. [33]

**Sexual dimensions and gender bias in ecological ideology**

The serpent power and its potential to reside in woman is not merely a Christian or Jewish cultural paranoia. Returning briefly to our biological roots – as an ape, along with 99% of our DNA, we share with the Bonobo (a species of chimpanzee) a remarkable aptitude for pleasure and sex. The two are most clearly connected at the female pleasure centre – an organ wherein human evolution has placed the greatest number of pleasure receptors known to the animal kingdom – far greater even than in the male organ.

In this respect, the opinion of the evolutionary biologist, Elisabeth Lloyd, is of some importance. In her book *The case of the female orgasm*, noting that humans may be quite unique in this facility, determines by process of logical exclusion (for example, of the discredited uterine ripple effect and enhanced probability of pregnancy) that the orgasm has no evolutionary function whatsoever! [34]. She likens it to the male nipple – in the sense that it is homologous to the penis, but without an ejaculatory raison d'étre.

To be fair – which is hard, Lloyd states at the outset of her research, that she never asked women *what* they experienced. She was more concerned with whether and when and for how long. Psychology was not included. This is par for the course in biological sciences and sadly, often anthropology too. It is not a blind-spot, of course – it is a social taboo. Had she done so, and in particular, widened her social remit to include tantric adepts from Tibet, or even some Chinese or Thai courtesans, she would have had to document their fantasy that sexual power enabled consciousness to expand, to leave the body, to perceive things at a distance and to return. And had she interviewed the husbands or initiates of such women, she could document their claims that their women knew not only what they thought and felt, but at some distance and even, the thoughts of whom they were with. These psychic abilities would resonate with Brody's observations and have obvious early evolutionary significance – not just for hunting, but in social relations with other perhaps hostile tribes, and eventually within the hierarchical structures of city life. [34]

Had Lloyd then extended her cultural horizons to include ancient Vedic 'science' she would learn that one advanced culture at least, created a disciplined training that harnessed the serpent power such that it energised the basic abilities of the human – and contributed to a general sense of wellbeing: of rootedness, belonging and security, of powerful sensuality, a strong will centred in the belly, and a heart that was aligned to a greater spirit perceived as suffusing the world with a blissful magic! [35] Finally, that unused part of the brain receives a subtle current that opens an inner seeing, a dreaming power that is, in itself, powerfully creative.

When we now come full-spiral, it is obvious that all of human civilisation is *dreamed* first – every temple, every artefact, every engineering solution, and mostly, those dreams are of the *passive* form – they are intuitions, they are not logically derived. Even Newton's famous laws came by way of dreaming under an apple tree! Logic simply hones the law and applies it systematically.

And full-spiral comes to Newton in other ways. The father of the mechanical Universe was himself not a mechanist – that dubious honour belongs, perhaps unfairly, to Descartes. [36] Indeed, Newton had to hide away from the latter day inquisition and keep his experience of oneness to himself. For him, as a practising alchemist (derived from *al chem,* out-of-Egypt), duality was not the ultimate reality. [37] After Newton, came the institution of the Royal Society, the public burial of unified consciousness, and the final take-over in society of the animal power that resides in the cloud cuckoo – that of deception, trickery, and enslavement. Aristophanes knew very well the mentality of the slavers, and the play is rather more apt today in the *absence* of sky gods. The cuckoo parasite is invisible to the toiling little birds – they simply cannot see that it is not one of their own. [38]


## Toward a Unified Field in Ecology

With the demise of alchemy and its replacement by modern physics, the psychic realms disappear into the backrooms of Victorian party séance. In terms of educational norms, the Goddess Psyche, her consort Eros, and the interplay of the cosmic serpent and creative powers, are relegated to mythos. And with the typical amputated world of biologists such as Elisabeth Lloyd, the psychic importance of sex is completely lost from view. Only the shamans and the indigenous lament.

When attending the 10th World Wilderness Congress in Salamanca in the autumn of 2013, I had a particular mission to make contact with the considerable invited presence of indigenous peoples – especially those invited to share their experience of cooperative ecological management. I was struck by their stories of accomplishment – of sons and daughters sent to learn the ways of the White Man, of mastering law and the science of ecology and then returning to the camp. There was a message from them to the assembly – but strangely, it did not seem to register much. One Iranian nomad (with PhD) put it well – that what was needed from the White Man was a 'change of consciousness'. Of course, very few knew what he meant and no real interest was shown. [39]

*This* is, for me, the real nature of cultural severance. It is the severance of the right brain from the left, of the female from the male mode of knowledge, of inner and outer worlds, of spirit and matter, of human from the cosmic, and above all the separation of *heart* from mind. Indigenous cultures knew that the heart had to be educated as much as the mind, and with it the whole bodily system.

And if we are to be political – which of course, as ecologists we always *are*, then it is beholden upon us to look closely at who are the *cloud cuckoos* of today. Let us study how they camouflage their purpose. We are well aware that ecosystems are dependent not just on ecology, but on human management. Indeed, it is fashionable to suppose that the global ecosystem in a new era of the *Anthropocene* is to become the object of a more exact and predictive *ecological* management. Redemptive science strategies are now about to transform much of the world into an electro-technical landscape in an ideological sea of fear-based policies of survival. Even the world of finance is talked up as an 'ecosystem' in need of a more advanced strategic management.

And at the core of global strategies lies the Canutian war on climate change. However, just as the evolutionary biologist ignored the psychic realms of the female mind, so do modern day climatologists systematically exclude all cyclic phenomena from their computer models. They cannot handle the irregular periods, the dark side of the solar system, the hidden magnetism and the chaos factors, and above all, the spiral nature of solar mathematics. As a linguistically inclined anthropologist I note that these are all elements – the hidden, the dark, the unpredictable, the irregular, the periodic and cyclic, the chaotic and the destructive – of the *feminine* polarity of consciousness! [40]

What then does this mean for practical rewilding! For Monbiot's band of transformers of upland ecosystems, or the Dutch rewilders of abandoned land in the European Union? For the return of the bear, the wolf, the beaver and the boar? For naturalised black panthers or future genetically reconstituted mammoths? Not much, of course! [41] This modern Rewilding may be headed for conservationist territory – and the land of the dead parrot, rather than the trance-dance realms of the shaman.

A section of the modern youth dance culture knows the shamanic power of animals as reflected in western mythology as well as Native American natural lore: the bear as *keeper of the dream*, in both native American culture and in the legend of Arthur (Celtic for bear-king) who keeps alive 'The dream of Albion' [42]; or the wolf as pathfinder, the beaver as laying of foundations and the boar as sacred sow with its lessons of mystery and abundance? Not yet a while! We are still spell-bound by the Christian heretics who led us away from 'consider the lilies of the field', 'take no thought for tomorrow' and 'love your enemies'.

And if we break the spell, what would a rewilded human be like? It certainly cannot be reverse engineered! He and she would walk upright and tall, like a lion-king with a lion's heart. Sexuality would be free of guilt or shame and directed toward a higher journey – through strengthening of free-will and a personal empowerment where no man or woman would be slave to another or to the 'system'; where the heart would be full and open and celebratory; where everyone's voice would be heard; where there was music and dance and songs to acknowledge this long evolutionary journey with a real vision for the future based not on fear, but on the prospects of union. All the academies of recovery exist – in the forests of the Amazon and the mountains of Tibet, and the indigenous soul is crying out for this transformation.

It won't happen, of course. Things are too far gone – the system has ossified. The academies of science are in collusion and not just on climate change. Conscious bankers I have berated have helplessly replied – that they cannot make the system ethical nor sustainable – that they are trapped within it. The system has to be broken – and like all Empires of the past, it must eventually come crashing down – either the banks will fail, or the satellites, or a viral plague or a massive magnetic pulse from the Sun will disable the electrics.

There have been warnings – that the whole of our very modern scientifically engineered civilisation could be ended by a cyclic pulse of Carrington Event proportions. [43] And if this system does not crash – then say welcome to the rewilded mountain surrounded by turbines, the wild estuary bound by barrage, the forests cut down to palm oil, the deserts shining with silicon photovoltaics, and only the military, the bankers and their green advisors able to afford the biofuels.

**Notes:**

1) Estimates of the first appearance of *Homo sapiens* vary, but a figure of 100,000 years concurrent with the last ice-age would be generally accepted.

2) Of all of these evolving traits, one of the most neglected has been *cooking* food as a driver both of increased populations and social structure – see Harvard primatologist Richard Wrangham's *Catching fire – how cooking made us human* (Basic Books, 2010)

3) I am using this term to describe the nature of human consciousness before alphabets, writing and mathematics – which are all essentially left-brain activities. For an insightful treatment of the impact of alphabet on consciousness, see Leoard Shlain's *The alphabet versus the Goddess* (Penguin Books, 1999).

4) Anthropology favours the *objective* approach – with the ethnographer as separate from the culture under study, but learning by some level of immersion and participation, before emerging with the challenge of communicating to a professional world sceptical of shamanic realities. The anthropologist Carlos Castaneda famously used his personal experience, perhaps in part fictionalised, as apprentice to a Yaqui shaman, to communicate what he termed non-consensual realities (see *The teachings of Don Juan,* 1985; and *A separate reality,* 1991 (Washington Square Press).

5) I began my contact with shamans of varying traditions following ten years of intensive training in the Himalayan yogic tradition. That tradition is actually quite shamanic. I was under the direct tutelage of Herakhan Baba. (https://en.wikipedia.org/wiki/Haidakhan_Babaji).

6) He urged me to take the yogic knowledge to the 'religion' of my homeland and I joined an initiative known as the Oak Dragon Project for the recovery of indigenous knowledge in Britain. In that initiative I worked alongside Druid teachers as well as Buddhist, Sufi and Christian mystics. We all owe a tremendous debt to Native American teachers in the rediscovery of shamanic techniques such as Vision Quest; and to Amazonian shamans for working with Ayahuasca as a visionary herb. See Martin Prechtel's *Secrets of the Talking Jaguar* and

various books on Druidry by Philip Carr-Gomm (*Druid Mysteries: ancient wisdom for the 21st century* & *Druid Animal Oracle* (Touchstone, 1995)

7) *Scientific and shamanic perspectives on a world in crisis* Supporting paper for seminar to the panel on Invisible Cultures, Congress of the Royal Anthropological Institute, *World of Anthropology,* British Museum, June, 2012.

8) For example, George Monbiot in the Guardian takes several entirely out-of-context quotes from my autobiography *Shiva's Rainbow,* with the intention of showing some form of 'madness' in the embrace of non-scientific 'beliefs'. In fact, I recount experience and ask questions – and it should be plain that I do not embrace any belief-system. See: http://www.theguardian.com/environment/georgemonbiot/2010/sep/21 /climate-sceptics-evidence-gullible

9) See: Nicholson *The environmental revolution: a guide for the new masters of the world* (1971)

10) The original Club of Rome's *Limits to Growth* has recently been followed by *Fair Economics* Irene Schoene, which 'seeks explanations of why the global economic model continuously over-rewards the few'. A parallel text would be Tim Jackson's *Prosperity without Growth* in which restructuring of global finance involves the new world of carbon taxes, credits and derivatives.

11) A fundamental shift occurred with Lord Stern's inquiry, commissioned by Tony Blair, into the economics of climate change, where the future costs of non-action were held to outweigh the costs of action, which were estimated at 1-2% of GDP. Proponents of re-allocation of resources, new taxes and subsidies seem oblivious to the plight of modern western industrial nations that struggle to maintain growth of 2% and experience severe social disruption should growth become even slightly negative.

12) *Ibid* Club of Rome

13) see *Conservation on its last legs: the prospect for rejuvenation* (ECOS, 2015, *in press*)

14) I can point to no single exhaustive impact assessment of global renewable energy strategies – but they are clearly massive. At last year's conference I presented graphics of hydro developments proposed for all undeveloped mountain areas – such as Andes, Amazonas, Himalayas and SE Europe; in one country alone, Colombia, 400,000 acres of subsistence level agriculture were converted to oil palm production, 50% of which was imported to the EU for biofuels – there is a world-wide largely undocumented 'land-grab' for biofuel and hydro intrusion into indigenous territories.

15) For example, the writings of Christopher Booker in the Daily Telegraph.

16) There is a growing disjunction between the new professional organisations such as Rewilding Europe and the proven grass-roots initiatives, some of which are 10-20 years in their evolution. For example *Wild Ennerdale* eschews definitions and targets and involves all members of the local community, such as farmers and walkers, to participate in the formulation of land-use changes in this upland ecosystem. (See: P.Taylor, ed. *Rewilding* – Ethos. 2011, for detailed discussions and the history of rewilding in Britain.)

17) The recent *Lynx Trust* – a professional initiative of scientists and veterinarians, plans to apply for licences to release lynx at a number of sites in England, despite no track-record of involvement with communities or effective communication with the farming communities. See also comments by George Monbiot on the destructive effect of upland farming subsidies. http://www.theguardian.com/environment/georgemonbiot/2013/may/22/britain-uplands-farming-subsidies.

18) Modern science divested itself of all attendant non-physical realities in the mid-17th century with the birth of the Royal Society and the embrace of Cartesian logic. Before that time, no respectable 'scientist' (Newton, for example) would limit study to the purely physical realities of Nature. Thus scientifically 'educated' men took over medicine and agriculture and technicians applied themselves to creating an industrial economy that moved millions of people from living on the land to life in cities and factories.

19) My compatriot in the Oak Dragon Project, Ivan McBeth, for example, studied Engineering at University; Martin Prechtel is an accomplished writer as well as a painter.

20) My friend, the Australian Ayahuascero and musician, Vimal Darpan, was once arrested on drugs charges and it took several depositions of a legal and anthropological nature to clear the charges; likewise Adrian Freeman, also an accomplished and internationally recognised musician, suffered arrest and a year-long prospect of prosecution by the UK authorities, who similarly were eventually persuaded to drop charges. The police handling was repressive, undoubtedly targeted and in full knowledge of the real nature of the substance of Ayahuasca, which has legal standing as a religious sacrament in Brazil and recently also in the USA. The UK has punitive and irrational laws relating to plant and fungal entheogens, directed at commerce rather than actual users, thus closing off supplies.

21) See: *Shamanic wisdom in the Pyramid Texts* by Jeremy Naydler (Inner Traditions, 2004)

22) Thus was born the Hermetic Tradition – the main western esoteric practice that was subject to rediscovery during the Renaissance, having been hidden due to rabid persecution by the Roman church. Elements of this inner tradition were practised by Medieval

Alchemists – for example, by Newton and Elias Ashmole, founder of the Royal Society, and exist, though still hidden, within Masonic teaching where they are combined with the Caballa.

23) One of the most basic shamanic techniques is the incorporation – the bringing into the body, of the animal powers through a process of dreaming and invocation. The first-level of this experience involves thought-like communication or 'messages', and the more advanced, the transference of powers such that human faculties are sharpened or extended. The latter has to be experienced to be understood.

24) In the play, Aristophanes satirises the need of citizens for some authority above their own – for which a priesthood of Gods had evolved as intermediary. The birds deceptively take over this function and translate the wishes – often rather venal, of the lampooned politicians. Thus, rather than a play on the silliness of the 'cuckoo' (an altogether human projection), the playwright has selected a species that is a master of deception and a consummate parasite.

25) The faculty of 'dreaming' that involves a projection of a conscious 'energy body' or 'double' able to 'remotely view' objects is well known in yogic training as well as advanced shamanic practice. The American military famously tried to train operatives (rather unsuccessfully) in such remote viewing – an enterprise lampooned in the film *Men who stared at* goats!.

26) *What mad pursuit: a personal view of scientific discovery* Francis Crick, Basic Books, 1990.

27) The Bonobo has far less violence in its daily life. Wrangham theorises that female grouping inhibited male violence – and that territorial defence would often involve females approaching intruding groups with intentions of making 'love' rather than war.

28) There is in fact such a nascent movement in the American mid-West, extolling the virtues of carbon dioxide as plant food, sceptical (or in denial) of its greenhouse potential, and rather unfortunately antagonistic toward evolutionary science and human origins.

29) Punctured early human skulls found on skeletons in South African caves were at first taken as evidence of human intra-species violence, until careful measurements revealed the marks were made by leopard. It is noteworthy that the very first remains of human 'houses' at Catal Hyak, in Turkey, were extensively decorated with wall frescos of leopards.

30) for example, we looked at Gore's investment portfolio entitled Generation Investment Management that had heavily bought into carbon derivatives and renewable energy – a conflict of interest not noted in his award winning documentary *An Inconvenient Truth*

31) It does *not* work with tigers in the jungle – a Buddhist humility has proven more successful – there is a famous monastery in Thailand that rehabilitates orphaned tigers without cages, and which wild tigers regularly pop in for a visit!.

32) The serpent of *kundalini* power is little-understood in the West, and barely also in India, as it is often described as a *current* using an electrical analogue. It is much more than that and should not be thought separate from *psychic* realities. It empowers the dreaming faculty and the Highest Yoga Tantra involves union of male and female practitioners entwining their respective energy currents *and* psyches.

33) The ultimate serpent powers are cosmic in the sense of interplanetary and trans-galactic streams of plasma and magnetic field lines. Indigenous myths often refer to sky-dragons and 'feathered serpents' and may well refer to snaking streams of plasma caused by solar eruptions or galactic waves. Likewise, there are geomantic components of an Earth grid, recognised originally in Chinese *feng shui* and landscape planning, and also within the Druid traditions of stone-circles.

34) Sexual repression by the Roman church demonised serpents, dragons, Pan (as the Devil) and women suspected of consorting with such devils – with quite horrific punishments. What is generally not recognised is that female teachers of the equivalent to Hermetic practice were systematically eradicated (as of course, were many men – the celebrated astronomer Giodarno Bruno being a prime example). When asked why women were so much better at projecting their consciousness, Castaneda replied that 'consciousness i*tself* is female'. Modern science has apparently separated consciousness from matter – but in actuality, it has separated female consciousness from male.

35) An evolution of remote viewing, or any kind of extra-sensory ability related to intuitive knowledge of territory, would also extend to perception within complex social groups, hierarchies and power structures. Myth and literature (patriarchal for over 2000 years) abound with stories of the 'wicked witch' and her 'destructive' ways.

36) There is a vast literature on *kundalini* yoga and the 'chakra' system, largely dismissed by Western science and philosophy. The highest developed forms are to be found in Tibet. See *Highest Yoga Tantra* by Daniel Cozort.

37) Descartes evolved his philosophy of separation whilst observing the defeat of the Alchemist King and Queen of Bohemia by a Catholic crusader force at the Battle of White Mountain, Prague in 1618.

38) Alchemists practised sexual union as a meditation on the essential union of opposites – in order that the psyche could *experience* the realities of non-duality.

39) In an age of trade unions and worker's right, even occasional workers' control of the means of production, it is easy to forget that early industrialisation and even evolutionary science developed parallel to the slave trade, the genocidal occupation of Native America, Carib and South American territory, expansion of corporate Empire in India and the Far East and the hunting and eradication of 'sub-human' indigenous peoples in South Africa. The modern term 'economic slavery' applies to people disenfranchised and subject to the most extreme forms of cultural severance. All, upon which, the accumulation of 'western industrial' wealth or capital was based.

40) For further observations, see 'The Road to Salamanca' ECOS, 34 (3/4) 21-27, 2013.

41) See 'Perspectives from Anthropology' for further comments on these gender issues in climate science - in *Chill: a reassessment of global warming theory.*

42) See latest discussion in ECOS on the prospects for rejuvenation of 'conservation'. I am concerned that 'rewilding' will become a new sale-pitch for fading conservationism.

43) The Arthurian myths were laid down in the 13th century by French Troubadours, the inheritors of Cathar wisdom teachings only partially eradicated by the Catholic crusade against them and the Inquisition that followed. Albi, in SW France, was a centre of such teaching based upon the union of male and female, with the forest as church.

44) Amazingly, this became public knowledge only as recent as 2008, following a US National Academy of Science Report on the subject. Eventually, the UK Parliament conducted an inquiry on vulnerabilities to solar pulse. In July 2012, NASA observed a 'mega-pulse' capable of disabling electrical grids – that missed Earth by only 9 days of solar rotation.

**Bibliography**

Brody, Hugh (1982) *Maps & Dreams* Pantheon Books.

Carr-Gomm, Philip (1995) *Druid Animal Oracle* Touchstone.

Castaneda, Carlos (1985) *The teachings of Don Juan,* Washington Square Press.

Castaneda, Carlos (1991) *A separate reality* Washington Square Press.

Cozort, Daniel (1986) *Highest Yoga Tantra* Snow Lion Publications.

Crick, Francis (1990) *What mad pursuit: a personal view of scientific discovery* Basic Books.

Dunbar, Nan (1998) *Aristophanes, Birds.* Clarendon Press, Oxford.

Dodds, E.R. (1951) *The Greeks and the Irrational,* University of California Press.

Jackson, Tim (2011) *Prosperity without Growth* Routledge

Lloyd, Elsabeth (2006) *The case of the female orgasm* Harvard University Press.

Narby, Jeremy (1999) *The Cosmic Serpent: DNA and the origins of knowledge* Putnam.

Naydler, Jeremy (2004) *Shamanic wisdom in the Pyramid Texts* Inner Traditions.

Nicholson, Max (1971) *The environmental revolution: a guide for the new masters of the world.*

Prechtel, Martin (1999) *Secrets of the Talking Jaguar* Tarcher.

Sams, Jamie (1999) *Medicine Cards: the discovery of power through the ways of animals* St Martin's Press.

Schloene, Irene (2015) *Fair Economics* Club of Rome.

Shlain,Leonard (1999) *The alphabet versus the Goddess* Penguin Books.

Taylor, Peter (2005) *Beyond Conservation: a wildland strategy,* Earthscan.

  (2009) *Chill: a reassessment of global warming theory* Clairview.

   (2011) *Rewilding: ECOS writing on wildlland and conservation values* (ed) Ethos

   (2015) *Conservation on its last legs? The prospects for rejuvenation* (ECOS, 2015)

Wrangham, Richard (2010) *Catching fire – how cooking made us human* Basic Books.

Wrangham, R. & D. Peterson (1997) *Demonic males: apes and the origin of human violence* Mariner.

110

# PART 2

*These three essays were published in shorter form:*
*Return of the Animal Spirits in Reforesting Scotland (1995);*
*Coed Eryri in a chapter in Beyond Conservation (2005)*
*and The Healing Forest also in that volume.*

*The first essay illustrates the belligerence of mind that possessed me at that time. Perhaps it was a consequence of two decades of environmental campaigning on nuclear risks and chemical pollution of the oceans - despite my avowed wish to leave that world of perpetual conflict where the 'enemy' always set the agenda, and move toward a more creative endeavour. I had also grown very cynical about science - at least, environmental science with its history of abject failures in the 1980s.*

*I have softened since - perhaps not as much as I would have liked, but the chapters on changing orientation from purely scientific to first steps into shamanic realms and the healing powers of nature in Beyond Conservation, whilst perhaps still somewhat combative in relation to science, argued for a creative marriage between science and shamanism.*

*It is ten years or more since these essays were written and as will be evident from the following Part 3, some small progress is being made.*

# Return of the Animal Spirits

The civilised mind sees animals as objects. But then it sees everything as object, including itself. We, the civilised, have been systematically schooled to see ourselves as separate from nature, and separate from each other. Our sense of individuality and boundedness has been elevated to the only politically acceptable reality. We look out on the world, organise and manipulate it, including each other. Only lovers fleetingly dissolve that boundary. For the rest of the time, we are alone and only semi-conscious.

In other cultures and in other times, deeper realities were experienced and understood. That consciousness can be expanded and boundaries dissolved. That there is an inner eye, a single point of awareness behind this bounded consciousness, that is aware of itself, can shift, can leave the physical body, and in its expanded state, merge with any and all form, rock or mountain, ocean and whale, even witness the birth of stars.

There is a consciousness that is not bounded by time and space, which are illusions of the mind, of the eye and the hand that measure and the logic that interprets. In the bliss of their union, lovers sometimes touch this and the knowledge remains. Yogis and shamans train to enter this consciousness at will and to work within it. In the lostness of modern youth, many touch it through drugs but the confusion remains.

The civil mind relates to animals through this crippled sight. It may still love them, desire to protect them, study them, catalogue them. The heart is moved, but the sight is not extended. Logic informs, 'you are one with them, there is an ecological web, their fate is your fate', but it is fear that motivates conservation, and conservation is a global half-heartedness, for fear always drains the heart. All science, all ecology, is half-hearted, and therefore fated. Our science is founded on separation and separation is inseparable from fear. In that world, the animals will always lose, as will we. It is a world now dominated by fear-driven imagined needs and wants, a dynamic far more powerful than logic can persuade, whose only end is death. The civil mind will destroy itself in time. In nature, boundaries can never persist and what is birthed, must die.

At its apotheosis the Judaeo-Christian orthodoxy not only separated individual consciousness from nature in the spatial sense, the resultant individualised soul was also cut off in time, born with no ancestry, but with a future beyond its single life in some eternal and ethereal form, a happy and holy ghost of the personality. For the holocaust centuries and even after, you didn't make the heavenly resting home if you didn't toe the line and the hell of eternal torment awaited you if you didn't appropriately pay homage to the image of God as patriarch and sacrificial son. Thus, was the last of Celtic spirituality, with its shamanic relationship to the animal spirits, expunged from western consciousness.

112

What is it then to restore an ecosystem? Bring back the boreal ancestors: wolf and bear, lynx and moose, boar, beaver and bison? It has been argued that their fate is our fate, that the interconnected web will fail if key species are missing. This is ecological romanticism and not founded in science. These animals are not necessary for our survival. And in these isles, there would be little question of living closely beside them, for they will need undisturbed space. We shall have to separate an area, a 'wilderness', into which we may walk, but not live as our ancestors lived. And let no one pretend it will be a 'natural' space, a monument of pure nature unaffected by man. Even in Scotland, as elsewhere, the rain is acid with sulphur and enriched with nitrogen. There is a fall-out of synthetic organics, solvents and biocides, refrigerants, fillers and fire retardants. The soil is still contaminated from Chernobyl. And with fossil fuel burn driving the greenhouse effect, what was once boreal, may in twenty or thirty years be something quite other. And these animals wander. The little natural park will soon begin to export its offspring to the sheep-filled pastures and fields of oats, and out will come the gun and the poisoned bait, monetary compensation to farmers or trophies for hunters.

Either way, we will not be able to leave the animals alone, so if we want them back, we need to understand this: there is no complete sanctuary for them and there is no secure precedent for their ecology. We do not know how far we can recreate suitable habitat or how it will change as the climate changes. What we have lost cannot be totally re-instated. The British wolf, bear and lynx would have been genetically separated, perhaps distinct races, and they have been lost forever. Do we now take wolves from Poland and Russia, Spain or Croatia? Or from all of these and create some 'hybrid' vigour? The Scandinavian lynx, the French or the Czech? Beavers from the Rhone or the Elbe?

Science can inform, but it cannot decide, and it is therefore an error to let scientists make decisions for us, for they simply play out their own subjective aesthetic or political judgment. And besides, they will want to test their models, equations and computer programmes. Not for them now the 'suck-it-and-see' successes of the Brittany beaver re-introductions, the Lynx in the Vosges and Jura, or the bear in the Austrian Alps.

There is a beautiful puma in the natural history museum in Inverness, shot in the highlands many years ago, doubtless set free from a boring pet-hood (although there are some who believe Britain still holds an as-yet-to-be discovered puma-sized native big cat!). Would one to advocate the introduction of the puma to our highland megafauna, there would be more than a kerfuffle from the sheep farmers: such a proposition would meet opposition and even derision from most scientific conservationists, for they are just as much a community of cultural traditionalists, holding to the past as if what has been, ought to be.

*Three lynx: bottom: Iberian; middle: Central European; top: Scandinavian*

Science can only follow our political will, our policy. If we want to re-create the past, then it can tell us what to do and possibly how to do it.. Science is about what was, what is, and how to change things, with all of the knowledge of the first two being focused, these days, on how to manipulate the 'things', the outer objective realities. Science can only ever see animals as things. Yet the majority of us are scientifically illiterate. Another impulse draws the millions to safari parks and zoos, an aesthetic, a wonder, and a race memory perhaps. This has no place in the Sites of Special Scientific Interest, born of a protectionist mentality that freezes a recent past of man-induced landscapes, heathland assemblages of rare moths and twayblades, or treeless marshes and wetlands, and pores over them in studious Victorian mentality.

For wilderness to be valued, there has to be a wildness in the heart. If we are to recreate the majesty of continuous forest, alive with large predators, a place where the heart can taste the primeval thrill at the distant howl of wolf, or the adrenaline surge at the rustle of a big animal unseen but close in the underbush, we will have to break through the stranglehold that civility has placed upon the value of nature.

But why wilderness? What about a funicular? A safari-lodge with special drive-through non-polluting electric vehicles? After all, if there is no real purity, why be purist? It would bring much needed jobs, and the youngsters would be educated, and the animals would not mind at all. Surely that is the only way to safeguard nature, make it pay for itself?

Civil and scientific. Does your heart not sink? Is there not an impulse deep and inexpressible from which the 'please, no' is generated? What is it we seek with this wilderness? Why do we really want them back? Is it not a plain and simple love forgotten, or faintly felt but does not now dare to speak its name? I mean not the surface sentiment upon which the zoos feed - and who, after the awe and wonder, has not left those enclosures with heavy sadness in the heart? Is it perhaps an inkling that they are a part of us, a dim awareness that our fragmented soul was once at one with them?

Boreal ecosystem restoration is the cloak of reason. Is not the wellspring of this desire our long lost knowledge, our long suppressed love? Yes, you may say, whispering close, but here lies danger, we are surrounded by civil minds in fear of the very word. We shall be called cranks. Better to keep the disguise of science, obligations under the European Union Habitat Directive, UN Biodiversity Convention, and such like. Born of the survivalist's fearful mentality they may be, but lets stick to the guerrilla tactic, in the open it would be war and we're bound to lose.

The druids, Siberian shamans, Amerindians, North American Medicine Men and Himalayan yogis all have or had techniques of merging their consciousness with animals. Certain species were revered as teachers and each had qualities it could impart, or particular teachings and meaning should it appear either in dream, meditation, or physical encounter. The fully awakened mind of the shaman does not have the same boundary of inner and outer reality, everything is imbued with meaning. The animal powers were always available for healing of the soul and they are approached with humility. In later European culture this healing tradition was held by women herbalists and survived until the Christian holocaust when, over a period of 500 years, an estimated nine million practitioners and other 'heretics' were branded as 'witches' and ritually executed.

But for what would then be the fight? For the animals? Worthy as that may be, it leaves something out - *us*. Separation again. There is a higher objective, and I would argue we must go for that now, for now is not only when the animals need us, but when we need them. We are lost in a separated consciousness. All around us the world of beauty is disintegrating. Fear predominates and love is weakened by romance and sentiment. If we cannot strengthen love, humanity will destroy beauty. There will be survivors and they may even call it a civilisation. This is not about physical survival it is about the retrieval of soul.

It is for this that we need the animals. Firstly, imagine that we, that is this little island, say to the world, we are bringing back the animals because they will make us whole again. And to do it, we set aside land and spend large amounts of money, and put parts of our economy aside. We signal that something matters other than material growth and physical security. It will be a small signal, because, after all, we are rich and can afford it, and the physical risks are small.

And then, in addition to the ecology of animals, we teach our children to reach out to them in shamanic reality. Instead of looking at the new beaver colony through binoculars from the hide, beaver comes to them in the awakened dreamspace of the inner eye. They ask beaver for help, to show them the qualities of the founder, the builder, the industrious one who cares not that the winter floods carry away the dam. Beaver works beneath the surface water, symbol of the unconscious, where the vision must be anchored. Beaver dams are masterpieces of anchorage and the foundation is always intact for the new spring build. This work creates still water, fertile wetland for growth of willow, aspen and alder (plants with dream medicine of their own) which will then feed not only their own new children, but the other animals.

Each animal has its own medicine. Their habits and ways impart this knowledge. To the beaver's pool comes first Moose. Moose is the power of earth drawn to the waters to feed. The bull roars, unafraid to signal presence, power and sexuality. Following Moose is Wolf, the pathfinder, the teacher - so much to learn from Wolf, social and predatory, it is very close to human, and indeed, our mythological mother for the civilisation born at Rome. The animals teach by what they do and the energies they carry.

Once, I watched a sitting Osprey, a young bird on passage one September at the estuary by Ynys Giftan. I watched the still bird for seeming hours through the telescope, only its head slightly moving, judging distances and time. Then it launched, flying straight toward me and the river, talons outstretched, perfectly timed to snatch a fish from the surface. In that moment I was one with the bird and something of the encounter remained. It was about effort and timing and skill. The fish has to be on the surface before you try to catch it.

116

Who now knows that Bear is the keeper of the dream, and of its import for the island that is Britain? Bear sleeps through the barren winter. There is a time to awaken. In vision I once saw Bear charging through the woods, stumbling and half erect, and then the upper half was Arthur with his sword, half-man, half-beast, half-awake before his time. Where the Bear lives in the name of Arthur, (Arth, Welsh for bear), who sleeps yet, as the mythic hero in the neo-Druidic tradition, Lynx is the holder of secrets, enigmatic as ever. There is no record of the smiling one in the memory of Britain.

Now if we taught this: that anyone can in waking consciousness invite the animals, that they know our story, our quest for knowledge and our journey in love, that they are not separate, that they are already at one with the Universe and that the consciousness of the Universe moves through them; then we can learn from contact with them of who we are, for the Universe moves through us. If we have forgotten the quest, they will remind us. If we have lost our love, they will lead us to love. That is the deeper ecological restoration.

The irony of science is that modern physics draws toward the same conclusion as the yoga of 2000 years ago! Worlds are born out of and disappear into emptiness. Beneath the objective reality of perceived form, there is only wave form, like a ripple in the aether. All is vibration like a primordial sound. But the physicist has observed and deduced, where the yogi and shaman have experienced.

There is a higher journey, a journey home, that is not for the animals and in that final quest they cannot help. The animals are our past, the animal in us, our foundation. Out of this animal world, has been born a consciousness and a love that reaches back into the very heart of the Universe. At present, it is faltering and fallible. The animal powers can support that journey by strengthening the love that is here, for this planet, for all the lifeforms, for each other and the knowledge that we are one being. They do not question. It is as if they know that we are the outcome of this long evolutionary experiment - it lies with us, and they are in that, as if we are their heart and they our feet. Even the great whales, whose consciousness and joy permeate the galaxy, support our journey for they know we can go further.

A children's television programme explains the origin of the universe thus: 'scientists believe it started with a big bang' and the smiling enthusiastic female presenter pops a balloon and graphics show bubbles interacting with each other in a melee of atoms, electrons, coalescing stars and planets and spiralling galaxies. When I was a schoolkid I would have been amazed and totally hooked. Now I am appalled. I feel like Jung Chang, in her autobiography, describing what it was like to wake up from a lifetime of communist indoctrination and feel the alienation. At least for her there was a subsequent exhilaration - that there was another world that beckoned.

'Scientists believe'! Such a loaded thing. The presenter announces it without a hint of reservation. Indeed, the slight undertone of 'they are not sure but.....' is presented as a positive thing, as if you can trust them even more because they work by hypothesis and don't assume anything until they are absolutely sure.

This is not seen as indoctrination. It is not seen as a political ideology. It is simply the passing on of pure knowledge - that which scientists have discovered about the nature and origin of the universe.


Is there no sociological term for it? Where whole realms of the human experience are marginalised by non-reference, as if they did not exist, and by a process that is so unconscious that it doesn't even do it deliberately. Indeed, so complete has been the process of indoctrination, that it doesn't have to be deliberate. The enemies of materialist doctrine were vanquished so completely that they no longer find cultural expression.

I want to rage. Who cares what scientists 'believe'! They are a thoroughly boring joyless lot. Astronomers may be harmless, but the others, the physicists that brought the bomb and radioactivity, and the geneticists now manipulating the future, the engine makers, road builders, forest devourers, makers of pesticides and biocides, and the psycho-pharmacists.........science is full of madmen, yet the ordinary person still pays them due, more, honours them as the fount of knowledge, even to the origin of the universe. How pathetic is their creation story. There was a big bang! The universe is like a balloon. Atoms are

119

like marbles, positive and negative and neutral billiard balls, and gravity attracts and creates a universe of one hundred billion gas fires.

Where is consciousness? Not there at the beginning, for sure. Only billiard balls. The question doesn't even feature. What was before? Well, sensible question, but unanswerable by science - of course. It has got to the point where the non-answer is enough. The whole story is ridiculous because it tells you nothing of any relevance to your life now. And it doesn't hold water even by the standards of science. The big bang could not have been the beginning, because there had to be something there to go bang in the first place, and no amount of saying, well, it was very dense, unlike any substance known, alters the point that before the beginning of 'this' universe, there must have been something to initiate the bang, a *source* of all that energy, and that even when you have spent two hundred years, and thousands of man-years of thinking and calculating and computing even, that ultimate source remains what it is and always has been - a great mystery!

So in the beginning there was Great Mystery.

But what really matters is that 'scientists' and their camp-followers have determined what is 'real'. The human journey has become the outward looking conscious analysing action - what is seen, measured and manipulated. The person who does the looking - the consciousness that has become aware, has been relegated. This is not a personal journey. Only those impersonal and repeatable, replicable, elements of discovery have become currency. It is called 'objective'. Do not tell of your feelings. Do not tell of your personal journey in love. Do not tell of your relationship to Great Mystery. At least not in this temple. That stuff is for the home, the marital bed, the church and the hospice.

The yogi tells that in the beginning was consciousness itself. Like a great sound, it penetrated everything. And before that, was that which cannot be known. Which the ancients call the void, Great Mother of All. And the vibration that was the great sound has been called the Word, which has been always. And whatever the fossil history of this planet, our star the sun, our spiral galaxy, and everything that our instruments can yet perceive, these are the merest scratches that human perception can make on the surface of that mystery.

It is a great arrogance to assume that this small minded mathematics has any importance in the great scheme of things. Yet this arrogance is so big. It teaches the children what 'scientists believe' and expects them to sit still, to accept, to write it down and churn it out in exams. Those who will never get to peer through these massive telescopes or interpret the signals of radio-dishes, unquestioning, write it down as if it is great knowledge they should know, or simply concur, in petty resentment, because the marks are needed for the jobs that are going.

The whole of inner life has been marginalised. Love has been marginalised. Mystery has been un-named - that which is currently beyond our method deserves no name. Only the method has power. And for us, dear children of the Universe, robbed of our mystery, there is a joyless future in a planet devoid of soul. The fields of our longing have been squared and resown, the grass engineered, the wildtrees tamed in their rows. And we will not want to rebel, to look again inward, because first there will wait on the threshold, the pain of our loss. Who will willingly choose pain?

We cannot see the enormity of this crime. We turn from mystery and love and the true riches of human life toward the paltry reward of material power and control. We call our pathetic scratching at the workings of the universal energies 'science', and we follow the emotionally crippled characters that pose as its priesthood, scrambling for the crumbs at their table, crumbs that will make us competitive in the world market, give us a chance to be a merchant with a fine house and a ticket to the beach.

# Coed Eryri

The emblem of the Snowdonia National Park is the arctic-alpine Snowdon lily *Lloydia serotina*, and this refugee from the arctic is found nowhere else in Britain. But the Welsh name for these hills is Eryri, the place of eagles. To the modern mind, an eagle, however spectacular, is just another species, but to the older culture of these hills, it held a special meaning, it represented visionary power. Eagles were eradicated in North Wales in the 16th Century. In February 1992, I wrote a pamphlet for a small group to work on a vision for a Forest of Snowdon, Coed Eryri, inspired by Alan Featherstone's work in Scotland and by the success of Community Forests in England[1]. We aimed to draw together a number of disparate initiatives for rewilding Snowdonia, but we had to work against an entrenched antipathy to natural processes. The National Park (see Figure 2.1) held no core-area of wild land, virtually no naturally regenerating forest, due to the presence of sheep, and indeed, despite 30% forest-cover (mostly plantation), only 1% remained of the ancestral indigenous oak[2]. After three years of discussions I concluded that we were dealing not just with the economic interests of farmers and foresters, but a deeper psychology relating to the need to dominate nature and bring wild land into productive use:

...... the primary thing, the fear of listening, is a fear of Nature herself. In the Forest there are no voices but hers. This is not the Chapel to the Son, who will be our salvation, to a Father who will guide the righteous and judge the wicked, or to a Holy Ghost that forever sustains and promises a personal immortality. It is not a Cathedral of solid immovable stone set by architect and mason. Here there is darkness and constant motion. Here we may be reminded of our physical frailty, our death and decay. Here is the dark mother, not Mary the sustainer, but Ceridwen or Hecate, the destroyer. Here is where the male mind must surrender and meet its greatest fear. Here is the rebirth of consciousness.

What began then was very much a personal rebirth, a personal journey of reconnection for each of our group, but particular for myself, blinkered by years of scientific training and policy analysis. In our small group we began to uncover ancient practices of listening, of storytelling, of drum and dance and vision quest, and in so doing, sought our teachers among the Native Americans, the yogis, and those few women who had kept alive the ancient spiritual traditions associated with a deeper healing connection to nature,

*......from other cultures we have long sought to suppress and exterminate, we are now learning that this great mystery of nature cares for us, that her voices speak wisdom, that her servants, the animals and trees, have spirit voices that speak of love, with love. All along it was so, but we could not see through the mist of fear. The wolf and bear have medicine as deep as any herb. Raven and*

*beaver will speak if we cup hand to inner ear. In dreams or quiet wakefulness they will come. They know our journey, they know love. Of course, how could it be otherwise? How could the divine not be everywhere, not be with them and with us unbounded by concept, by language, by time or space? This is not 'mysticism'. It is honouring the great mystery and is a deeper reality, a deeper ecology.*

And of course, that made it difficult for mainstream conservation, National Park committees, or farming communities, to embrace our vision! My friend Eric Maddern, however, developed 'Cae Mabon', near Llanberis, to become a centre for education and the spiritual connection to the wild land of Snowdon[3]. The vision of a wild forest is held firm in many hearts and we must trust that what we have shared will influence those with responsibilities for land management in Snowdonia. Coed Eryri's activities have been primarily a 'visioning' process involving the core group, educational outreach and discussions with various 'stakeholders' in the National Park, and that has been ongoing in relation to a core area in the Rhinogydd (see Figure 2.2).

However, in the slow metamorphosis from ecological vision toward cultural change, I have also undergone a personal transformation in understanding and values and in this account of Coed Eryri, I will depart from the normal accepted form of conservation discourse and objectivity, as I believe we, as conservationists, have to make such a transition on a broader political level – we have to become central to human values in areas in which we are now marginal. I do not believe we can do it by embracing economic 'services' nor through some quasi-scientific conservation ethic. I have come to believe that through our work with wild nature, we must restore something central to the human soul, something that has the power to over-ride selfish and short-term motivation, as well as the great fears of nature still rooted in the psyche.

When I moved to Snowdonia in February 1989, I was struggling to live with a severely split personal world. I had a scientific training in biological sciences and had worked as a professional consultant in ecological policy for over 10 years: ranging over the fields of radioecology, chemical pollution, climate change, renewable energy impacts, and various industrial policy issues. I also had further degrees and academic training in social anthropology that had given me a perspective on man's relationship to spiritual and natural worlds. But I had become mired in these systems of thinking, and was already engaged in the process of redeeming another more intuitive part of my self. This other self trained in yogic 'sciences' with a Himalayan master, worked with Native American teachers, and ran groups developing techniques of spiritual purification and vision-quest. My spirituality had begun as an essentially eastern quest for the purity of heart and absence of mind, and much later I had confronted the reality of living in the west, the place of creativity and dreaming[4].

I was to spend seven years slowly reconciling my two worlds and working with some remarkable people. The Coed Eryri group consisted of local artists, sculptors, storytellers, shamanic healers, community workers, foresters and woodworkers, about half of whom were native Welsh speakers.

On previous encounters with the bleak mountainous terrain – in the 1970's I took my students for hikes above Cwm Idwal – I had looked upon the land with the manipulative eye of a zealous ecologist – 'if only we could get the sheep off, rejuvenate the flower meadows, reforest the slopes. This place should by rights be forest. After all, it is a National Park where nature should be paramount.'

Instead, it is a national sheep reserve, overgrazed and ecologically impoverished. The answer was to re-create the forest, with its ecological web intact. I set about making plans and finding allies. There were already many small independent initiatives, and if we combined, we could argue for major policy changes and the funds for ecological restoration. What Alan Featherstone was doing for the Caledonian Pine, we could do for the Welsh Oak!

Only about 1% of Snowdonia National Park is remnant semi-natural woodland, yet there is 30% 'forest' cover consisting of plantations, largely of alien Sitka spruce, Japanese larch, or Scots pine. Outside of these plantations, almost every nook and cranny is grazed by sheep or cattle and very little of the remnant ancient broadleaf woodland is regenerating. Wild herbivores are few: there are some ancient feral goats in the rockier parts of the hills, and fallow deer (not indigenous to Britain), in the Forestry Commission's Coed y Brenin in the south of the Park. The red deer and roe deer are extinct in the region. The grazing pressure from domestic stock prevents re-colonization of the bare hillsides by natural regeneration, and large areas have been invaded by alien rhododendron scrub.

The first response of conservationists in protecting existing woodland or planting new, is to aggressively fence out domestic stock. I had opportunity to compare open and fenced woodland along the ancient woodland ridge of Harlech near my home. Almost a third of the wood was fenced, another third or more heavily grazed, but the immediate area of about 20 ha around the house was lightly grazed by sheep and a small suckler herd of eight or so Welsh Black cattle. That third which had been fenced off from all stock had a thick shrub and herb layer of bramble and ivy, with few flowering plants and little regeneration; the heavily grazed section held little other than grasses and mosses with no young trees; whereas the lightly grazed area was alive with flowering plants, regenerating young trees and a large variety of shrubs and ferns.

## Llety'r Fwyalchen, abode of the Blackbird

That area of active regeneration surrounded my home Llety'r Fwyalchen, the abode of the blackbird. Whilst I set about my plans and alliances, largely around the traditional model of conservation – how to get stock off, erect fences, combine planting and natural regeneration, take care over provenance etc., I would walk daily around the meadows and woods. I kept a diary not of the times of flowering or numbers of species, but of the moons and the inner dreams that came. I would walk out on a circuit from the house and visit first the old crab-apple, casting her dense shade, a space below barely high enough to crouch, surrounded by the bracken and bright sunlight, to quietly feel the day's concerns drain away in the cleansing darkness.......

*These woods are special in ways that cannot be measured. The scientist would find nothing unusual here, for here is a poetry of the commonplace. Yet a poetic masterpiece, a symphony of the most divine.*

*We begin with Crab, the Old Lady, Hecate, alone in the witchy dark, to crawl beneath her black wings on the damp moss, she is the purifier and the entrance and here we ask the shadows to cleanse us of the dross we bring. On then to Grandfather Oak, its youth saw Glyndwr's rebellion, the securing of the Bardic land, if momentarily. Fissured bark. Huge girth, giant arms, broken and horned. Heart of Herne. Old Druid. Lend us strength for the journey.*

*On to Holly. Boughs pink flushed grey tickling the sensual centre with erotic curve, a thigh to touch, delicate arm, rounded breast, or muscle bulging with power, flexed and waiting, man or woman? Here is mysterious coupling, knowledge beyond the veil.*

*To the Alder grove. Ground sodden first flush of golden saxifrage. Her place. Red bleeds her wound. Kingcup in pools where the moon strikes through. Iris bed. Yellow her favourite. The owls nest here, bird of the coven. We come with no requests. This is not the place for asking, but of gratitudes, the return of love. Bathe deep in cold waters. Open to moon's silver, alders' shadows. Come when Luna is full and dances on the surface of her pools. Slip softly under, let the water embrace. Here there is no asking. Kiss the moss between her thighs. She loves you, you are welcome, always. Then listen. She tells you how long she has waited, knowing your wild heart.*

*It is a bluebell spring. The foragers are late and the blue comes to full bloom. Beltaine brings a carpet of wonder, whites of anemone and woodsorrel, stitchwort and pignut, tiny stars of sanicle, woodruff and a foam of ramsons heavy with scent, and everywhere yellows of celandine, pimpernel, spearwort, buttercup and marigold, blue violets, pink herb robert and campion. So quick now. Each week brings someone to seed. Meadows of dandelion heads, daffodils long gone, snowdrops bent back to the earth, burying their green swelling womb.*

125

*Soon will come foxglove, meadowsweet, woodsage and valerian, tall to outpace the vigorous summer grass, the spreading ferns. And honeysuckle, queen of the woodland night high above her carpet, the enchanter's nightshade.*

*She is bright now with song. Mwyalchen opens the gap between the worlds. Winter loyal thrush, dunnock, robin and wren, joined now by throaty blackcaps, flute-warblers, flycatchers and jeweled redstart. You have come a long way for this. Pan's garden. Wild heart*

Every species was regenerating – ash, oak, willow, birch, alder, rowan, holly, hawthorn, crab apple, spindle, blackthorn, gean, and all holding their own against the prolific sycamore; yet the meadows were grazed and there were no barriers to entering the woodland. The small sloping fields among the woods were alive with musk mallow, marsh orchid, cranesbill and betony and in the wet woods, in one small patch, in May, I counted 13 species of woodland flowers, with many medicinal herbs such as valerian, wood sage and lady's mantle. You can walk for hours elsewhere in the National Park and not see a significant flower.

In the long-fenced section of the ancient woodland, you were also hard-pressed to find any flowers – the whole place was a tangle of brambles and ivy. However, it took several years for the significance of all this to sink in. Meanwhile the plan unfolded: draw maps of land use categories, - the planning authority had maps of presumptions for forestry (admittedly old-style commercial); develop strategies to get rid of the stock over large areas. The solution was clear: buy key bits of land (approach John Muir Society, National Trust, Woodland Trust, and even raise money locally), then fence and plant, or regenerate where sufficient seed sources existed. It might also be possible to get agreements from landowners (the National Trust owns significant acreage) to fence and regenerate small areas on the higher ground, especially stream- sides. It would take a long time, but if all parties cooperated to a grand design, in fifty years we could see a new forest on the barren slopes.

Not much happened. The National Trust did great work on the upper reaches of streams by fencing and planting, but balked at purchasing redundant Forestry plantations with the aim of re-conversion. The agencies of National Park and Countryside Council for Wales thought our long-term plan 'unrealistic'. And of course, they were right. The difference between Caledon and Eryri, is that Eryri has hundreds of small scale sheep farmers, myriads of stone walls, and several centuries of human domination of the landscape. The traditional Welsh speaking communities are also insular, rather cool toward incomers with ideas, deeply religious, and totally dependent upon agricultural subsidies. Many of today's farming families were quarry workers in the Victorian heyday of slate mining, and attitudes to the land by some had not evolved greatly.

In modern times a 'traditional' Welsh upland farm has no trees outside of the odd single-aged copse, with no regeneration; billiard-table green swards of improved meadows of in-bye land; and access to the moors where heather has

126

largely been replaced with acid grassland. The farmer's kitchen are bare of dried herbs or bottled anything: no jams, honey, fruit, cobs.....the culinary forest is smaller than the remnant ancient oaks. World-weary National Park ecologists and other assorted nature conservationists long settled for protecting what is left – the bats, and the twayblades hidden in the heather. Otter were getting scarcer, pine marten hadn't been seen for years, black grouse were on the verge of extinction. Though there was no detailed species list and limited monitoring data for the National Park[5], it was plainly obvious that the old concepts were not holding ground and that the agricultural economy was both the historical villain, and the main obstacle to change.


## The ancient forest, cattle and the Celtic heritage


If we were to transform Snowdonia, however, we had to have the farmers on board. This would mean a fundamental social and cultural shift. In realizing the need to integrate current farming communities in the vision, the 'forest' came to mean much more than my earlier scientific ecological training had provided for. Earlier concepts of primeval woodland replete with re-introduced herbivores – boar, roe deer, red deer, and beaver, and maybe the odd lynx (Scotland was the only place big enough for bear and wolf), now gave way to the 'cultural' forest as a place where people dwelt and intimately used the forest whilst respecting its natural sanctuaries and wildlife. This was the forest of the original Celts. They were a cattle people and a forest people and respected the wolf and the bear, as much as any tribal people in other parts of the globe respected the big cats and other dangerous species in the forest around them. Theirs was also a shamanic culture. The relationship between the human psyche and the creatures and plants of the forest was a two-way communication in the furtherance of healing and spiritual growth. The tribal healers entered into communion and alliance with the healing spirits of the trees, herbs, birds and other animals.

It is at this point that the superior western scientific mind starts to include tribal peoples in the same category as the twayblades and red grouse: objects for study. Social anthropologists make wonderful patterns with quaint comparative tribal data. Following the work of the anthropologist and popular writer Carlos Castenada, there have been a few dissenters, but generally, the world of the shaman is relegated to the realms of personal experience and cultural delusion[6]. Modernity knows where reality begins and ends. Yet, truly modern and open science knows that it co-creates the reality it purports to study objectively. Physicists tell us quite clearly that there are no boundaries to physical reality – that underlying everything is electro-magnetic wave-form and gravity field. The occasional psychologist has put this scientific mind under scrutiny – but few scientists know their work! The scientific worlds of measurement and metaphor, with their glorious technological spin-offs, have gained not just primacy as knowledge, but primacy of culture: the objective and consensual over the personal, and the rational above the intuitive.

And despite the fact that everything we ever conceive and make must first be dreamed, the dream is relegated. Our schools do not encourage dreamers, nor teach intuition. No one is taught to expand their consciousness beyond the boundaries of their own personal mind. Odd really, considering Galileo, Kepler, Copernicus, Mendeleyev, Newton, Einstein and Tesla were all dreamers, gaining their breakthroughs by deep intuition, and most of them were ostracized for it at some time by their narrower-minded scientific or political fraternity.

In my mountain retreat I began to relate to the underlying reality rather than the surface form. The forest began to take on another light. Slowly we became conscious of what the forest had meant to the mythical ancestors of Snowdonia. It was a place of healing and spiritual retreat. In meditation, a communion was reached with animals and trees. They talked by reflection, but that reflection always held a greater wisdom. And in return came gratitude, respect and ceremony.

**A mythic bear**

At the mythic heart of Britain, lies Arthur the King. He sleeps, sometime to awake. He is the keeper of the dream, the essential soul matter of this land. Noble yet flawed, ever in service to the Grail Goddess, his sword of truth now long lost beneath the waters of human consciousness. Something we know and treasure has retreated from this land.

'Aart' is bear in Celtic languages. Native American teachers call bear 'the keeper of the dream'. The mythic bear-king thus keeps the dream of Albion alive, a time when there will be a true relationship to the land, of honouring, respect, reverence and celebration. The Grail is the deep feminine mystery, which the masculine must touch and be touched by in order for the land to be fertile (and the honourable man to be healed of his aggressive masculinity).

As I work on this book by the banks of the Artro (the bear-river) that runs from the heart of the Rhinog mountains, where Robert Graves went to primary school and later first dreamt of the White Goddess[7], there is now a yellow digger grinding out new drains. All over the National Park, furiously religious men dig and scrape, hurtle about in four wheel jeeps or quad bikes, part of an 'industry' of producers, businesses, service providers. New conservation subsidies rebuild the walls that the Goddess has weathered, erect barbed wire as if at war. We are so far from the balance of masculine and feminine.

But the blackbird still sings at Llety'r Fwyalchen. In the druid oracle, blackbird's song heralds the gateway between the worlds. Many people came there for that journey into the Otherworld of dream. Four days and four nights in the woods, with no food, and some would take no bedding and just sit, still, quiet, until the forest revealed itself in the quest for personal vision. The ancient Celts and Native Americans knew that in meditation, in active lucid dreaming, with nature all around, a unity of consciousness can be reached where the presence of animals and plants influences the dream. The ancients would ascribe to each participant in the dream, a spirit reality, an essence of their medicine and healing influence drawn from direct dream experience.

Ten years ago, the scientific mind would scoff more than it does now. The arrogant edifice has crumbled a little – the ozone hole, global warming, acid rain, dying seals and forests, gender bending chemicals, BSE, HIV and the funeral pyres of Foot and Mouth. The techno-world is vulnerable to nature as well as its own follies. But there has to be something more – perhaps a realisation that science elevated itself too far above the personal and subjective, wherein dwells the soul, and through which man reaches to the soul in all about him.

Yogis and Native American medicine teachers, and Shamans of all cultures have no problem with this. Not because of some theory, but because it is their practical experience – they can dwell in the unified field of consciousness. In that field, the voices of oak and ash, raven and eagle, are not separate from our voice, and each has its own particular character – they do not simply reflect, they heal – they hold 'medicine'[8]. We return to this theme in Chapter 9, *The Healing Forest.*

And in that realm of healing – God is not a postulate, a belief, an hypothesis, but the direct experience of *presence,* a feeling, a seeing, of connectedness, of beauty, and above all, of love. There are no cultures that have nurtured this expanded consciousness and have not felt and named this presence, be it Great Mystery, Great Mother, Wakan Tanka, Pancha Mama.

This, of course, takes us even further from the problem of the cultural tradition that is Welsh sheep farming – and which in its current form of smallholdings and enclosed land is only a few hundred years old. Here, God is definitely a man, and a very orderly one: a shepherd, a husbandman, a guardian, a steward. Nature conservationists settled on the latter and tended to disappear when talk came round to re-creating wilderness – to have done otherwise would be political and perhaps even social suicide. Nevertheless, in this unpromising environment, the small group called 'Coed Eryri' was formed, with the intention of holding the vision and promoting discussion. Our time would come when the CAP dissolved and the uneconomic farms went to the wall. Only in times of decline and distress are communities open to new ways. Meanwhile we needed to develop the vision to address the political realities of our community.

**Integrative Regeneration**

In this respect, an opportunity arose in the form of a derelict but very fine building in the heart of Snowdonia. The former slate mining town of Blaenau

Ffestiniog (a major tourist attraction with the former deep mines and caverns), now an enclave of industrial dereliction, had growing social problems of unemployment and disaffected youth. The building in question was an old market hall. It was stone built, with a huge vaulted roof housing what had been at times a ball-room, a cinema, and a war-time production unit for uniforms. The old market was on the ground floor and the upper story, supported by pillars, held a magnificent sprung wooden floor. The roof and walls were still sound, but all the windows were gone and boarded up, and significant repairs were needed. The council could not afford the costs, and had decided to knock it down unless a buyer – or custodian could be found.

We had already witnessed the parents of the Snowdonia Steiner School design and build a 'science unit' for the school – a large and wonderful building on wooden piles, with shingle roof, where all of the timber had been cut from local larch forests and shipped in using the 'tourist' railway (formerly built for transporting the slate). We approached the County Council with ideas of restoring the building using local materials (slate and timber) and local skills in carpentry. The eventual use for the building would be as a community and educational centre, perhaps with its own theatre group. It would provide a most excellent performance space. The youth theatre project could focus upon issues of regeneration and the relationship to nature, as well as issues of dereliction and social dysfunction (drugs among young people was fast becoming a problem in rural Wales).

We began researching the feasibility of an idea that had great potential for regenerating links between the urban areas of Snowdonia and the natural resources as well as the natural beauty of the Park. I visited a pioneering project in mid-Wales, where the National Trust was restoring a large country house and estate it had been bequeathed. There, the local director of the Trust had eschewed immediate large inputs of money to renovate the derelict buildings, in favour of smaller, timed allotments to finance a community-based programme of restoration. Timber from the estate was to be harvested and milled to provide for a team of locally recruited craft carpenters who would replace the fittings. Such old skills were in short-supply and many retired people were enlisted to train modern apprentices. When I visited the site – Llanerchaeron, it was a hive of activity, a ready example of integrative regeneration of skills, meaningful work, cooperative endeavour, and connection to the land.

Sadly, what was an innovative opportunity for one National Trust director, was a potential headache for another – the North Wales regional director, after much consideration and site visits by some of the Trust's more forward thinking officers, would not take on the Market Hall, though it was offered by the Council for a nominal £1 and there were obvious sources of funding for its renovation and management.

The interest in the Hall sparked alternative schemes by local interests centred around a 'heritage' experience – effectively a pay-at-the-door tourist attraction.

130

At least our involvement was instrumental – the building was eventually preserved and renovated by the Council, and serves now as a community arts centre, but the opportunity for a truly 'integrative regeneration' was not taken. This brief attempt to reconcile urban life with the forest, the past with the future, and to reach a disaffected youth, taught us the important role that individual personalities and politics play in any history.

In many respects, the former industrial history of Snowdonia affects current policies – there are large communities within or on the edge of the Park who look to a future of high technology companies, energy resources or tourist developments such as narrow gauge railways and artificial ski-slopes, rather than any kind of relationship to nature itself. Indeed, since its inception, the National Park has been blighted by major installations – such as the nuclear power station at Trawsfynydd, an above-ground hydro-pipeline on the very slopes of Snowdon itself, a massive pumped-storage scheme, power lines, 'improved' roads and a plethora of new applications for small scale hydro schemes on the rivers, many of which were in use in the industrial past. If the future of the National Park is to include a re-wilding, a way ahead must be found whereby there is an integration of development with local resources and skills.

### Re-evaluation and vision

The time at Llety'r Fwyalchen thus evolved as a dance between the two worlds of personal initiation and a community ecology. Occasionally the one world would inspire change in the other. Values began to change. My own political ecology became more human-centred. I came to learn that the essence of shamanic relationship is the human journey of love and caring. All ideas of the expulsion of humans from nature, to leave it as pristine, were thus long gone. But what then of domination? Of over-use and the acute lack of honouring of nature's processes? We began to formulate a more integrated approach to a wildland ecology, and at the same time, to untangle an ideology of the 'natural' forest.

The forest must be grazed to be natural. A sapling that has grown tall and never in its youth been munched, is as unnatural as any alien Forestry Commission plantling. Its form will never be natural. Tulley tubes may gain a few years growth, but the seedling will be weak and untested by wind or nibbling teeth. The vital growth spurts of young trees, shrubs and herbs all evolved in a battle against the forces of innumerable nibblers – aurochs and tarpan, wood bison, moose, two or three species of deer, boar and beaver, and as we were later to realise, mega-herbivores such as temperate forest elephants and rhinoceros

The primeval forest had a plethora of grazers, browsers, diggers and dammers – beaver created wetland, boar opened ground for seedling development, roe deer, red deer, forest pony and forest cattle kept the balance between glade and thicket, and the wolf kept them all moving around such that no one place was overgrazed. Where then our English Nature Reserve? The process has been emasculated, evolution interfered with, alien minds are in charge! Grazing and browsing, crushing and trampling, damming and flooding – they are integral to the beating heart of the forest.

So – why make the farmer redundant? If Llety'r Fwyalchen had such a rich flora and the patchwork maintained itself, this could be a model for all the valley woods and farms. The open moorland would remain fundamentally open and kept under lesser grazing pressure by removing sheep, introducing wild cattle and red deer and licensing culls for the local organic meat market. Beaver could be introduced to the wetter valley bottoms, and again, cattle farmed on the meadows. Ultimately, a grazing system based upon cattle would be robust enough to bring back the lynx and the eagle. Initially this could be done in one large area. The Rhinog hills, with no major roads running through, nor settlements in its heart, looked ideal.

A vision began to form that sought to maintain a balance of land-use within the National Park -the northern areas of Snowdon (the peak) and the Carneddau would remain under hopefully less intense grazing regimes as recreational areas for walkers, ramblers and climbers, and support the remnant populations of moorland birds; the southern areas of Cadair Idris and Coed y Brenin would remain as open hill country and commercial forestry, but hopefully with a more enlightened choice of indigenous species, but in the centre, at its heart, there was space for a re-wilding.

**Cultural shifts: from grass pasture to wood pasture**

The vision as articulated, may be fanciful on a cultural level, but is economically and ecologically feasible. Virtually all Welsh upland farmers are effectively paid by the state. Their inputs cost as much as they earn from their output, and any real income is courtesy of the European Union or the UK taxpayer. The average income on UK farms in the 1990s fell from £10,000 to £4000 in ten years, and in Wales that is likely to be significantly lower. In addition to agricultural subsidies, therefore, most farmers are on income-support. If the average farm size is 100 ha and a decent new forest covers 20,000 ha of wood pasture-mosaic then the cost of maintaining farmers as managers of such an area would be £800,000 per annum – which they are being paid now by the EU anyway! More realistically, double that income and twice the farm size would be required, with the farmers encouraged to supplement that income as managers with eco-tourism or craftwork. This sort of money is available and paid today either under the CAP or various Welsh stewardship schemes such as Tir Gofal to provide for marginal food production, land management, woodland creation, rural economic and social aid[9] .

There is no a priori reason why the same farmers could not be retrained to manage a regenerating forest, the introduction of former species, eco-holidays and conservation work camps, as well as shepherding small herds of prime organic beef (the last three activities confined to the buffer zones around a core area). There are models of silvo-pastoral systems in Portugal and the famed *dehesa* of Spain. Shepherding communities co-exist with bear, wolf and lynx in both these countries, as well as France (lynx in the Vosges), Germany (lynx in the Bavarian forest), Austria and Slovenia (bears in the alps), Italy (wolves in the Abruzzo National Park) and the great carnivore stronghold of Romania. The key to success is adequate wild prey, and effective guard dogs. We would not advocate the wolf and bear for Snowdonia, but there is certainly room for the lynx.

However, we cannot assume that the current level of social subsidy will persist under the free-trade dominated international market conditions that are only now beginning to make their presence felt. Food subsidy has somehow maintained political favour, as it apparently led to cheaper food – something the international market now purports to provide. Social subsidy for an uneconomic industry is less attractive – and there are adequate precedents, even in Wales, of whole communities, such as the coal miners in the south, having to face redundancy and adapt. Whether a social subsidy could be sold as maintenance of landscape, recreation, ecosystem restoration, and obligations under the EC Habitats Directive remains to be seen. Current Wales-based stewardship schemes exist (Tir Gofal, see later chapter on strategy), but have only a limited vision: primarily of maintenance of the social and environmental fabric as it currently exists, but with a marginal improvement in meadows and woodland.

But of course, the real barrier is not ecological or economic – it is cultural. Re-wilding is seen as a step backwards. Farmers have seen themselves as producers, an 'industry', and operate as self-employed small businessmen. They are fiercely independent, yet massively dependent! Few know their flowers or birds, though every field has a name and a history. Much as their heart might belong to a bygone Celtic poetry, their minds are focused by chapel and the protestant work ethic. At Harlech the highlight of the young farmers' year was the banger-racing fest. Chemicals are macho, organics are for dreamers. One successful neighbour of mine worked all hours but took two weeks in Florida before the lambing. The unsuccessful work all hours for little reward and severe stress is common with broken marriages, disaffected children and a rising suicide rate. If wildland advocates are to orchestrate changes in land use over wide areas such as the Rhinogs, they must address the disintegration of the present cultural framework. The repair work began for us at Cae Mabon, but such centers are far removed from the inclinations of most indigenous working people in North Wales.

**Cae Mabon and Rites of Passage**

When I first visited Muriau Gwynnion, Eric Maddern's home and centre for new approaches in education, located above the lake at Llanberis, it was to participate in a gathering of 14 men intent upon recreating something once integral to human psychology, and like our ancestral ecology, long lost in the past. As men there was still something within us that had never become adult, though we ranged from mid-thirties to mid-sixties in age. We had come to realise its absence when confronted with the task of guiding 14 year-olds through powerful initiations of vision quest and the scary ordeals of being alone with the mountain and forest. We all felt at ease with nature's wildness, but the initiations we were working with involved boys gathering together with men where their trials and quest were witnessed both by their peers and their mentors. Few of us had had the same opportunity when we were young. Or, in my case, that opportunity had been on a God-forsaken Scottish moor, with a Lee-Enfield rifle and a platoon of rain-soaked would-be commandos in the Army Cadet Force. I recall, on the long forced-march into headwind and sleet, glancing down-slope at some hawthorns amid which huddled dozens of exotic Waxwings, rare vagrants from the Russian boreal forest, and then cursing our intrepid leader. No time to stop.

*Stone and thatched round-house with central fire for storytelling*

In my misguided youth, I lost all poetry, all sensitivity to love, any hope of a truly open meeting with the opposite sex, and the natural landscape became simply a backdrop to the endless games of ego. Initiation there *had* been, but into the blind world of men separated from their women and from the land. At Cae Mabon, with my friends Eric Maddern and Iwan Brioc, we came to appreciate that the real barriers to realizing our visions were laid down in our uninitiated youth.

Meeting Eric and his co-conspirator, Alex Wildwood, provided an opportunity to work with two great pioneers in the enormous task of providing an initiation for young men into the mysteries of their divinity, their relationship to the land, to each other, and to women. In that first gathering in Eryri, we, as grown men, set ourselves the task of rediscovering 'initiation' – firstly, of who we truly were, and secondly, of how we relate. Each of us recounted our life history, its hopes and fears, trials and successes, and crucially, of what we felt was missing, or unhealed and unattained. Then each of us in turn left for a two-hour sojourn in the woods, and whilst away, the group devised a ritual, a piece of theatre, a task, perhaps even an ordeal, that would address our need. None of us would know what to expect. All were participants in the initiatory process, everyone a witness.

In some sense, we were developing a school of 'male mysteries'. We were already well aware of the pioneering work of our women friends and teachers in developing their own 'wild women' courses and initiations. The women were rediscovering their sisterhood and the deeper feminine power so long abandoned in the western world[8]. We had shared with them the sweat-lodge, the shamanic journeys and the Vision Quest process, and for some, even the fire-walks and earth-burials. Yet, something always divided us and eluded us, some level of meeting. It was as if the mysterious elements of deep feminine power that were being liberated bred a separation. As men, we had all learned a great deal from female teachers. Some men had suffered an oppressive guilt of maleness in a world devastated by the mentality of domination. We were now involved in an inner process of rebalancing, and in that the discovery and liberation of the feminine within ourselves.

At its heart, we had to learn to mother ourselves, to liberate ourselves from deeper psychic needs that inevitably prevented a truly equal meeting with woman. As long as we had not, we were still boys. I came to believe that without this inner liberation, whereby a level of acceptance, receptivity and trust in the essential abundance of life, men will always seek to dominate Nature, to control her, and even take out some unconscious revenge upon her. In some sense, it was as if their own mother had let them down – they were still her boys, for she had not taught them to find the mother within themselves, and this had bred a vicious resentment now projected out upon the earth itself, and all too frequently, on deep psychic levels, upon the women in their lives.

I know of no sociology to support these suppositions, other than the obvious correlation of such deep imbalances within 'western' materialist culture, and its continual rape of the earth's resources. I cannot prove by scientific means that rebalancing such disoriented psyches will lead to stability and satisfaction such that the goal of 'economic' growth and ever greater consumption is replaced with less damaging values. These things are perhaps beyond science – for how would it be possible to conduct appropriate surveys, isolate factors, and ultimately prove causes and effects? Science has always been limited when applied to the human psyche, and for that matter, the complexities of human health and the environment.

Eric Maddern's centre slowly became Cae Mabon, a cluster of low-impact dwellings in the forest clearing above Llyn Padarn, and below Elidir Fawr in the western mountains of Eryri. An Iron Age Roundhouse has been built for gatherings, music and storytelling, and over the years, Eric has added a straw-bale Hogan, and some nomadic tents. It is an ideal setting for gatherings now devoted to, 'creative expression, healing and spiritual wellbeing, traditional arts and crafts, environmental awareness, rites of passage and personal transformation'[10].

After 12 years of development, Cae Mabon produces a rich programme of events, with activities taking place most weeks of the year. In 2001, the John Muir Society held its third camp there for young people between the age of 16 and 24, exploring the deeper 'magic' of the wilderness. My friends, Iona Fredenburgh and Elisabeth Brooke held workshops on 'Plant Spirit Medicine' exploring the healing power of plants. There are workshops in 5-rhythms dance, masked drama and clowning, Zen, Yoga, and the perennial Rites of Passage for men. Cae Mabon has become a place where East and West meet, and where the ancient Celtic heart of Wales is being re-created.

In Eryri the wildwood is still a remnant. For it to return amid all the competing needs of a farming community, 'economic' forestry, and a tourist culture, the forest must first grow in the hearts of the people who make their living or find recreation in Snowdonia. This is the essential work of Cae Mabon, but as I put forward at the outset, I believe that elements of initiation are essential if we are to liberate ourselves from the fear and denial that drives our current relationship to nature, our culture's essential disrespect for the wild.

**New green shoots of change**

There are some new signs that our vision has not been entirely dismissed. The Countryside Council for Wales recently put out to tender a contract for ways of implementing a doubling of Snowdonia's natural forest cover. The National Trust recently bought three thousand acres on Snowdon and is committed to re-establishing woodland up to the natural tree line. The Trust also has an active interest in applying minimal intervention in large areas that it owns elsewhere – Ennerdale (see Chapter 5) and of large-scale habitat restoration in the fens of Cambridgeshire, for example. Coed Eryri lives on as a vision – now held by a motley assortment of educationalists, artists, writers, poets, sculptors and the occasional forest ecologist. It is an open and evolving concept that must embrace culture, community and ecology.

We are now more acutely aware that the temperate forest ecosystem evolved in the presence of the now extinct 'megafauna' and the forests of Snowdon in that former natural totality cannot now be restored. In all of my earlier work I had failed to appreciate the extent to which the mega-herbivores processed the forest – keeping it open and free of accumulated vegetation. Parts of Europe must have resembled the wooded savannah of Africa and been teeming with game. If we now wanted to restore the primeval ecology, we would need to

136

genetically manipulate some safari-park elephants and rhinos, re-create the tarpan and aurochs from their descendants, and import a few Asiatic lions!

What now the argument against alien species when Snowdonia's hills are covered in rhododendron and Sitka spruce, the streams colonized by Japanese knotweed and Himalayan balsam, large numbers of the planted oaks came from Poland and there have even been sightings of escaped panthers? Our benchmarks have been blown away. What we now create can hardly be justified by the narrow confines of a rather mutable ecological science.

It had been part of the Coed Eryri dream to bring back lost species. A small group of us began to think about beaver, and in 1992 in the company of Alan Featherstone and the more adventurous agents of Scottish Natural Heritage, we visited re-introduced colonies in Brittany. After 8 years of contemplation, the Scottish authorities have agreed to a re-introduction programme and there is a small scheme in Kent (see the later sections on species in Chapter 7). Beaver is a builder at the base of the ecosystem. In the animal medicine of North America it teaches the value of a strong foundation and industriousness. Ecologically beaver transforms habitat and provides a foundation for a web of diversity.

If there is success in Scotland, then we can ask again for Snowdonia. The bear and the wolf may one day return to Scotland, but for Wales, the dream is of eagle and lynx. Eagle is associated with poetic 'vision', and lynx is the 'keeper of secrets'. Only when there is a poetic vision to match the divinity of the Welsh language, and when the great mystery of nature is hallowed and not hounded by science, will we have the will to bring them back.

In Wales I learned that our soul and our future are intimately bound with the wild. As we rediscover ourselves, we shall safeguard and sanctify the wild places, and not out of some ecological sense of doom if we don't, but because of our love and expanded awareness. In the ancestral Celtic forest, I learned that the animals, trees and herbs held healing powers, the whole environment was alive with spirit, and there was no boundary between the human mind, the forest and the greater cosmos. I came to see that we had lost that consciousness and in so doing, we were moving toward the endgame of a planet-wide destruction of our very life support systems.

Coed Eryri taught me that there is no environment to be studied, managed, conserved or restored – the environment is not a thing, not an object, other than as a human concept. It has been a category mistake, something we have separated from ourselves, set apart from other categorized things, such as 'the economy', from industry, or business. As such it will always come second, as something we must protect while getting on with what really matters now that 'the economy' has become God.

The major part of Coed Eryri's work now lies in the projects at Cae Mabon: to apprehend the truth that we are a part of nature, to rediscover the rituals of appreciation and the joys of reconnection. But the vision is held and will one day help to integrate all of the disparate workings of foresters and nature conservationists who strive gradually to enhance the wildwood of Eryri.

However, immediately to the south of the Rhinogydd, in the North Cambrians, there are signs that 'wildwoods' and the concept of core-areas (see Chapter 5 on the work of the Land Use Policy Group) are gaining local advocates, and this may yet revitalize proposals for the Rhinogydd, which has the advantage of a cluster of 'public' lands in the form of Forest Enterprise holdings and National Trust land in the south-east corner, and one or two large estates in the center and north. These may yet provide focal points for management of wild areas with the introduction of deer, ponies and wild cattle; the conversion of plantations and regeneration of upland vegetation.

To be whole, we must be able to experience wholeness. To be able to experience wholeness, we must be whole. It is a paradox. The soul-less will enter the wildwood and experience their soul-less-ness, it will be an empty place. But to those just awakening, the forest will sing the song of awakening. And to the weary and humble, it will offer solace and strengthening. And to the joyful and playful, the questers and explorers, it is a gateway to the stars.

# The Healing Forest

In an ancient past the forest was not a place to visit. It was not separate from daily life, and in that time before civilisation, our language would have had no word that categorised nature as other than ourselves. The earth beneath our feet merged imperceptibly into the land of rivers and mountains, swamps and grasslands, open areas and thickets. It was the dwelling place and provided food, clothing, and shelter. It was *mother*, rather than *other*. Only gradually, as man settled into agriculture, did the forests recede to be named as something beyond our normal life, though they remained as providers of game and timber. The medieval English word 'forest' did not necessarily imply trees but referred to an area designated as hunting reserve. It has its linguistic roots in the Latin for 'outside'.

It is as if the outside began to shrink, first as humans settled and cities grew, and then finally as the wild remnants of forest became 'royal' preserves. A dichotomy of town and country, civil and wild, artifice and nature gradually led to a duality of concept: nature and the natural, set apart from man and the man-made, and where once the divine had permeated everything, new religions evolved that would confine it to one realm, that of the human. Gradually the old ceremonial connections to wild nature were demonised, and those that lived beyond the boundary of the civil world – the *pagans* (literally, those outside who had no protection), and the *heathen* (literally, those who lived on the heath) were then classified as without God.

Curiously, our eventual word for that outside wildness *nature* and *natural* – which were first used in the 13$^{th}$ Century and derived from Old French, having their origin in the Latin, *Natura* – birth, and were first used in relation to bodily processes and restorative powers of the body, and later as innate character and disposition (about 1380), and as *human nature* in 1526, only later, in 1660 as meaning the material world, its features and products (Chambers Etymological Dictionary). Thus have we termed the wild 'that which gave birth'. Had we not substituted the Latin for the ancient Scandinavian and Germanic 'birth', we would conceptually refer to our surroundings as 'the birther' and be rather closer to our divine mother!

It is as if we are only half-emerged from the religious paranoia of the past – where pagans and heathens were slaughtered not only as ungodly, but as sub-human – the words and concepts live on in mass consciousness, and the habitual assumption remains, that the divine, though one spirit, only exists within the human heart. It is this that must be healed. We in the West are beginning in this last century to emerge fully from the old fears, such that the one-spirit is seen to pervade all of life, something that many other cultures did not lose sight of.

At least, those who do acknowledge spiritual realities are making this transition. Others have yet to emerge from the later stages of our cultural history where scientific modernism took the separation a stage further – neither nature nor man presupposed a divinity, and hence what man willed and desired became central. Modern man looks to the forest as a resource. Modern forestry sees itself as delivering multi-purpose public goods in the market economy – recreation, wildlife conservation, and landscape quality as well as marketable timber.

Thus have forests shifted in meaning according to the culture of the times. They have become a metaphor and an icon for that which lies outside. At times a place of dark threats and a refuge for bandits, outlaws and dangerous animals, places with special laws to protect the privilege of royal hunting grounds, and now in recent times, as the planet faces a crisis of climate change, human population explosion, soil loss and water scarcity, the restoration of forests has become a major tool for the protection of life-sustaining ecosystems. And discernible as the Millennium turned, an icon for the restoration of a deeper thing lost, a sense of wholeness.

In Genet's poetic story '*The Man Who Planted Trees*', a barren land is restored to fruitfulness by the human sower, slowly, selflessly, with an eye to future generations. As the trees come, the dry winds cease, the dust settles, and the mountain streams begin to flow again. Flowers and butterflies and birdsong return to the villages, and the human soul begins to smile and hold hope for the future. It is more than metaphor – the trees carry a living power that impacts the human psyche. By their presence, their growth, their strength, their different characters, as well as the life that they foster about them, they imbue the human psyche, as if quiet teachers by example. In James Redman's world bestselling mystical novel '*The Celestine Prophecy*', the presence of old trees, with their massive girth, is held almost as a prerequisite for the wholeness of the land and the happiness of people.

This relationship is nowhere better articulated than in the practical conservation work spearheaded by Trees for Life in Scotland, but it also surfaced in unexpected form in the work of government agencies. The Forestry Commission in Scotland was already engaged upon restoration of the ancient Caledonian pine forests, and became Alan Watson Featherstone's very supportive ally.

In England and Wales, with forest cover long reduced to a paltry few percent of its former glory, the Forestry Commission had, until recently, become a by-word for crass economic mass production and the alien destruction of treasured upland landscapes. In the past century forests had become ugly. For many who value the aesthetic of landscape and wild places, plantation forests were a scar upon that land. Campaigns were mounted to limit the impact upon wildlife and tourism, and to educate city-dwellers into what should be or could be in their place. Hitherto, nature had only ever been beautiful – and it was doubtless the commercial 'forest' that led the realisation that human intervention in nature when on a large scale and devoid of feeling could be such a soul-less enterprise. In the 21<sup>st</sup> century, however, we are witnessing a startling rebirth. Its antecedents were in the late 1980s and early 1990s – BANC caught the shift in consciousness with its conference, '*21<sup>st</sup> Century Forests*': conservationists and foresters were beginning to bring beauty back into the landscape.

There is now a discernible movement toward a new perception of the forest as healer of the wounds inflicted by urban and industrial civilisation's ugliness. In the early 1980s the Countryside Commission embarked upon a remarkable programme of 'Community Forests' – twelve areas, each of the order of 100,000 ha being targeted, and each within easy travelling of large centres of population and urban dereliction, such as Newcastle – the Great Northern Forest; Swindon: the Great Western Forest; East London: Thames Chase Forest; Bristol: the Forest of Avon. The idea also sparked the Scottish Lowland Forest between Edinburgh and Glasgow. These 'forests' would aim to create new woodland at about 40% overall cover in a patchwork of agriculture and villages on the edge of the urban areas. Forest development offices were set up and staffed, with cooperation from Local Authorities, local businesses, wildlife and community groups. Each forest would have an identity, with the communities contributing toward fund-raising, planting and educational work. Within this concept, the arts, such as sculpture, music, poetry and theatre added meaning to the endeavour, and ancient crafts, such as hurdle making and charcoal production were re-activated. Whether articulated or not, the underlying ethos was of a forest as a potential healing experience. Since its inception, the idea has generated further initiatives that now include 'urban forests' that penetrate the city, for example, in Cardiff and Belfast, and Urban Forestry Unit in Birmingham and a large New National Forest in the English Midlands.

However, the conception of the forest as a healing power is ancient knowledge, and what has surfaced now is perhaps an unconscious rediscovery of that force. For millennia the forest has been a source of healing herbs and medicine. In our modern culture we tend to think of that healing in terms only of medicinal effects: some herbs have healing properties, and once discovered, they can be harvested, perhaps even processed to extract the 'active' ingredient, and then administered. But this is to limit our understanding to those areas accessible to science. Scratch even the most scientifically qualified medical herbalist of today, and you may still find a deeper understanding, often deliberately hidden. Talk, however, to a Druid practitioner – and several I have known have also acquired their Bachelor of Sciences in medical herbalism, and the deeper picture emerges of the forest and its denizens as part of a greater spiritual reality. Each individual herb may cure this or that ailment – and doubtless there are active ingredients which can be extracted, but the place of that herb in the forest, and its intimate relationship to the broader healing not just of physical, but emotional and spiritual malaise, is a matter not of some accident of evolution, but of deep process and design.

To the Druid each plant has a spiritual place in a community of spirit that includes humans as part of the forest – though now somewhat lost in their wanderings from the ancient home. This extended reality stretches to the very vastness of our cosmos. Our current science is not entirely ignorant of this: we know that the sun is the source of all life in the forest, but we measure only the rays of its electromagnetic spectrum. We know that without its gravitational field, we would all be lost in space – but it is a mathematical belonging, without gratitude. And the vibrant life around us, with its millions of years of evolution, is due not to spirit, but to the biochemical processes of photosynthesis. The diverse beauty, the song of the forest, the panoply of anemone and orchid – all the soul-less consequence of genetic mechanism! The scientific world-view elevates the mechanism as the most meaningful reality, and although the more humble would then say this does not denigrate what may lie beyond science, they still collude in the separation.

## Science as separation

We understand the superficial consequences of the relationships of plant and animal life to each other, to the geosphere and to the solar system as ecological or physiological process and evolutionary history, but that is to stay on the surface of the reality. Superficially, we know that the heart of our planetary system is the sun – without its rays there would be no life on this Earth. Our sun, as a star, has a stellar life measured in billions of years, and our own evolution is thus bound to that lifetime. We also know that the sun is part of a larger galactic system and as such, part of a galactic lifecycle. Just as the Earth has rhythms as part of its relationship to the sun, so the sun has rhythms as part of the galaxy.

If we stay focussed on the physical levels of reality at the current limits of science, then we cannot explore further the intricate relationship that plants have to the sun, our planetary system, and indeed, the galaxy beyond. One day, but perhaps not soon, there will be instruments sensitive enough to reveal to ordinary eyes the complex web of energetic relationships. Objective science could then begin its exploration. Though, if we were to dwell in depth upon the scientific endeavours at the boundary of current knowledge, we would see that the boundary is always in a state of flux, and it would be there on the boundary, as always, that the accepted knowledge of the future would now be evident. And, as always, there is resistance to that future knowledge – a phenomenon I can only describe as a boundary effect, as if some self-erected social fence, electrified by fear, guards the periphery.

Sociologists of science have long recognised that what grows as 'knowledge' is socially constructed and influenced by political and economic interests. In Barry Barnes' analysis '*Interests and the Growth of Knowledge*', even the apparent objective world of mathematics and geometry is not immune – how much more so then the complex world of fundamental physics with its huge expenditures and implications for weapons technology and the competitive economy? The scientific world view is like a powerful microscope – it reveals structures we would otherwise not see, and relationships that have been productive of the most amazing technology and apparent mastery of nature. But take one simple step back from the microscope, and we would see that a bipedal ape, an animal with complex instincts and intelligence, is what is looking down the tube. That human world, of concepts and collusions, is also part of the process of science. It is ongoing and ever changing. The ultimate science is to gain knowledge of that process, but few make the inquiry! And again, there is great resistance to that particular area of self-knowledge! Huge resources are devoted to the microscopic quest because of the rewards attendant upon developing technology, then to be wielded by the cleverness that devised and financed the quest. It is not a quest for self-knowledge but poses as it seeks nobility of purpose, as a quest for ultimate reality, the nature of nature itself. Noble purpose, if it ever existed, has long been swamped by the instincts of manipulation and control - of enemies tribal or natural.

It would take a work of great scholarship to lay bare the scientific quest as political and even psychological process and sadly, in my lack of such scholarship, I can provide little in the way of signposts. I trust, however, that one day, science as self-knowledge will provide the all-encompassing language of a unified reality. Objective science still seeks such a unified theory of every force that moves the universe – and of course, it is sought 'outside' as measurement of something we can all agree on, or at least, the majority of scientists can agree on. But whatever reality is there described, it cannot be the whole. The ape that peers down the tube, has another reality behind the eye – an immense world of poetry and song, art and beauty, love and the struggle to love, as well as a world of shadows, of fear and loathing, histories with resentment, jealousy and anger, and the dark will to dominate, humiliate and abuse. The shadow as often directs the microscope as any nobler purpose, and for the most part, unacknowledged.

If science has been a separation – a looking 'outside' of ourselves, and with an ulterior motive of manipulation, then in a curious sense, that medieval 'forest', that which lies without, is what science has all the while been looking at. The 'forest' has been a symbol for the natural world that is a separate reality, to be studied and manipulated. Yet now something new is happening. Our sense of loss and our love for the trees and wild places has opened us to the power of that which appears to lie outside, where in that openness, we let something *in*, something of the healing power that is nature, and it inspires us, it awakens the children to joy, to art, music, dance and poetry, and it awakens the child in the adult to awe and natural majesty.

That the forest has this dimension to its healing is evident even within our current material culture. A perusal of the many brochures for the Community and City Forests, and attendance at the art, sculpture, poetry and drama events instigated by their programmes will readily display a sense that the forest has come to represent the healing power of wild nature from which an urbanised man has become separated. It is as if the wholeness of the forest itself has the power to recreate wholeness within the human spirit. In the forest that is outside of our selves, there is no judgement, no right and wrong that frets out vitality, and where trees are old, where the process of death and decay is evident, there is an obvious sacredness.

## The soul's healing

Not all science has been concerned with the outside. In the last century science as 'psychology' began to explore the world of the 'unconscious', finding its most erudite expression in Carl Jung's '*Modern man in search of the soul'* and the development of humanistic psychologist (as opposed to 'behavioural' psychologists - those regular scientists still focussed upon the apparently objective realities of mammalian physiology and cognition for all manner of managerial purposes). This study of man's inner world built upon the psychotherapeutic beginnings of Freud and began to elaborate the patterns of both the individual and collective mind. What started as an attempt by 'doctors' to heal the emotionally dysfunctional, developed into a broader and more positive view of the psyche as possessing a will to 'individuate' and grow.

Jung's lineage of psychotherapy works primarily with verbal expression – counselling and analysis, and where dreams and symbols have come to figure strongly in the landscape of the mind. It is nevertheless still a world for the healing of trauma – from childhood abuse, rape, violence, and oppression in its grossest form, to the more subtle worlds of dominance and hierarchy. In its most developed, it has a purpose in the healing beyond trauma – as the rebirth of the individual soul in its power to love and to participate creatively in the social world.

In its early days, psychotherapy suffered as any other scientific endeavour from social and political interests. Wilhelm Reich, a student of Freud, was the first to break from a system that he saw not as healing, but simply patching the damage without addressing the very social forces that created that damage. Reich's critique went to the heart of the 19th century inheritance that Freud had attempted to work with – the repression of sexuality, but addressed it not with mental palliative, but with the energetic life-force of the primal body. Through the healing power of touch, deep tissue massage and bodywork Reich discovered that the stored memory of the mind, with its consequent resentments and other negativities, was mirrored by stored energy in postures 'held' by the body. If these energies were released in the body, there was feedback to the mind, and vice-versa. He went on to link disturbances in energy flow to the onset of diseases such as cancer, and interestingly, to take up the microscope as an aid to studying this dysfunction at a cellular level. His 'biopathy' was the final straw for a scientific community not able to extend itself to someone who moved from psycho-analysis (then desperately keen to garner an image of scientific credibility), to body-work (a taboo area in middle-class middle Europe of the time), to political critique (of the rising fascist societies and their repressive industrial mentality), and eventually, to biology and the pathology of cells.

Reich's studies of 'energy flow' are widely accepted and respected by 'hands-on' healing professionals working with the human body, movement and creative expression. However, he extended his work to environmental energies that he termed 'orgone' – not separated from the energies at work in the human body, but with great influence upon it. He began construction of devices to harness these energies for healing – so called 'orgone accumulators', for which remarkable results were claimed among terminally ill cancer patients – not of 'cures' as such, for the body's physiology was not able to cope with the flux of dead cancer cells, but of a heightened sense of wellbeing before death. In the 1950s, having relocated to America, he was prosecuted for fraud and died a broken and paranoid man in a US prison. Much of his work on human biopathy disappeared. His research on the manipulation of environmental energy flows, in which he claimed the ability to induce rainfall, was to be buried with him 'until such time as humanity was mature enough to handle the knowledge'.

Reich's work at the outset was that of a pioneering genius, and it may have ended in the ramblings of a persecuted crank – but there was always a simple method to test his work: repeat it with an open mind. This did not happen with the later work when the scientific community closed ranks against him. It is a fate that many pioneers faced, only for time to prove their truth, and there may yet be a resurfacing of Reich's work.

The studies of Freud, Jung, Reich and others, utilising some elements of the scientific method – cataloguing and case studies, the search for patterns and correlations of cause and effect - though not readily amenable to experimental methods, have been among the major developments of 'western' culture. The 'unconscious' mind has been mapped and related to organ dysfunction and disease, psychological stress and spiritual growth. Our concept of 'soul' has expanded in the last fifty years, as has our concept of personal individuality.

However, our approach to psychological damage as 'soul' damage (from the Greek *psyche,* the soul) is still compartmentalised and not yet integrated with medical science. The prevalent paradigm still views the physical body as a mechanical system prone to invasions or breakdowns. Almost every doctor's surgery now has access to counsellors and therapists and the relationship of psychological stress to illness is well appreciated, but the linkage is usually through the presentation of physical symptoms, and the motivation largely that of performance management. If an individual wishes to pursue the healing of psyche at a deeper level, then he or she must enter the private realm of 'therapist' and client. Society as a whole has no motivation to help in that quest.

Once again, there is much in the language: *therapist* in its Greek origin means one who administers healing, and in that ancient time had connotations of 'giving the Gods their due'. We live now on the threshold of a unifying world view. The frontiers of physics have led to the boundary of scientific method where the presence of the human as well as the perceptions of the human mind are clearly seen as both affecting as well as defining the realities that would be described. But the boundary is not yet crossed. Modern medicine still holds to a largely mechanistic world view, though it has bridges not only to psychotherapy, but also to the hitherto spurned worlds of homeopathy, developed in the west, and acupuncture of the ancient east.

It is here, in the interweaving currents of modern and 'complementary' or 'holistic' medicine that we may find a small bridge to a future more inclusive science. My problem with trying to build such a bridge across the realities of current day medical practice to the realm of soul and its connection to nature, is that even humanistic psychology has its perceptual limits and compartments. Psychologists still deal with the human entity as if it were a bounded individual. Human consciousness is perceived as residing totally within the individual and presumed to reside at some relevant bodily level. Current favourite for its location is the 'brain', but that has not always been so – other cultures having presumed a more gut-level location. Certainly, studies of brain damage will readily locate functions of the mind in particular regions, but this is about as relevant as trying to locate the orchestra one listens to on the radio within the circuits of the little electronic box on the windowsill. If you damage particular components of the receiver, the music will distort. And if elements of the orchestra are missing, there is no symphony.

It is the same with the plants and animals of the forest. Each species exists within an orchestra of form that goes beyond the mere physical. There is a symphony that is playing beyond the human ear. In our long departure from the forest, our culture has lost the words to describe it. For such language we can turn to other cultures that have not wandered so far from that which birthed them. Little more than a hundred years ago, native peoples were hunted as animals of the forest by the Victorian products of a scientific education. In Southern Africa, tourists could apply for licenses to hunt bush-men. In the American west, we are now only too aware of the massacres fuelled by 'civilised' man's view of the natives as sub-human. Yet now, there is a turning. For the past twenty years, Native American teachers have been travelling to Europe to impart their knowledge. Laurens Van der Post retrieved something of the divine from the lost world of the Kalahari bushmen.

In their teachings, native peoples have many naiveties of perception that can lead us to dismiss everything they perceive. They know little of the chemistry of photosynthesis, or history of the ice-ages. But in other respects, they have developed techniques of perception that far outstrip our limited scientific methods and the world view spawned thereof. Where we have made outer realities our journey ground, they have voyaged inward. These journeys inform

146

their world and language and have built a consistent body of knowledge. They have tuned the receiver inside to finer frequencies, and above all, they have been willing to listen to the whole orchestra.

In all of these different cultural assemblages – with their varying myths of creation, causality, purpose, perception of disease, and techniques of 'medicine', there is one common factor – a perception of spirit. Every being, human, animal, plant, mountain, river and even stone and crystal, exists within a world of spirit. The sun is not just a heating and lighting unit – it is grandfather to some, father or mother to others. The earth is not simply soil and rock, but fertile mother, sentient, loving and at times, fiercely dark in lessons to her errant offspring. In our past and too often present arrogances, we have pretended to know better – yet in even our science, we know there to be truths in these perceptions. We are quite comfortable in acknowledging apes as our ancestors, but not frogs. And though we are made of ancestral dust and water, not without the sun could we have been birthed. We just don't celebrate these facts. We take them for granted. That is to say, there is no gratitude.

Native peoples have not come to hold these worldviews from belief – a common misperception – though they may now be maintained as such in what is left of the original communities. The fine tuning has led to direct *perception*. It is Western civil society that has built a world of belief, mediated by priesthoods, whilst 'reality' is honoured largely as economy, commerce, and warfare. Into the world of 'belief' are projected images of God and human purpose. Those who, within this material culture, have any direct experience of God, are regarded as 'mystics' and for the most part ignored, though historically often cruelly persecuted, and at strangely pivotal points, embraced as the harbingers of great social change. In societies where direct experience of the divine presence is fostered as the norm, there are no histories of messiahs or redeemers. The world of the divine spirit as experienced by native peoples is a world where the divine and the human are not separated anymore than father and son, or mother and daughter are separated. The creative power is not projected *beyond* nature – it resides within nature, and is *represented* by the sun, the moon, the ocean, the earth and the forest.

For civilised man, who has broken free from nature, who has come to see the human story as an evolving dominance, free from her cycles of scarcity as well as abundance, there has evolved a hubris, a sense of liberation by the power of intellect and technology, and hence, where gratitude lies is in what we have become grateful for. How many can now feel the simple gratitude to be alive, to be bathed in the sun and surrounded by the miracle that is consciousness and life? With such gratitude comes celebration and what the civilised have dubbed 'worship'. Thus the Druid is seen as 'worshipping' the sun, or the oak, and 'believing' in this or that element of a religion. In truth, the Druid is no more than a person dedicated to celebrating the great mystery that is the forest, or showing gratitude and organising celebration. Belief may have crept in, empty ritual may have resulted, appreciation of the magic that is ordinary life may

147

have turned even long ago to sorcery and the manipulation of other minds, but fundamentally, the medicine quest in Celtic times, and in the Native American teachings, was and is about honouring our deepest nature, which is love, and realising the natural world that surrounds shares in that deeper nature as surely as our mother and father share the same blood

The so-called primitive human psyche knows from whence it has come, and that its brothers and sisters live in the same forest. And for the individual, redemption is not a promised land beyond the boundary of this life, it exists only in the here and now, the present moment of the very present forest. If one looks to the writings of Native American teachers, such as Jamie Sams, that redemption is about love in the face of all of the human frailties that are not love. It is the same story as that of civil society, but with one major difference: nature is an ally not an enemy.


**Wandering from the garden**

Our own civilisation's somewhat jaded creation myth has us wandering from the 'garden' of our innocence. After a birthing process for the human psyche that has taken several million years to produce our outer form, and about 250,000 years to produce the first semblance of language, art and craft, all within the cradle of an intact forest, we have in the short biological time of only 8000 years created an alternative reality for human existence – the civilisation that is the city, the state, the functional entity now so distant from the wild – a world where nature takes second place and the evolution of the human is proposed as an unfolding of purely human concepts and values. Whether conceived as the highest of arts, craft, science, poetry, or literature, these ultimately revolve around the freedom of the human soul from the oppression of nature both outside of itself, and within.

There has always been that dark  soul, the oppression within – our supposed animal inheritance, the baser instincts of violence, greed and the will to power, hierarchy, injustice, and enslavement. Against this unfolding drama, the natural world has become merely a stage, and very much taken for granted, at least in the west, where part of the drama has been the will to conquer nature in all its irritating and dangerous intrusions upon that human story. We have been swift to consign these darker elements of ourselves to the animal realm – yet any observation of nature 'red in tooth and claw' will find a curious calm even amid the most intense of predatorial chases. There is no malice in nature, and no mercy either. Aggression may be common among mammals, but seldom in the chase: it is primarily a dance of territory and sexual display, a fire that flares up and is gone. Only the human soul has the qualities of resentment and hatred that have evolved such a formidable degree of intra-specific killing. With our clever technology and the liberating science of the past two hundred years, we now stand on the threshold, not of communicating with the stars, but of annihilating all sentient life on the planet. Thus far have we wandered, and so great is the need for healing.

## Denial of the shadows

On a personal level, the conscious psyche is always afraid to confront the shadow side of itself and the most powerful way to avoid the shadow is to deny its existence. As long as the psyche is not whole, it will function in a disturbed way. The person so afflicted holds firm to certain views and values and judges their opposites as seen in others very harshly. In truth, those opposites exist in the depth of the person perceiving and reacting to them, but pushed down deep and denied as part of that particular human. A person may hold a particular image of themselves – as upright, morally correct, pure, honest, just and generous, but so often their actual behaviour contradicts and they may even when confronted not see themselves as they are. The unconscious part of the psyche always has more power than the conscious and if there is any deep contradiction, it ultimately sabotages the self-image.

As nations are made up of individuals, and individual unconsciousness relates to others just as readily as conscious mind, then denial also works on a collective level of nations and cultures. We are living, I would contend, at a time of deep cultural 'denial'. It is not possible for 'western' societies to face a fundamental reality of their structure. Our culture is founded upon the principle of freedom of the individual and expressed as representative democracy. This is its conscious face and its conscious will is directed to upholding that freedom. It is essentially 'humanistic' rather than theistic, and focuses upon the rights of the 'individual' to freely choose their path in society, though there are also obligations. The economy is then supposedly structured by this freedom and choice and presumed by theoreticians to be the by-product of a myriad individual decisions within the market-place.

Western culture is not entirely material and consumerist – there is also an ethos relating to freedom of individual expression that works through an education freely available to all and in which a person may bring out the best of their creativity and strengths. In more recent decades, there has evolved the essentially western concept of individual 'growth', a kind of soul-maturity where the individual becomes ever more conscious of motivation and pattern and strives to become a better more loving human being.

On an historical level this ideology of individual freedom experienced a great rebirth in the 1700s when individual human rights were embodied in laws and institutions following the French revolution and the founding of the United States of America. Prior to that was a long transition from tribal consciousness, through settled agricultural hierarchies in city states – varyingly theistic and at times, as in ancient Greece, partly humanistic; then through the nation states with their power structures of 'royalty' and 'church', to the final liberation of individuals in the pursuit of 'freedom'.

In all of this evolution, there has been a shadow. In the great struggles for liberty and humanity, supposed opposites, such as the 'royals', and the later 'counter-revolutionaries' were shown no brotherly love, but cruelty and execution. In the American 'lands of the free', native peoples were deceived and dispossessed, and finally hunted and slaughtered to make way for settlers.

However, this is the 'Western' story. In the East, ideological evolution took a different route, more fundamentally theistic, retaining hierarchies of priests or mediators into modern times, as in Islam and Hindu cultures, or embracing the dissolution of the 'individual' as in the Buddhist traditions. In the eastern ideologies, the individual is subsumed not into the State, but into the 'godhead' and becomes an instrument of divine will. In Islamic culture, that divine will could be warlike and imperialist (and was largely accessed through mediating priests), whereas in Buddhist culture it was introspective and compassionate, and accessed through personal experience. There were no Buddhist imperialists.

We could explore many aspects of the collective psyche and its shadow within these cultures, but what is evident in the gradual evolution of *global* consciousness is the polarity that has emerged over the past two thousand years as represented by the eventual evolution of 'the West' and 'the East' as superpowers. The polarity has not been fixed. Ideas have flowed between both poles and been taken up in powerful ways. In the 1700s the liberation ideologies of the West penetrated the East – in three hundred years the process has advanced considerably, with Japan, Russia, and finally China embracing western humanistic ideology. Buddhist ideas and practice have penetrated western cultures, but in a more 'underground' way.

We could extend this analysis, but we are here concerned to identify deep currents of a global malaise, and we need at this stage to lay a context for that part of human consciousness that is caught up in a process of evolutionary change, a process that generates great stresses within the collective psyche and over which the average individual has little conscious control. These forces have enormous destructive and disruptive power. If we are to engage upon *any* local or global endeavour of ecological restoration, they have to be addressed. It is the deepest human affliction, the deepest level of soul disturbance, and the greatest healing crisis.

As I write this, the leaders of the 'Western' world have begun what they call the first $21^{st}$ century war, and what may become a 'world war'. In a sense , it is already that – a global phenomenon, with global 'terrorist' networks and global alliances to combat them. And while the western leaders do their utmost to disclaim that it is a clash of civilisations and not a 'war on Islam', millions of 'eastern' people perceive it as exactly that.

Conservationists, meanwhile, plant trees, protect butterflies, recreate flower-rich meadows. A wacky geneticist hunts for mammoth remains in the Siberian wastes. Zoos build up their Asiatic lions and Amur leopards. Climate Care restores a few hundred hectares of Madagascan forest and thereby soaks up a few tonnes of an industrial conglomerate's carbon emissions. Everyone hopes the war will end and they can get on with restoring the planet. It appears the issues are not related - that conservation is a peacetime activity and a luxury of the rich. Yet what happens on a global level impacts every local initiative. Restoration of the earth requires a massive commitment of resources and an international focus far greater than any world war. And the consequences of delay could far outweigh the human losses directly consequent on the conflict. Where then is the relationship, the connection between global conflict of civilisations and the healing power of nature?

We come to address these questions at the apotheosis of a western culture that has systematically ostracised the soul from daily life. Soulfulness has no expression in the normal business world. Homes and workplaces struggle to maintain a quality of soul in architecture and building, but everywhere, from offices and airport terminals, sprawling housing estates and motorways, we are afflicted by a built environment without soul. People who are born and grow up in these urban environments have little contact with the natural cycles that sustain them. There is born a culture of consumerism without depth that spawns its global icons of fast food and cinematic entertainment. And just as its most obvious global element is the Hollywood film, it is founded on fantasy: the freedom of the few enslaves millions in mindless repetitive 'jobs' at minimal wages who then hunger to escape into some consumer paradise; but above all, it is not sustainable, it is slowly destroying the very ecosystems that support it.

There has always been a 'western' shadow culture. It has now reached such massive proportions that it can no longer be denied. One in ten citizens will suffer debilitating mental illness. Suicide is the biggest killer of young men. Narcotic drugs are so prevalent that the United States devotes billions of dollars to a 'war' on supply. The medical use of anti-depressant drugs is a normal feature of urban life, especially among woman. Violence to women and abuse of children is endemic. Obesity, especially in young children is a 'western' disease that is now spreading to Russia and even China. In Southern Africa seven million people will die of AIDS by 2010 and life expectancy will drop to 41 years. There is a clear relationship between the AIDS epidemic in Africa and the fragmentation of communities, migration of males to find work, and consequent breakdown of social and sexual mores. The western model of economic growth, global markets and freedom of choice is built upon economic slavery and misery in large parts of the newly industrialising world, and upon a great deal of social distress and poverty within the old industrialised nations. For the less intelligent and socially disadvantaged, there is no real choice but to work in dull, repetitive jobs with some small hope that by their own economic struggle, they may make life better for their children. It may take some little more time for these masses to make the realisation that almost all ecologists now know – that the global ecosystem will not support any significant increase in the number of people now enjoying what has become known as the western 'standard of living'.

If we took even the most basic standard – that of living just above the poverty line in England today and extrapolated that to the populations of Russia, India, China, Brazil and Indonesia – countries that perhaps *do* have the resources to attain those levels, the global climate would be destabilised, and food and water resources would be compromised. Large areas of the globe, particularly Africa, simply do not have the natural resources to support such growth.

Some may argue, (as Lomborg has done in his widely publicised book '*the Skeptical Environmentalist*), that technological change and market forces will ensure that such future growth is based upon renewable energy systems and non-polluting technology, and that even climate change brings both pluses as well as minuses for food production and water resources. Few informed scientists agree, and especially not those of the UN scientific committees to the Climate Convention. The problem is that there is too much inertia within the system – certainly the technology exists, but even in the rich West, it is not being deployed. The system of production as it now stands has too many vested interests for it to embrace the initially expensive option of paying for the current 'externalities' of production – the cost of pollution. There is thus now a growing attempt to enlist scientists in a denial of the problem.

The ecological issue is one great shadow of western consumerist culture that at least has an open discourse. There is another not so easily discerned: wherever individual freedom has been espoused and fought for against the repressions of the old order ( of church and king ), the resultant 'brotherhood' has erected some of the most repressive of State regimes where the new social order has sought to extinguish the creative freedom of the newly liberated individual. The 'Aquarian Age' began with the scientific and cultural revolutions of the late 18<sup>th</sup> Century, but led to the great 'Aquarian' social enterprises of Hitler, Stalin, Pol Pot, and Mao Tse Tung. Individual thought and freedom of expression were ruthlessly suppressed in the name of the greater social good. The humanistic quest had lost contact with its soul – that is, the totality of its being. In astrological terms, the psyche had polarised toward Aquarian values, whilst reacting against its opposite, which is Leo, the symbol for individual will and creative self-expression.

The western psyche now stands victorious, having fought in the name of individual freedom *against* Hitler and other totalitarian States, having gone through the 'Cold War' with eventual success, and finally it looks on expectantly at the commercialisation of China. But the shadow is as active as ever – and there can be no peace until it is healed. Shadows are visible only when highlighted by polarities. No sooner have the Aquarian extremists been dealt with, than Islamic fundamentalism raises its head. Its terror is like a fierce fire that threatens to consume 'western' civilisation – though it is in fact rather narrowly targeted upon the hegemonic aspect of control and power symbolised

152

by the USA. The 'alliance' against 'terrorism' is an alliance of all of those states, including many Islamic, who support and gain from not just American leadership, but the whole 'western' economic superstructure. Sadly, the concerted focus upon the fire means few will look at the shadows cast by its light. The shadow is of a humanity that has embraced consumerism and the 'free market' and made it God above everything, above love, above community, and suicidally above the health of the natural ecosystems that support human life.

As I intimated earlier, the human psyche in wandering so far from nature, has concocted a world where man is 'god', where it is the creations of technology that feed and clothe him, protect him from the winter, from flood and storm, parasite and disease, and where he may strut and compete for his sense of fulfilment in a marketplace of goods and services. In the world of business, the dominant force in a global culture, he has abandoned even the ethics by which, in his personal world, he would otherwise live. That there can be special funds (which are but a fraction of normal funds) that can be termed 'ethical and environmentally sound investment' is testament to the betrayal of humanity inherent in the normal practice of business.

That the western psyche is sick, disturbed and dangerous cannot be admitted. That is the force of denial. Thus it is that the superpower states can, over fifty years, amass enough explosive power, estimated at 5 tonnes of TNT for every man, woman and child of the planet, to annihilate civilisation, and all in an ideology of 'freedom' that would sacrifice itself rather than surrender. Similarly, dangerous technologies such as nuclear generated electricity were developed in secrecy because it was well anticipated that the public would not necessarily share the faith that such technology could be controlled by the experts. Before Chernobyl, there was denial that reactors could melt down. After Chernobyl the denial was narrowed to only 'western' reactors which could not melt down.

It cannot be faced that there is not enough of a global resource to sustain western societies, and also it cannot be faced that the market can never deliver global equity.

Rather uncharacteristically and to its great credit, western science has not colluded with the environmental denial – though it has done with few exceptions in relation to nuclear weapons and nuclear reactors.

All is not however hopeless. That the emperor has no clothes was realised by many in the early 1970s and grew to a mass movement by the mid-1980s. What was an initial movement of resistance against soul-less, centralised and dangerous technology, symbolised by nuclear power, became a progressive and creative culture embracing renewable energy, organic agriculture, sustainable forestry and the protection of wild areas. In recent years a new organic architecture seeks to bring habitation and nature together in marriage of form and sustainable building materials. Organic agriculture, whilst loudly focussed

153

upon food safety and soil conservation, also has an underlying ethic of animal welfare and an honouring of natural cycles and processes. Even the business world stirs – a recent article in the Financial Times headed 'spirituality in business' recognised the soul destroying nature of a corporate world that had lost sight of the core values of humanity, and reported that Price-Waterhouse, a leading management consultancy, had started to send its managers to the Findhorn Foundation for courses in personal discovery. Meaning, purpose and identity crises are surfacing and these apparently affect the all-important efficiency of business affairs!

These early attempts at retrieving the soul in the corporate world may begin as a response to failing motivation, but at least they are a recognition of where the problem lies (see Richard Barrett's *Liberating the Corporate Soul: building a visionary organisation*). If such seeds can prosper in the thorny ground of corporate finance, then it is but a short step to conservation biology and economic forestry!

The disjunction between conservation science, resource economics and the 'sacred' is not now as great as it was. Whilst few scientists have attempted to bridge the divide on a personal level, ecologists and anthropologists have at least begun to realise the value and potential of native systems of 'ecology' and 'conservation' that are based upon deep observation and rules of sanctity.

### Steps toward a sacred ecology

One such is the anthropologist Fikret Berkes, whose recent book, *Sacred Ecology*, provides case studies of Cree Indian culture in sub-arctic Canadian 'wilderness', where aboriginal peoples have used and shaped the most apparently pristine of environments. He argues that 'conservation' ethics needs to take on board the cultural dimensions of such use and further, that traditional knowledge – in this case, that of the Caribou migrations, numbers and health of animals – though based upon oral history held by certain elders, and not strictly scientific in form, needs respect not only in its own right as part of a cultural heritage, but also as a successful system of predictive knowledge complementary to ecological science.

Indigenous knowledge is not, however, romanticised. Some of the weaknesses of indigenous practices have been revealed by scientific ecology and he acknowledges the mass extinction phenomenon when aboriginal hunters first encountered the mega-herbivores, but in the eastern James Bay area, there are documented studies of the Cree exploitation of beaver, goose, black bear and caribou which demonstrate stewardship and respect, and there are no records of any species extinction since the end of the Pleistocene. This material provides a useful counterpoint to the arguments of Krech and Flannery on the role of indigenous peoples in mass extinctions, and particularly where writers have set out to debunk the myth of the 'noble' savage living in harmony with the environment. Early indigenous peoples may have wiped out their competitors and exhausted the supply of very large animals, but they quickly learned to husband the mid-sized, lunch-sized creatures that were left.

Berkes argues that an enlightened management system for natural resources would include indigenous peoples not only as part of the ecosystem, but part of its management at both a practical and philosophic level. It might be expected that the arguments would end here – he is Professor of Natural Resources at the University of Manitoba, and so far the 'sacred' has been merely a descriptive element in the anthropology of indigenous knowledge and practice. His final chapter, however, is entitled 'Toward a Unity of Mind and Nature':

'Until only a few years ago, the spread of modern, rational, scientific resource management was considered a part of "natural progress". The problem is that Western scientific resource management, despite all of its power, seems unable to halt the depletion of resources and the degradation of the environment. Part of the reason for this may be that Western resource management, and reductionist science in general, developed in the service of a utilitarian, exploitive, dominion-over-nature worldview of colonists and industrial developers......best geared for the efficient use of resources as if they were limitless, consistent with the laissez-faire doctrine still alive in today's neoclassical economic theory. But utilitarianism is ill-suited for sustainability, which requires a new philosophy that recognizes ecological limits and strives to satisfy social as well as economic needs'.

He goes on to argue that traditional ecological knowledge and practice demonstrates that worldviews and *beliefs* matter – 'almost universally one encounters an ethic of non-dominant, respectful human-nature relationships, a sacred ecology, as part of the belief component of traditional ecological knowledge.' This necessarily challenges the dominant positivistic-reductionist paradigm, and where given status and respect, becomes a 'political ecology' which alters the power relationship of hitherto marginalised people toward the dominant culture. He articulates a compelling argument for conceptual pluralism, a more participatory, community-based alternative to top-down management, and the injection of a measure of ethics into the science of ecology and resource management, thereby restoring (Bateson's) "unity of mind and nature".

This latter claim may seem rather fanciful in the light of the speed with which indigenous peoples are embracing a globalised exploitive culture, and it is an optimistic person indeed who sees the potential to challenge utilitarianism, as characterised by an amoral approach and commodification of nature, with an ecological ethic where -

> 'the relationship is not one-way, and there is explicit human-nature reciprocity in which animals have obligations to nourish humans in return for respect and other proper behaviour'.

But Fikret Berkes has the advantage of having *experienced* the reality of an indigenous relationship to nature, and perhaps therefore, the very personal reality of that reciprocity. My feeling is that this alone is the key to a fusion of sacred and scientific ecology. The latter may have grown more humble in the light of its now very obvious limitations of prediction and control, but until a largely urbanised political and scientific corpus get to experience the sacred dimensions of nature other than as romantic idyll or recreational frolic, scientific ecology and resource management cannot begin to incorporate the sacred other than as a marketable attribute of some indigenous culture ripe for eco-tourism.

## Deep ecology and the medicine wheel

So far, the sacred may not have found much practical expression in conservation policy, but at least it is not dismissed. Perhaps that is because ecologists are more acutely aware of the deep malaise inherent in 'western' culture that has not only separated people from the land, but led them to erode the fruitfulness of the earth upon which they depend.

Ecologists have become increasingly conscious of the failures of predictive environmental science – the ozone hole, gender bending chemicals, loss of immunity and large scale deaths of sea mammals, forest die back, the consequences of global warming. If we start to talk of becoming more at one with Nature, or living within Nature's cycles and learning from her processes, as a former British Prime Minister once exhorted her people to do, most will listen with an 'open' mind. However, we in the rational 'West' are not used to opening the mind *fully*. (We must find a better term for the 'western' tradition of rational philosophic, scientific and economic thought that is now hardly confined to the 'west', and which has its most radical counterpoint in the deeply 'western' traditions of Native American and Druid tradition). When we talk of open minds we are still talking of minds open to differing opinions, on a rational level. The deeper 'west' of the Native Americans and ancient Celts is a deeper level of opening.

We may find some guidance in Native American and neo-Pagan *systems* of relating to Nature (re-invented Celtic Druidism draws heavily on Native American experience). In these, and also in many other indigenous cultures, the 'four directions' have a primary place. North, South, East and West are honoured in ritual. Each has a ruling power, a set of symbolic co-ordinates. In the Order of Bards, Ovates and Druids (OBOD) with whom I have worked, the East is the realm of the sun, symbolised by the dawn, the element of air, and the flight of the Falcon. The West is the setting sun, the element of water, ruled by the Salmon of wisdom. To the Native American the West was the place of dreams, the realm of the unconscious, of death, ruled by the Bear, and the East, the place of the teacher, the light of enlightenment. It is in the North that the colder realms of thought and reason lie, and to the South where the fires of passion burn and the joys of children and nurturing and sexuality are to be found.

I recall, how, on my first sojourn in the great forests of Africa, on a long walk with a young and educated forest ranger, he referred to the North, a continually warring imperialist spread of homogenous culture that embraced North America, Britain, Northern Europe, Russia, and Japan. East and West that had meant so much to my own student psyche, meant little to him – the world was split into North and South.

It is not hard to see the superficial truths in the differences between Northern European and Southern European cultures, or between North and South America, Europe and Africa, Japan and Polynesia. The South holds the fires of passion, of community, children and nurturing, whilst the North holds the frightening power of intellect, categorisation, separation, and action based solely upon reason and perceived wisdom. In the deep intuitive teachings of Druid and Native American 'medicine wheel', the task is to honour all four directions *within* the individual and hence to create balance and harmony.

And so with East and West – the east holds the power of the clear light, the guru, the zen-mind, the monad wherein there is no separation, whereas the west holds the dream, the unconscious sea of archetype, a multiplicity of gods (and demons), where the personality eventually surrenders, or dies, and wherein also lies the powers of rebirth – the creation of new life. In this latter sense, our culture has been very western. It has been a culture of new inventions, new thought, new ways of looking at the world, and more, a culture that has translated thought into action, most obviously in the progression of technology. It is curious, however, that this progression is celebrated (and ritually honoured) as a process of the rational mind – science and technology are juxtaposed. Yet science has progressed largely by insight, and all that has been built, must first have been dreamed. Curious that we place so little store by intuitive modes of thinking and train our children so intensely in rationality, almost to the point where the intuitive is educated out of them. The intuitive mind also requires a long training, and this is not neglected by indigenous peoples. It is in this realm that they find meaning, purpose, healing and the deepest connection to Nature.

Of late, I have walked with practical woodsmen and estate managers, though admittedly the more holistic kind that work for the National Trust, and been moved by their openness to new (or, really, the very old) ways of looking. People who are close to nature and not bound by needs of economic exploitation, are more open to the great mystery that surrounds them daily. It has been in conversations at what is now the cutting edge of conservation – how to integrate the cultural with the ecological, the old and the new, how to hold what is of value, yet accept the management of great change to come – that I have, somewhat surprisingly, found parallel interests in the *shamanic* world and the healing power of Nature.

157

There are also signs of a new spring in what have hitherto been the barren grounds of the scientific medical professions. It was, after all, here that the soul was first 'excised', liberating the body to become the mechanical android of pumps, valves, circuits, pressures and temperatures that appeared a far higher order than the ethers and mists and ill-defined agues of the dark ages. In this reasoned architecture, largely male 'doctors' could take over from their largely female antecedents of herbalists and spiritual healers (but not without a five hundred year pogrom on 'witches'). Curious how 'doctors' shy from the term 'healer'. Healing is restricted to something that wounds do. Essentially it is a natural process. This might at first indicate a certain humility within the medical profession – where medication is simply a support for nature's own process of healing. However, doctors do just what the name implies, and there is a definite negative connotation to 'doctoring'. They also see themselves as waging 'war' on disease, with a language of fight and combat, as if illness was always an outer enemy, never a possible inner friend.

## Curing the sick and healing the soul

When something is 'doctored', it has been interfered with and got at in some way, and the medical profession lost itself in that coldly reasoned world of mechanical doctoring. For every great gain in patching up the machine, there arose insidious losses as science sought ever more zones of conquest – the immune and hormonal systems were treated in much the same way as the circulatory and skeletal. Where the latter had responded to the knife and the mechanical model, as they were essentially mechanical systems, the chemical scalpel was the tool of intervention in disease and mental imbalance, as if that too were simply a chemical system.

The medical world has suffered almost as much as the environmental from mishaps and miscalculations, especially with regard to the use of chemicals. And just as environmental health has declined, so the 'health services', in Britain at least, are perceived as in decline, though perhaps more for reasons of bureaucracy and overload than medical effectiveness. The overall impression has become one of disease management, rather than the promotion of health and healing, and only in recent decades has the service begun to focus upon preventative health as a way of avoiding the overload. Overcrowded hospitals are a symptom as much of the failure of doctoring in the population at large, as of any bureaucratic error or lack of adequate funding for the hospitals themselves. However, just as the old framework begins to decay, there are signs of rebirth as new knowledge surfaces - and very old knowledge resurfaces.

Initially, in the 1960s and 1970s the new knowledge called itself 'alternative', but has now grown sufficiently to be 'complementary' to science-based medicine. Sadly, too many of the conventional medical practitioners still regard the realm of 'healers' with distrust, especially areas that involve touch, or the 'laying on of hands', or mediation with spirits. Yet we can talk of 'healing herbs' as well as 'healing hands' and of emotional wounds 'healing with time'. We know about psychological as well as physical trauma. We have long bridged the divide of mind and body, and learned that emotional and mental states affect physical well-being. We have begun to understand that children deprived of good housing and green space are likely to become disturbed and delinquent. We can now talk about a more holistic health that includes stability within the family and harmony in the environment. Children are taken 'pond dipping' and tree planting, and school grounds are planted up. Adolescents are exposed to the risks of extremes in nature, with white-water rafting, canoeing and rock climbing. In the last few decades, health has become more broadly defined and there is an integration evolving. Not all doctors and nurses are closed to the world of deeper healing. Perhaps we are now ready for the next step.

We need to explore the dimension beyond 'doctoring', where conventional medical practice very largely deals with symptoms and has a limited perspective on causes. The scientific mind, constrained by training in the methodologies of experiment and controls, tends to think of single 'causes' because that is what the methodology best deals with. This was the undoing of predictive environmental science. Faced with multi-factorial environmental reality, the methods failed to deliver. Even where mechanisms and linkages were understood, the complexity of interaction made prediction all-but-impossible. The medical profession is still decades behind – and still held within a paradigm that sees, for example, infectious diseases as 'caused' by viral, bacterial, fungal or amoebic agents. The ecology of these agents shows us clearly that most of them are present at all times and that 'causation' must then include a second cause, the failure of an otherwise competent immune system.

Such 'second cause' thinking would naturally lead to greater awareness of those inner elements that affect the competence of immune systems.

We should add that there are now enormous vested interests at stake in the billions of dollars worldwide that have been invested by multinational drug companies and the pressure they bring to bear within the doctoring framework. The drug companies are geared for combat with the invading entities. Far less effort is devoted to diet, essential vitamins, exercise, stress relief and emotional wellbeing – all of which impact upon the immune system.

Most doctors are well aware of this, but within the constraints of time and resources of conventional medical practice, they cannot treat the primary cause with its plethora of contributory factors. Like Wilhelm Reich half-a-century before, they are asked simply to patch up the working machine and send it back into the environment that made it so sick in the first place. These limited responses apply to such chronic ailments as arthritis, back pain and headaches which perversely, seriously impact upon the working efficiency of the population. In the case of cancers and heart disease, which eventually kill the majority of us in old age, doctors have long recognised the role of diet, pollutants, stress, lifestyle and attitudes – but again, can do little about it, and ultimately return to the magic bullet of drugs and radiation therapy. These diseases cost society enormous sums in inefficient management – they overload the hospital system, and make huge profits for the drug industries concerned.

'Healers', on the other hand, exist within what is known as a 'complementary' or 'alternative' system, and as we shall see, this 'system' is much more fundamentally concerned with causes rather than symptoms. However, the two systems have begun to co-operate, especially over the last two decades, and whereas most observers would agree that the health service problems continue to mount, despite technological advances and successes with individual diseases, complementary medicine in contrast is growing rapidly. This is particularly the case with Homeopathy, Acupuncture, Herbalism, and some of the hands-on therapies such as CST (Cranial Sacral Therapy), Osteopathy and Chiropractic. These disciplines deal with the protracted problems of chronic disorders that are not so amenable to treatment by medical drugs. We might also add the fields of family therapy, counselling, and humanistic psychology. There is also a gradual blossoming of dance, movement, drama, music and art as therapies for the sick and disabled (and even the healthy!).

What then has all this to do with the forest? The underlying reality of many of these complementary techniques is the same underlying reality we have tentatively begun to approach in the forest. It is the causal layer – that which has birthed us, that which lies beneath our perceptions of outer and inner. There is also another link: there can be no true healing if the cause of the sickness is not fully addressed. Humanity is made sick by soul-less enterprise and the forest has the power to restore soul not only to the damaged psyche, but to be part of a new and soul-full enterprise. But first we must know more of causality itself.

**Complementary maps of reality**

To explore the causal layer, we can turn to some of the very oldest systems of medicine concerned most fundamentally with cause and which do not perceive the body as superficial mechanical and chemical systems. Traditional Chinese Medicine is a mixture of careful observation and listening, detailed case history, and intervention with herbs and acupuncture needles. Most people now know that acupuncture 'works'. Since the mid-1970s numerous schools of traditional Chinese acupuncture have been training students in Britain.

My own involvement in the healing professions began in Oxford in the late 1970s where the first and one of the best of Britain's newly trained acupuncturists began to practice. Peter Mole was a fellow graduate of St. Catherine's College, and during a period of declining health, I became one of his first patients. On his clinic wall were intriguing maps of the human energy system, of meridians, channels and nodal points that bore no relation to the maps of blood vessels and nerves that I knew. His work turned around my chronic health problems and may well have saved me from far worse deterioration as a result of what he called major imbalances in energy flow. The needles were inserted to channel and modulate, slow or invigorate the various flows of *chi* energy and achieve a healthy balance. In traditional Chinese understanding, the distortion in the energy field was the primary cause – physical and mental disease would follow. All manner of things could distort energy fields – thoughts, resentments, oppressions, environments, diet.

Though I had just gone through an intense scientific training – I was open to alternative maps of 'energy' through my practice of yoga and reading of yogic texts.

Yogic knowledge often used parallel metaphors to the world of atoms and electricity, a feature highlighted by the biologist Rupert Sheldrake in his *New Science of Life*, where he proposed 'morphic resonance' as a phenomenon of interacting *fields* that lie beyond the electro-magnetic spectrum, and also by the physicist Fritjof Capra in comparing the science of vibration with the yogic descriptions of sub-atomic reality. To the yogi, all matter is vibration: the slower, the denser, and many of modern physics' deepest revelations, are paralleled in yogic knowledge gained not through instruments but by direct perception. In yogic reality, the pervading vibration is *consciousness* and by meditation and spiritual practice the yogi can raise his own consciousness to that all pervading level and thereby gain direct perception of such realities.

My own interest in the power of yogic breathing techniques lay, however, in its ability to heal emotional trauma, and I had begun a professional training in order to make the techniques more widely known. In 1980 I came under the tutelage of the Himalayan master, Herakhan Baba (known my many simply as Babaji). By the mid-1980s I was teaching breathing techniques in seminars to alternative health practitioners, partly for their own healing, partly as additional tools in their practice. From this work I had the privilege of knowing several excellent practitioners of acupuncture. I once watched a video of an operation where a patient was 'anaesthetised' by needles in the neck whilst undergoing a hernia operation, and who then walked away with no pain. Several of my students working with deep transformational techniques in yoga turned their lives round to become healers, and among them some now leading acupuncturists, homeopaths and herbalists. I have had opportunity to watch and to discuss with them the healing processes, as well as being rescued from various unhealthy states of my own.

Though these practitioners may limit their explanations, and even their goals, to relief of symptoms, and there are 'medical' acupuncturists as well as 'medical' herbalists and homeopaths (those who learn simply which remedies tend to effect a relief of symptoms), the traditional practitioners have both a different map of reality, and a wider goal of healing.

Firstly, the map. We need not go into detail, and it differs for each discipline, but essentially it concerns the 'energy' body. Acupuncturists have mapped the subtle pathways and nodes within the human body as exactly as geographers would map the streams and tributaries of a great river system. It is into these 'meridians' that the needles are inserted. All of the organ systems of the body receive vital energy from these flows, and if the flow becomes blocked or clogged or slowed or feint, then the organ system will suffer. A practitioner requires months of training to locate and identify the pulses and their varying qualities – a sensitivity as yet beyond the most sensitive of technical instruments – there are six pulses in each wrist and each pulsing with one of a dozen different qualities. These pathways can be affected by emotional and mental states, trauma, stress, attitude and accidents. At the deepest level, a person's spiritual integrity and well-being helps to energise the pathways, and conversely, the emotional and physical world feeds back, through these pathways, to their spiritual health. In traditional Chinese acupuncture, the ultimate goal of the physician was to help align the spirit to the divine presence.

Herbalism has had much the same rather secretive goal. In recent centuries it has had to hide itself under the guise of 'doctoring' physical and emotional health, but gradually, some of its practitioners are beginning to admit that for them, it is the 'spirit' of the plant that effects the healing, and for some there is even the admission that they no longer work with the infusions and decoctions, but simply request that the plant spirit intervenes and does the necessary healing. Such admissions may be scoffed at by medically qualified herbalists, though, even there, I have the acquaintance of some who have gone down the road of academic qualifications and now fully embrace these spiritual realities.

In herbal medicine, the scientific mind has continually failed to grasp what is on offer. It limits itself to seeking the 'active' ingredient, the magic bullet that will cure the symptom. And certainly, active ingredients *are* isolated and *do* work – the compounds of the Periwinkle that have aided recovery from leukaemia, the extracts of the Yew tree that have benefited AIDS and cancer patients. Extracted *cannabitols* are set to legitimise the medical use of cannabis for relieving chronic pain, without the 'high'. The greatest pain reliever of the western world's medical chest is still the extract of opium poppy. Undoubtedly, one reason for this myopic vision is the industrial pharmaceutical imperative of business and profit. If the extract can be refined and simplified, patented, tested, manufactured and bottled, distributed and transacted with the minimum of involvement on the part of others – then it makes money. If the herb remained whole, with the added complexity of regulated doses, careful monitoring, additional remedies to moderate side-effects – all of which require time with an experienced practitioner, then the economics would flow in a rather more decentralised way. For this latter reason many such complementary methods *are* expensive at the point of use, even though the remedies may be cheap.

Thus it is, that for reasons of scientific prejudice and economic stricture, conventional 'western' medicine does not address ailments of the spirit, and barely touches the emotional and mental states (other than in the management of depression). It perforce limits itself to seeking 'cures' rather than seeking 'healing'. These plants offer far more than cures for the symptoms of disease, but we need to wade slowly now into the deep end of this inquiry.

In this respect Homeopathy may guide us into that deeper water. It has a much more recent history than either herbalism or acupuncture, both of which go back thousands of years. It was birthed in the modern western scientific culture – by Hahnemann in Germany in the 19th Century, and so it is to a great extent sanitised of spirits, and does not concern itself with maps of cosmic energy flows. Like acupuncture and herbal medicine, however, it is founded upon detailed observations and trials of what 'works'. Few homeopaths have been much concerned with the physics or mechanism, as healers their interest has been confined to the speed and modes of recovery. As with acupuncture, I have been fortunate to know several accomplished homeopaths, and my children have all had homeopathy as their primary medical care. I have watched them respond through all their childhood illnesses and had my faith tested time and again through the risks of infection and fevers, contagious diseases in the tropics (they have never been immunised), and the vicissitudes of emotional upset and trauma. I have seen fevers abate within hours, stomach upsets clear, emotional states transform, and I have seen some failures where physical symptoms run their course unabated. Homeopathy requires early diagnosis and treatment, and as with the other complementary medicines, the remedies are cheap and natural, but the practitioner's time is expensive. However, the remedies have seldom failed where directed at a 'constitutional' level and led to general improvements in chronic conditions and emotional stress. There is now a growing scientific literature of double blind trials showing the effectiveness of homeopathy in treating chronic ailments, such as asthma. It is also effective in the veterinary field.

### Concepts of energy and information

Though homeopathy is essentially practical, it has one basic tenet – the doctrine of signatures: like treats like. A remedy is derived from any substance – be it herbal, animal, inorganic or organic, that produces a reaction in human physiological, emotional or mental states – and the nature of that reaction, for example, an angry reddening rash, is a guide to the remedy's potential healing of an ailment that shows *similar* symptoms. For example, the Nightshade, *Belladonna*, when given in low doses produces a fever and in higher doses, it is fatal. It is used in homeopathy to treat fevers. New remedies are sought and 'proven' by teams of people who catalogue the symptoms at low doses. The remedies are then 'potentised' by repeated dilution and secussion – a process of shaking.

All this would be to some degree acceptable to conventional thought, were it not for the process of producing the homeopathic remedy. The substance is 'diluted' by such a huge amount that chemically, no trace of the substance remains (below the Avogadro number, that point at which statistically, no molecules would be left in the sample). Homeopaths have never had a problem with this because they are open to the possibility that the 'signature' of the substance is left in the water. Indeed, the procedure of secussion whereby the substance is vibrated whilst being diluted is meant to enhance the uptake of the signature in the solution. The resultant dilutions, which may range from 6x – that is, $1/10^{th}$ dilution carried out six times, through 30x and 200x, to 1 or 10 million times, have different properties. At 6x the remedy treats mainly physical symptoms. At 30x and 200x it treats emotional and mental states. The larger dilutions affect changes on the spiritual level.

For the scientifically trained medical mind this is too much. Homeopathy is often accorded the same treatment as astrology, and regarded at best as the placebo effect and at worst as quackery and mumbo-jumbo. But times are changing. Homeopathy has become big business in France, and in recent years, companies that produce the remedies have undertaken scientific trials. The most famous of which were carried out by Jaques Benveniste in the early 1990s. He claimed to have demonstrated the effects of potencies in an elegant experiment where a clotting agent was diluted to homeopathic levels and then applied to phials of blood in such a manner that the effectiveness of the agent could be accurately determined by spectrometric analysis. His work showed peaks of effectiveness at the 'step' dilutions used by homeopaths, and the effectiveness appeared to increase with the dilution. His work was scientific enough to merit publication in the prestigious journal *Nature,* but there followed the fiercest of establishment backlashes. His laboratory was visited under the pretence of fellowship in science, but with the expectation of fraud, and the team included the well-known debunker of magic and superstition, the magician, James Randl. The investigative team rubbished the methodologies as self-delusion, yet uncovered no evidence of fraud in the standard scientific methodologies used by Benveniste. The affair was a scandal. *Nature* at least published a letter from me that condemned the witch-hunt. In response to that letter, I had correspondence from several physicists worldwide that were working on the capability of water to retain 'information' within its electro-magnetic structure.

The jury is still out on the reality of the mechanism, but modern physicists are now open to the concept that water can carry complex information in the form of 'memory'. I have always found the defamatory and plainly emotional response of the scientific establishment somewhat of a mystery. A true scientist has an open mind. All of the great breakthroughs in science have been made not from the editors of journals, nor from the ploddingly banal repetitions of the technically correct abiding by the rules and theories of the time, but by creative and intuitive minds in often deeply spiritual individuals, many of whom faced unbridled hostility and denigration before acceptance. This has applied to many of the truly great biologists, physicists, chemists, astronomers, and even geologists. Galileo, Kepler, Copernicus, Newton, Mendeleyev, Tesla, Einstein, and Darwin – all struggled against established prejudice. In this century, Wilhelm Reich was shamelessly denigrated and persecuted.

A similar fate was to befall Walter Schauberger, an Austrian scientist studying the unique energetic properties of water, who was ruthlessly exploited by the American secret services in their post-war search for new propulsion systems, and then abandoned to sickness and an obscure death. In both Schauberger and Reich's case a new age mythology has developed which alleges the discovery and suppression of new science and technology that would undermine very large financial interests in medicinal drugs and non-fossil fuel propulsion systems. Sadly, intriguing experiments on bio-energetics by both these scientists have not been repeated for fear of ridicule.

Before we leave this issue, consider again the analogy of the radio as illustrative of the limits of scientific method. Though a scientist, I have little idea of how it works (narrow specialism), and even if I understood it in theory, I doubt I could build one (lack of practical knowledge). Had I the practical knowledge, I would not know where to source the components or their price (lack of market awareness). I do know, from first principles, that as I listen to the music, the complexity of the symphony has been encoded in very simple signals – in the amplitude and frequency of electro-magnetic waves in the atmosphere (science always simplifies). I do think it is an amazing piece of technology (scientific technology is always in awe of itself!). However, no science can interpret those signals. Science could tell me they were unusual, that there was a pattern above the general noise that is natural radio-background, and almost certainly from an intelligent source. But to tell me that it was Beethoven's Pastoral, one needs to abandon the realm of science. And to experience the feelings that I experience, there must be a surrender to the music itself.

However, if the scientist were to insist that the music arose from the complex electrical circuitry of the box before me, he would be laughed at. We know, a priori, that the orchestra produced the music, either in some other place at the same time, or even at some other time. Moreover, we know that ultimately, Beethoven created the music in his dreaming.

The world of 'healing' is rather similar. The totality of any individual human being is not held within the circuits of the body and the brain. That knowledge is not supposition on my part, any more than my knowledge that the music has an orchestra and a composer. That knowledge is experience-based. It comes from opening the perceptual field with tools of the mind that go beyond the personal realm and the limits of the senses. This knowledge is only denied by those who would rule, a priori, such realms as irrelevant.

Just as we can embrace with awe and wonder the fact that a whole symphony can exist in the ether about us, right now, even if I turn off the radio – indeed, a myriad symphonies, and conversations, and languages exist right now, all about us, encoded in great complexity and with the potential for emotional charge, mental interest, and spiritual uplift – all, that is, if I have the means to access them. Pictures and movies too! Yet the medium that holds the information and transmits it over great distances, has no substance and is not discernible to human sense organs. Were we to go back 200 hundred years, when it was beyond instrumentation, it would be beyond credence, even, and perhaps especially, to most scientists.

The relevance that this has for the 'healing' realms is more than analogy. The energetic body that responds to homeopathic remedies, that channels cosmic *chi* and *prana* (the yogic equivalent) through the meridians that vitalise the organ systems, exists on a similar plane to the electro-magnetic wave forms so capable of encoding and transmitting the symphony. That energy body is not totally beyond the sensitivity of technical instruments – there are micro-electrical instruments and Kirlian photographic techniques that can pick up changes, but it is most easily accessible through the incredible sensitivity of the human hand and brain – to acupuncturists and others trained to touch and sense energy moving in the human body. Deeper still, elements of its play *can be seen* by those who have a trained eye (though that is rare, and the gift is more often inherited)

However, there is also another shared reality, and far more easily accessed. As with all human art, the symphony first existed not in the orchestra, but in Beethoven's personal dreamworld. All human artefacts, from the paintings on the cave walls at Lascaux, to the monstrous Pompidou Centre in Paris, first had to be dreamt. The human story has become the dreaming of another reality.

**The unfolding dream**

It is a bizarre science that concerns itself so much with the circuit boards of life, the molecular structure of plants, the sequences of genes, the chemistry of the brain, and yet ignores the dreaming. The more bizarre when all of science's greatest breakthroughs came from those who could listen and act upon their intuitions. And intuition, which can be learned and perfected, is all about 'listening'. It is essentially a passive act of surrender, but it takes a disciplined mind to let go into that silence.

We are deep enough now to consider the underlying reality in the healing power of plants and animals. They exist *within* the dream. This *is* the *shaman's* reality. They have already been dreamt. They are at-one with creation, which is an unfolding dream. For them there is no atonement. We, however, are different. We are not at one with this creation. We have dissented big time. We don't like it. We think we are above it. We hate or fear each other and most of creation itself. We are not at-ease, and hence full of dis-ease.

The *shaman* enters that reality on a dream level and in the healing work, the animals and plant powers are allies in the process. The *shaman* effects changes in ordinary reality by first instigating changes in the underlying dream reality. Our scientific anthropology still regards the practices of medicine men, shamans and witch doctors as so much psychological trickery, however effective they may prove to be in individual cases. Rarely is it possible to gain any kind of trustworthy insight into shamanic practices - the shamans do not usually speak our language, and why would they bother? There is, however, a recent book that provides such a rare opportunity.

Imagine you are a good field naturalist and you love animals. An old man who knows vastly more than you, sets you a task. To prove how in tune you are with the natural order of things, you have to go into the Longleat game park and pluck the whisker from one of the lions. In the case of Martin Prechtel, it was the jungles of Guatemala and the whisker of a wild jaguar. How far we are, with our bird-hides, visitor centres and board-walks and signposted nature walks, from such a level of trust in the wild side of nature.

Prechtel passed his test, not so much by courage, of which there was an abundance, but by trust, when the jaguar came to him. Martin Prechtel's story is the personal history of a traditional *shamanic* training – of the medicine man healer, who communes with animal spirits in an alliance for the healing of the human condition.

He was born of Swiss and Native American parents and brought up on a reservation in the USA - a bit of a teenage misfit, who married early and met the all-too-common difficulties of an indigenous soul searching for meaning in such a damaged culture. As his marriage and community life foundered, he had a vivid dream of a village of unimaginable beauty, with its native community intact, by a deep blue lake surrounded by lush forested mountains. He set off on a journey south, guided by instinct, and when that failed, by the unseen hand of his dream. By 'chance' he crossed from Mexico into Guatemala, and found himself in the village he had seen in his dream - Santiago Atitlan, by the lake and the then intact forest. An old man jumped him from behind, accosting him for taking so long to get there.

Thus began his training. The old man was the most revered Indian *shaman* in Guatemala, and announced that he had 'dreamt' Martin to him to train as an apprentice. The training takes years. It is a training in all the old ways of the indigenous Mayan culture. Herbs and healing are central, but also we are given a window into the rich and astonishingly intricate world of ritual. The indigenous soul of the Mayan village, indeed, the Mayan culture, is kept vibrant by a constant stream of devotion to the Gods. This is perhaps the most difficult element to grasp, so far removed is it from our own cultural understandings and practices. These Gods are felt as real, with fierce consequences for getting things wrong, and great bounty for being in right relationship.

167

In weaving the story of his own evolution, Prechtel paints pictures of the intricate wonder and meaning of Mayan language, costume, dress, music, prayer, food and relationship to nature. What is at first an obviously simple and hard existence, is revealed in great depth, meaning and beauty. Despite the hardships, there is much laughter and great love. He wins his spurs through ordeal and constant practice of ritual, to finally qualify as shaman.

As the old man, his teacher, announces that he will die in a few days time - he knows the time and manner of his death, and that his work is now complete, for Prechtel has been passed the knowledge of the ancestors, he foretells that in a few months the village will be destroyed and the Mayan culture all-but exterminated. Prechtel is told to return to the United States and teach what he knows. Sure enough, after the old man duly dies, Guatemala experiences a military coup and a vicious ethnic cleansing. The old world of balance is finally laid waste in the name of modernity. Prechtel now lives and teaches in New Mexico.

In his final chapter he talks of the 'indigenous soul' and how it must be kept alive at all costs. Modernity is not necessarily progress. As we look at our own countryside, we know that only too well. There is an acute lack of soul. We have no jaguars - not the bear and wolf or lynx, reminders of the limits of our human power should we momentarily surrender our technology. Look also at our farms and villages - the old buildings had balance, harmony with the hill, the copse, the meander. Now, despite our huge wealth, we have a welter of corrugated sheds, tacky boxes and neat gardens, fields barren of birds and flowers, with 'nature reserves' on the edge, never central, hardly respected.

We have a lot of work to do. We might call it ecological restoration,' sustainability', 'conservation of biodiversity'. All worthily scientific. What is lacking is still soul. We have yet to grasp that fully. Prechtel makes a plea, that without a soulful relation to nature, a richness is lost. This we can learn from the indigenous soul of the shaman as healer. From so-called primitive cultures we can access a wisdom we have lost. My only question is, for Prechtel, this wisdom was won at great personal risk and huge devotion. I know of many trainee shamans in Britain, from neo-native Druid and Wiccan, to imported Yogi and Native American, but have yet to meet anyone who has broken through to the level of consciousness that Prechtel describes.

Yet, we *are* dreamers. We have the power of creation. No other species on earth has been given that. It was our gift when we left the garden. For good or evil.

So, to our healing. It is not a question of cures. My father died of a cancer that could not be cured. It was a painful ending. He almost drowned in his pulmonary fluid. The doctor had given him a few hours once his heart had failed to pump the blood from the lungs, and he was left alone. The ward nurses and sisters held a space of angelic quality, but it would not have reached him in his dire state. He was in great fear. He very nearly died with no healing. In those final hours, however, his spiritual dimension made its final push through the prejudice, fear, pride, the immense guilt of the years, and he asked for help. I count myself immensely fortunate to have been by his side at that moment, and to be able to offer the gifts I myself had received. He began to work with the ancient yogic breath and to embark upon the healing journey.

I do not know who and what he encountered, because he could not talk, but I could feel and at times sense the energetic work. Five days later, after no food or water and no medical intervention, his spirit crossed the threshold with a confident joy, shorn of guilt, self-forgiven and at one with life. His shrivelled body glowed with health, there was a smile on his face, and a deep peace in his final sigh as we kissed him goodbye. His death was a healing. His cancer was a healing. Had he keeled over with a heart attack whilst gardening and gone in seconds, there would have been no such healing.

Healing is about atonement, not about curing symptoms. Sometimes the physical symptoms clear, sometimes they don't. But for healing to manifest, the person must be at one with what is happening, however painful and whatever the outcome. In that space of oneness, of acceptance, miracles happen. It is not necessarily a passive space – it may be time to be at one with aggression and fight and the will to live. Healers are often aware that the disease is the cure in progress. There is a lesson for the body and the mind and the spirit. Guilt and resentment will lead to disease of the body, often to cancer, and if the guilt or resentment is not released in a healing process, then the body may be beyond recall, in which case, the cancer offers the prolonged state of heightened awareness of death and the potential for revelation and forgiveness. It is a *work* to be done.

Disease is a fact of nature, and its prevalence is well revealed in fossil bones of everything from big cats to gorillas. But in humans dis-ease exists at the physical, mental and *spiritual* levels, and the latter is our highest evolutionary expression. Most healers experience the spiritual level as primary cause, then mental, then emotional, then physical. The body is always the last to register the discord, and by then, it is often too late to affect a 'cure'. The healing process can engage at any of these levels. Bodywork releases stored emotional energy from musculature. Alignment work such as osteopathy and chiropractic corrects postural patterns that can arise from wayward attitudes and a lifetime of holding and tension. Analysis and psychotherapy can address guilt, resentments, fears and childhood trauma – essentially mental conclusions, which have gathered emotional charge that can also then feedback into physical and emotional release. We now have the immense heritage of Jung with its rich exploration of symbol and archetype in the unconscious mind – and perhaps the single most important articulation of our evolutionary destiny – the individuation of the soul.

In this respect, deep yogic breathing has the curious ability not only to release emotional memories from childhood, and feed back into physical and mental states, but to access dreams of 'past-life' trauma and patterns that appear to repeat in this lifetime (whatever the attendant reality of the past-life dream). In such explorations, the participant recognises the soul's long struggle to grow, to love and to have that love tested, *as an individual.* And for love to be made manifest in our work, we need to come into our full creative power as individuals as well as part of the social whole.

In these processes of healing, growth and personal unfolding, homeopathy, and at times acupuncture and herbal medicine, have the power to affect not only emotional and mental states (and hence the physical too), but also deeper underlying spiritual malaise. There are remedies that lift and strengthen the spirit in its constant battle against despair and doubt, and in the willingness to love, to be humble, to forgive and to trust in the divine unfolding. And it is in these realms beyond ailments and physical distress that the spirit powers of plants and animals can be most effective: where plants can strongly aid the constitution, physically, emotionally and psychically, it is the animal powers that lend the strength of will, courage, industriousness, determination, and divination of the path.

This goes beyond the impersonal homeopathic remedies made from the berries of deadly nightshades or the venom of dangerous snakes – a curious relationship where some of the most deadly poisons have healing powers (what my friend, the herbalist, Elizabeth Brooke calls 'dancing with death')! It goes beyond the doctrine of signatures and similarity. The animals and plants exist in the dreamworld. They may not dream as we do, and they cannot create, but they can join with us in *our* dream. Our mind has the power to include them, from choice. They already exist in the greater mind, into which we can expand, but until we do so, they cannot be other than what they are as animals and plants in the slowly unfolding dream of evolution. Once we enter that expanded reality, and invite them into our process of evolution they will respond as willingly and as readily as the faithful dog offered a run in the meadow. It is as if, when we make that move, we become co-directors of the film, and they are willing and very able actors who want the work.

It is a point that is hard for many eco-philosophers to face. The animals and plants may have evolved as far as they can – they have roles, powers and abilities that have been honed over millennia. Their qualities are as varied as the Universe in which they are immersed, but their greater purpose is to be there for us. The oak tree has many ecological functions, but when connected to the human psyche it becomes an expanded being of heart and strength, joy and light; the yew occupies the realm of death and rebirth, of darkness and the underworld powers of regeneration. All of the trees have different qualities. The Remedies developed by Edward Bach are decoctions of the essence of flowers, many of which are trees. They are largely used to treat mental and spiritual states. There are correlations with herbal medicine, and even with legendary and mythic Celtic lore - the Druids had a tree-alphabet that was also a monthly calendar, with each month having an association with a particular tree, and to them, the oak *Derwen,* was the *doorway,* as befits the heart, and the word Druid itself was derived from this. As with Beethoven, there is no scientific treatise thereupon. This is something all the dreamers know because it is a consistent experience of the spirits of these trees as met in the dreamworld. It is the job of the healing herbalist to know this. It would be no surprise to a Druid elder that the oils of the yew *Taxus* had provided a cure for failure of the regenerative powers of the blood and immune system. Everything connected to the yew is connected to that realm.

Lastly, almost any therapist and healer will hold that the key to healing is acceptance. There is a lovely new book on trauma therapy called '*Waking the Tiger: healing trauma*', that makes a point of observation – you seldom see 'trauma' in the animal world. I have always marvelled at the peaceful grace of a charging tiger – the absence of aggression, and even at the apparent absence of fear in the tiger's prey. Carnivores can be aggressive, but usually it is reserved for territorial battles and dominance among themselves. In the act of killing they appear quite at peace, and the prey almost mesmerised in the throes of death. The thesis of the book is that trauma arises when a person is not at one with the event. Animals are surrendered to the dream. We, as dreamers, are not. We create much of our own reality and in seeking to control our world, impinge thereby upon others, and upon the planet.

I can go no further now with simple words. To know further, you must be willing to enter the dreamworld. It is not difficult at all. It is a revelation. Knock, and the *door* will be opened. There you will find the most amazing friends. Whatever your healing quest, you will marvel at the wisdom of animal and plant spirits as they guide you, surprise and amuse you, and above all, how well they know you. How could it be otherwise. They are the handmaidens of the creative dream. A dream that has dreamt you as its eventual co-dreamer! It is the nature of the Great Mystery known to all peoples, even our own, that we cannot know the creator other than by the process we see unfolding. *Evol*ution in the language of its conceptual birth, carries within it the sign of its purpose, which we know anyway to be *Love*. In that word, love is reversed – for it is to love that we must return. It has always been the greatest human challenge to have faith in that process. All of creation knows our journey into love. The yogis teach that when all of our energies are in harmony, when we are at one with the divine source, the vibratory power that energises all life, then we can experience only love. Then are we one with the creator.

The healing journey is thus fundamentally a quest for harmony with the creative power. Where each of the animal spirits has a particular healing power to address the small disharmonies, the forest in its wild and natural state teaches the harmonies of nature itself. In the symphony of the wildwood there is no disharmony. In its wholeness it holds and reflects the Great Mystery. To be whole, we must be able to experience wholeness. To be able to experience wholeness, we must be whole. It is a paradox. The soul-less will enter the wildwood and experience their soul-lessness, it will be an empty place. But to those just awakening, the forest will sing the song of awakening. And to the

171

weary and humble, it will offer solace and strengthening. And to the joyful and playful, the questers and explorers, it is a gateway to the stars.

In the deepest truth of creation, all is well. Even now. The degraded forests that surround us, the absent bear and wolf, the pollutant run-off, exhausted soils……in Earth time, these are mere midnight fevers. Even the doubling of human numbers to eight or ten billion. In Nature there are truly no dis-eases, *all is harmonious*. Death and decay are matched by birth and new growth, expansion by contraction, new forms replace old forms. What may appear to be the disease, is the cure in progress. The Earth herself, is the most patient of physicians, and ultimately knows that evolution pays no heed to comfort or pain. Her ultimate goal is our healing. She, herself, is already perfected – the eternal mother, married to the dying star that birthed her.

So why do we struggle? If all is perfect, even the most cancerous growth and the plague that is AIDS and the awesome planetary destruction that humans are capable of, what then is to be done? This is where the yogi in my psyche meets the human ecologist. The sage keeps still in the knowledge that all is unfolding as it should. Is it then the unwise that would move to alter things? To restore this degraded ecosystem, whether for wildwood, or water supplies, species conservation or carbon sequestration? Is it simply the prerogative of youth that action is required, and I am not yet an old man? Is it less simply that to be still, is to sever the ties to youth and vitality, and thus to procreative life, and thus more, a fear of death? If I had answers, I would be suspicious of my conceit.

But there are few things I know as an ecologist, and which most of my life I have had to keep under wraps – not out of doubt, but out of fear of being misinterpreted. Ecological knowledge is not necessarily a prescriptive guide for humane action. There are two dangerous areas of discourse: the first relates to medical progress, the second to world population growth. In medical intervention, the over-riding impulse is to preserve life and alleviate suffering. Upon this are built vast edifices of action to combat disease – with all manner of imbalances related to the type of disease. In 'western' civilisation, billions of dollars are devoted to cancer interventions and research for cures, funds which vastly outnumber those available for worldwide diseases linked to dirty water and diarrhoea, which afflict far more people, especially the young, and funds which also dwarf finance for preventative health programmes, diet and fitness. A huge effort has been expended in the eradication of bacterial and viral diseases, even quite common and hitherto accepted childhood illnesses, such as mumps and measles, along with the nastier polio and smallpox. This is not to say any of this intervention is *wrong*, but it has consequences. World population has grown as more children survive – a combination of better sanitation and nutrition, as well as medicine.

In the South, where this population growth is 'young', the population is dominated by young people of childbearing age, and thus is set to increase further, whilst in the North, apparent environmental well-being has led to a

172

less-fecund and older population, that though relatively stable, is both out of balance with its immediate resources, and genetically vulnerable to disease. Part of that genetic vulnerability relates to having removed the selective pressures exerted by childhood diseases. Finally, as the world population accelerates to a doubling every 30 years, food production cannot hope to run parallel. Almost all humanitarian aid to avert famine and provide food and medicine, whilst at the same time not addressing the stability of the local ecosystems, is in danger of creating double the suffering it attempts to alleviate, but at a later date.

Ecological knowledge cannot provide the whole of guidance necessary for action in the face of immediate misery. However, we may learn from indigenous peoples who are closer to nature, and who have not had the options of technical intervention in nature's often fearsome processes. Though they suffer heavy childhood mortality, and their encounters with 'disease', death and grief are more numerous, there is for them a teaching that brings them closer to life. In my own experience of people living close to that edge, they seem more vibrant and more vital. In my own family, grief at the death of loved ones has been the greatest pruner of my pettiness in life, and suffering my greatest teacher. In those whom I have watched and held as they died, I have seen the power of acceptance at play, even in the presence of the most undignified and painful of circumstances. This is not to argue for an idle acceptance of the suffering of others – but for engagement in the process of death, loss and grief. Nor is it to gainsay the fruits of literacy, education and the provision of economic security, both of which when accessible to women in cultures where large families are the norm, have rapidly reduced the birth rate.

Nor is it to argue for a hands-off approach to international problems, such as famine, but for greater resources to be devoted to sanitation, habitation, robust agriculture, appropriate technology and education. As in nature, disease in the form of invasion of pathogens, parasites or agents of decay, is not random – it follows overcrowding, stress, and malnutrition, and it is nature's regulator of numbers. We are slow learners on that score, and have stored up immense ills for the future. Part of the answer is to stop fighting the dis-ease, and address the cause. There is time for ecological action. And it is time for greater acceptance of the power and wisdom of nature – including the wisdom of her pathogens, the bringers of death.

I am in deep water. It has been a choice. There is no point now in living in the shallows. Swimming is the only option. But to swim freely, with the peace of the whales and joy of the dolphins, and not out of a fear of drowning, I need to embrace the ultimate teaching of Nature. We humans are consumed by our fears: of death, of enemies; of suffering and disease; lack of resources; pollution and genetic integrity; and now, fashionably, the very weather itself. It is the price of consciousness that we can look into the future. Yet all futures are imagined. In the Yogic tradition, the master, Yeshua bar Yosef, Jesus the Nazarene, is revered as one of the greatest healers and teachers. He urged us to

173

consider the lilies of the field, adorned in all their glory, that do not spin or weave, and 'take no thought for tomorrow'. It is the toughest of teaching in this modern world – to hold no fear, no negative projections of tomorrow, to trust totally in life, and hence, to be fully present in the moment.

This teaching underlies all Eastern spirituality. But it needs to be balanced by embracing the West, which is the direction of the dream, of individuation and creativity. In the West we are creative healers. We have the great healing traditions of humanitarian medicine, ecological science, and depth psychology. Thus, at the risk of playing out the unwisdom of my years, my proposition is this: that we join together in recreating a wonderful sanctuary of nature. That we build a natural temple. That we gather together its components of beauty, the species that serve the processes of wild nature. That we create sufficient space in each of the nations of England, Wales, Scotland and Ireland. That we throw off the strictures of out-dated sciences and call the process what it is, a healing of ourselves – not a healing for the Earth, except in one sense, that a song of gratitude to our mother is as much for our healing, as for hers. We have called upon many nations to safeguard their forest temples, having appealed to all manner of motivations, to beauty as well as biodiversity. But our own house must be put in order.

And then, from this base in our consciousness of beauty, and the espousal of our co- creative place on Earth, we need to move Heaven in our endeavours to restore a natural resilience and beauty to the most basic realms of agriculture and habitation. It is the most important task of the Millennium.

**Bibliography**

Barrett R. (1998) *Liberating the Corporate Soul: building a visionary organisation*, Butterworth-Heinemann.

Beer T. (1984) *The beast of Exmoor: fact or legend?* Countryside Publications, Barnstaple.

Berkes, F. *Sacred Ecology: Traditional ecological knowledge and resource management* Taylor & Francis, Philadelphia and London.

Boitani L. (2000) *Action plan for the conservation of wolves in Europe.* Council of Europe. www.nature.coe.int/cp20/tvps23e.htm

Carr-Gomm P. (2002) *Druid mysteries* Random House, London.

Carr-Gomm P. ed. (2003) *The rebirth of druidry; ancient earth wisdom for today* Element, Shaftesbury.

Castaneda C. (1993) *The art of dreaming* Element, Shaftesbury.

Featherstone A.W. (1997) *The Wild Heart of the Highlands* ECOS 18 (2), 48-61.

Fazey D. (2003) *Seeing over the hill...a vision for community land ownership in Wales* ECOS 24 (2) pp51-56.

Forestry Commission (1998) *A new focus for England's woodlands: strategic priorities and programmes.* Forestry Commission, Cambridge.

Graham H. (2001) *Soul Medicine: restoring the spirit to healing* NewLeaf, Dublin.

Graham H. (1999) *Complementary therapies in context: the psychology of healing* Jessica Kingsley, London.

Harner M. (1980) *The way of the shaman* Harper, San Francisco.

Jaideva Singh (1979) *Siva Sutras* Motilal Banarsidass, Delhi.

Jung C.G. (1966) *Modern man in search of the soul* Routledge, London.

Kaptchuk T (1983) *Chinese medicine: the web that has no weaver* Rider, London.

Krech S. (1999) *The Ecological Indian, Myth and History.* WW Norton, New York.

Levine, Peter (1997) *Waking the tiger: healing trauma* North Atlantic, Berkeley, California.

Liu Y. (1988) *Traditional Chinese Medicine* Columbia University Press, NY.

Lomborg B. (2001) *The skeptical environmentalist: measuring the state of the real world.* Cambridge University Press.

175

Mason, Colin (2004) *The 2030 Spike: countdown to global catastrophe* Earthscan, London.

McKibben B. (1990) *The end of nature: humanity, climate change and the natural world* Bloomsbury, London.

Mech D. (2000) *The wolves of Minnesota.* Voyageur Press, Stillwater, MN.

Miles H. & Jackman B. (1991) *The Great Wood of Caledon.* Colin Baxter, Lanark.

Muir J. (1992) *The eight wilderness discovery books.* Diadem, London.

National Trust (1999) *A Call for the Wild* National Trust, Cirencester.

Perrin J. (1997) *Visions of Snowdonia: Landscape and legend* BBC Books, London.

Peterken G. et al (1995) *A forest habitat network for Scotland.* Research, survey and monitoring report No44, SNH, Edinburgh.

Prechtel M. (1999) *Secrets of the Talking Jaguar.* Element Books.

Pullman Philip (2000) *His Dark Materials* trilogy: *Northern Lights, The Subtle Knife, The Amber Spyglass,* Scholastic, London.

Ramsall J. & Murray N. (1987) *Questions and answers clarifying the principles of Bach Flower remedies* Mount Vernon Bach Centre.

Saks M. ed. (1992) *Alternative medicine in Britain* Clarendon, Oxford.

Sams J. (1988) *Medicine Cards: the discovery of power through the ways of animals.* Bear & Co., Santa Fe, USA.

Sams J. (1998) *Dancing the dream.* Harper, San Francisco.

Taylor P. (1993) *Restoration forestry & the global ecosystem* ECOS 14 (2) 2-8.

Taylor P. (1995) *Whole ecosystem restoration: re-creating wilderness* ECOS 16 (2) 22-28

Taylor P. (2002) *Big cats in Britain* .ECOS 23 (2) p56-64.

Taylor P. (2004) *Shiva's Rainbow* Ethos, Oxford.

Vithoulkas G. (1980) *The science of homeopathy* Grove, New York.

Walker, Barbara (1983) *Women's Encyclopaedia of Myths and* Secrets Harper-Row, San Francisco

Wilbur, Ken (1996) *A brief history of everything* NewLeaf, Dublin.

Wright M.S. (1988) *Flower essences* Perelandra, Warrenton, VA.

Yogananda, Paramhansa (1952) *Autobiography of a Yogi* Harper-Row, San Francisco.

176

# PART 3

## *Staying within the econometric and scientific paradigm*

*This section contains essays and papers that remain largely within the accepted econometric and scientific paradigm of modern conservation.*

*The Sheffield presentation in 2014 was an opportunity to present Rewilding to the community of old-school conservationists (where Sheffield Hallam under Ian Rotherham's guidance has a long tradition of professional education in nature conservation). I am happy to say that the presentation was well-received with much useful discussion and mutual understanding.*

*The same cannot be said for the community of Green economists, who have yet to respond to this submitted critical review of 'green economics' (sent in response to a call for papers to the Institute for Green Economics at Oxford University) – but then their tradition is relatively young and not at all established and they may yet be struggling with the incorporation of critical viewpoints.*

*My review of the first climate-change impact study on UK wildlife is very much a critique of computerised projections of change. It led to some strong reaction – which can be tracked on the BANC website. Since that time, the models have improved significantly – this criticism was received and acted upon, although I would still argue there is an unhealthy reliance upon 'consensus' estimates of climate change upon which all impact studies rely..*

*Likewise 'Rewilding the Grazers' arose from discussions with what was at first a sceptical community of conservationists wedded to the use of domestic grazing to maintain 'biodiversity'. I was eventually invited to address a gathering of specialists on this issue in Wales – with some resistance from both the farming community and the agricultural liaison officers within the conservation world. Discussions are ongoing and productive of change.*

*'Rewilding the political landscape' was originally published in ECOS and in the compilation Rewilding (Ethos, 2011).*

# Rewilding in Britain: lessons of the past fifteen years

*This is a background paper to an invited lecture given at the Sheffield Hallam University conference on 'wilder designs' in conservation, May 2014. A shorter version is published in ECOS 35 (3/4) 2014.*

Despite widespread public concern for wildlife, in these times of economic austerity the political and economic future for conservation looks bleak. Wildlife surveys report continued serious declines. [1] Yet, there appears a glimmer of hope with rewilding - a term that has recently caught the public imagination, penetrated to cabinet level in government, and is now moving with major initiatives across continental Europe. In the UK, rewilding is a growing movement, with a network of practice and experience that involves community and cooperation at local levels stretching back more than twenty years. However, as some recent and perhaps opportunistic players enter the field, there is a danger that the central message and transformational nature of these initiatives will be ignored.

My premise is that in Britain we have levels of 'rewilding' experience that are challenging to an old paradigm of conservation that is centred in scientific and econometric concepts of the world. This wilder experience of the natural world is developing at grass-roots level as an emergent community of practise involving both professionals and the broader public. I will argue that its achievement of a slow but steady progress in shifting consciousness toward a more creative relationship to nature is in danger of being ignored by new and opportunistic players in favour of a more glamorous, acceptable and fundable 'rewilding' agenda.

Rewilding, as concept, practice and potential social movement, may be capable of transforming our damaged relationship with the natural world in ways that traditional conservation fails to do. However, this movement may be in danger of capture by the corporate agenda of conservationists now seeking to break out of a defensive paradigm that is clearly failing. This attempt is without a strong connection to community. Indeed, the greater the corporate strength and ethos of these organisations, the less connected they are to the communities involved in rewilding. And although they may incorporate rewilding models of economic well-being supposedly of benefit to local community, they do so within the same econometric paradigm that has led to the ghetto status of modern wildlife conservation.

Community and personal experience of a transformational nature has no ready index and few champions – yet it is here that society most needs to register a

178

shift in consciousness. I have witnessed such shifts in all of the projects reported in the supporting materials {these were presented at the conference and are available by contacting BANC at www. banc.org.uk}.

## Corporate creep within a competitive economy

The issue I want to tackle is what happens to the wealth of grass-roots rewilding experience documented in the BANC and Wildland Network projects once other more corporate players develop agendas that include or champion rewilding but have little to no direct contact with that body of experience. Currently, there is a very professional high-profile campaign by Rewilding Europe where the lead is taken by WWF Netherlands, acting in partnership with eco-tourism interests. Rewilding is also attracting academic analysis as a concept to be categorised and subjected to theory. This academic interest and the interests of corporate bodies and associated entrepreneurs, see rewilding through the lens of their own designs, motivations and needs, selecting those aspects upon which to focus and discarding others.

Unfortunately, it appears that what is being disregarded is what I would consider the most important lessons and issues from about a dozen relatively large-scale 'rewilding' projects in Scotland, Wales and England. I would argue that at a grass-roots level, most of these projects represent a fundamental shift in 'conservation' values:

Each moves beyond the static concept of protection toward a more creative relation to the *processes* of nature wherein human agency is minimalised:

- Each challenges at different levels the concepts of biodiversity value such as priority species, or habitat protection, upon which many designated areas have been historically defined and 'preserved';

- Each involves a variety of 'actors', some in the state sector, some in the voluntary sector and even some in the corporate world (Water Companies, for example), working toward a common ideal – often with active managerial cooperation;

- Most have an educational and community component that extends beyond that of traditional conservation volunteers – for example, in the health and education sectors ;

- Some involve a more overt spiritual dimension to the project which informs some key objectives that lie beyond those of a traditional conservation-science approach.

I have visited all of the projects outlined in *Supplementary Material* over the past twenty years and know personally many of the managers involved. In 2005, with the support of a small project grant from the British Association of Nature Conservationists (BANC), of which I am a council member, we published *Beyond Conservation* – the results of surveying projects in Britain to

179

that date, and adding an appraisal of background issues such as agricultural economics, forest policy, and the 'rewilding' movement within conservation. I made an effort in that book to extend conservation thinking to include physical and mental health issues, as well as the spiritual dimension – arguing that the patriarchal, Judaeo-Christian religious perceptions of Nature, with its elements of dominion, control and above all, the absence of 'soul' in anything other than the human, when coupled with an apparently objective scientific paradigm of conservation biology, were limiting the wider appeal of 'conservation' – most especially to younger and wilder people.

## The Wildland Network

Just prior to that publication, a small group of us in BANC set up The Wildland Network with the intention of each project learning from others, and to gain a higher profile among government agencies and within the voluntary sector. The Network ran regional seminars and national conferences, along with site visits and invitations to the leaders of the Dutch 'flagship' projects that use feral herbivores. In the BANC journal, *ECOS,* we sought authors from all of these projects, as well as wider European schemes – for example, lynx and bear re-introductions. This body of writing (60 articles by 53 authors) was published as *Rewilding* (Ethos) in 2011 as a hardback and series of PDF downloads (with full colour) available from BANC. Additionally, BANC members were instrumental in setting up the Wildland Research Institute at Leeds University in 2009.

I make these points of history, first to emphasise that I carry hands-on activist experience which informs the views I will present, and secondly, because important elements of this body of writing and experience - with its very clear social, scientific and economic implications, have all the appearance of being wilfully ignored within much of the mainstream corporate conservation sector, as well as in academic treatise and popularising writings on rewilding.

## Avoidance of social issues

'Wilful blindness' seems to be a feature of early 21st century politics: it featured strongly in the Leveson Inquiry regarding corporate responsibility in the media as well as in the lead-up to the apparently unforeseen financial crisis. As a consequence of that crisis, government agencies in the UK are in the middle of a 30% cut-back in key staff. NGOs are also at the effect of this general austerity drive – both in respect of government funds and industrial sponsors, as well as with general membership. Academia is faced with the same general austerity, but more particularly, by government's further intention to make research contribute a proven (measurable) 'impact' to the general economic good.

This is the overall political and economic environment within which all organisations must now find sustenance. Such financial scarcity may work in either of two directions: lack of resources especially at the grass-roots may foster cooperation; but in the corporatised environmental sector, that same scarcity may work against cooperative ventures and connection to community – with a shift toward capturing private foundation or national heritage lottery monies. This is the trophic environment for several leading organisations, as well as academia. Authors of popularising books will likely also have an eye to gallery mentalities. In each case, I will argue, these opportunistic rewilders are deliberately ignoring the community and spiritual aspects of grass-roots rewilding – the very realms that do not play to the gallery.

Margaret Hefferman in her book '*Wilful Blindness*' draws attention to how executives isolate and insulate themselves from wider social responsibilities, and warns: 'To the extent that money is thought about a great deal in any group culture, social connectedness weakens or falls apart' [2]

I am concerned that such wilful blindness is emerging within Rewilding Europe – a major initiative across the continent [3]; in the media profile that is emerging from George Monbiot's highly successful *Feral,* following which the author is engaged upon setting up a small group intent on furthering the 'rewilding' of Britain [4] ; and in the academic approaches represented at the Sheffield conference (Wilder by Design, Sheffield University, May 2014).

As major, high-profile political initiatives, both *Feral* and *Rewilding Europe* initially ignored the *breadth* of British experience, selecting instead projects that support or illustrate their converging approaches, and failed to reference, discuss or debate any other models. Something similar operates within academic contexts – for example, at Oxford, Jamie Lorimer's sole focus upon the Dutch experience as indicative of rewilding and from which theoretical conclusions about rewilding might be drawn and where a broader appraisal might make an appeal to theory less convincing. [5]

The same limited vision serves conservationists who would defend their traditional objectives by railing against the more extreme projections of rewilding, such as appeals to rewild the British uplands *in general*. Much of Monbiot's wilder visions for the uplands and Rewilding Europe's large scale plans for abandoned farmland have serious political implications in relation to marginal farming, community life and rural economics. Monbiot argues, for example for the phasing out of 'perverse farming subsidies'. Such broad statements by players who have no communal responsibility are not representative of the rewilding movement that BANC has documented. Whilst having the potential to popularise and widen the constituency for rewilding, there is also the potential to alienate key players on the ground, such as farmers, game conservancies, fishermen, commercial foresters and even traditional conservationists – a negative potential that all of the grass-roots projects have worked hard to avoid.

Those rewilding initiatives that take a cooperative approach work within slow-moving generally conservative rural communities; they generally do not define their concept of rewilding or set fixed targets; and they engage in activities that reach beyond the scientific paradigms of ecology and biodiversity. Thus, they do not fit within narrow definitions or traditional academic discourse, nor does their experience on the ground support ideas of large scale political and economic change of the kind that would be required to fulfil the ambitions of a new rewilding agenda.

As this more ambitious agenda moves onto a bigger political stage – with potentially far reaching economic and social implications, it has begun to create organised political opposition. Its narrow focus upon big schemes, however imaginary, is readily taken up by opponents of rewilding – such as the Welsh farmers union in relation to Monbiot's attitudes to sheep in the Welsh uplands, and provides an excuse to ignore or side-line the cooperative, long-term, small-scale work *with* farmers, such as with the National Trust on Snowdon or in Ennerdale in Cumbria. The English National Farmers Union has taken a n aggressively defensive stance over Monbiot's vision of the Lake District, but ignores the cooperative work at Ennerdale, and such polarised attitudes feed back to the local communities and then act as political pressure against the more naturalistic grazing regimes within Ennerdale and against initiatives that would widen the scheme across the Fells.[6]

This myopic approach would be understandable if the hard work of cooperative endeavour, practical compromise and a willingness to eschew definitions was buried in unpublished managerial practice. This is not the case: the Wildland Network and BANC have worked to make all of this readily accessible. In particular, material has been made available to all of the above popularising initiatives well in advance of their public announcements and has been published and made available for students of conservation in the Ethos volume *Rewilding* and the downloadable material on the BANC website.

There is nothing wrong, of course, in only taking on board a particular part of the spectrum of rewilding: there are specialised groups for example working on river restoration or coastal re-alignment that involve engineering contractors and large sums of money; rewilding can create small-scale wildlife corridors in cities; even modern farming can be 'rewilded' in small ways.

There may be strategic value in *not* challenging an old paradigm with its entrenched interests – such as the academic focus upon biodiversity indices. Any approach that sits well within what Jamie Lorimer describes as the Neoliberal consensus in conservation is obviously a safer approach. But I doubt any new initiatives will prosper unless they establish contact at grass-roots level.

In this respect, Rewilding Europe, having produced glossy professional brochures and secured substantial lottery funding, as well as a team of chief executives, has acted on feedback and recently embarked upon networking. Monbiot has similarly engaged a team partly to continue the work of the Wildland Network. Whatever the neo-liberal tendencies, the more socially aware funders are looking for elements of inclusivity, grass-roots involvement and economic relevance to the rural issues of decline at the margins of agriculture. It is in this latter area, that the British experience is most relevant and where a number of us have been critical of the purist rewilding concepts, safari-land ecotourism and models of 'nature development'.[7]

My own views are of course as coloured as anyone else's. There is an unwritten academic code based upon the pursuit of objectivity, which assumes personal colours should not matter – of course, few sociologists of science would agree, but sociologists are also often rather wilfully ignored! All hypotheses are coloured – rather like Tinbergen's famous 'search image' from ethological studies of bird behaviour - once formed, it determines the field of view.


**Declaring personal colours**

My preference is for all endeavours that affect the countryside and wildlife to serve the broader community without prejudice. In that, I am slightly red with an orange tinge - I like to see decision-making that is inclusive and by consensus. If I have any blue, it is that I care for continuity and tradition, but dislike authoritarian regimes where local community decisions can be over-ridden in the 'national' interest. I become an 'activist' when supposedly national interest usually disguises economic benefits accruing to small elites of business, landed gentry, corporate or financial players. I am a deep green when it comes to living simply, keeping my footprint small and enjoying a wilder lifestyle.

And then there is a colour that would describe a spiritual connection and appreciation of nature but I am not sure what it is – it doesn't surface, of course, in the political spectrum. In India, it would be black – but, obviously, in Europe black has rather sensitive undertones! In Hindu symbology, black represents both the creative and destructive aspects of the 'mother' Universe. Opposite to this is white.

White is beyond the political spectrum, apparently, but I would ascribe it the colour of the scientific and objective mind, the calculator, the econometrician and measurer of all things. White, tinged perhaps with pretentious purple, is also the colour of the priesthood that accompanied all colonial and industrial scale expansions – including the expansion of sheep farming by the Monasteries of old England, a colour that also therefore gave us the current ethos of conservation. A white-beard, white-sky worship emerges – patriarchal to its core, where the dark feminine earth and waters are seen purely as natural *resource*. And further, by refinement, a business world develops together with a financial system that can claim only 1% of its investments as either ethical or sustainable. Thus the modern corporate world separates itself not just from the Earth, but in evolving the managerial concept of *human* resources, separates from *humanity* itself. This is now the common 'development' model offered worldwide to developing countries – one almost impossible for any state to ameliorate without considerable financial penalties.

White thus colours an empire of heartless exploitation. It exists separately and out-of-communion with all other colours, partly as a consequence of hierarchical structure, partly in defiance of nature itself, where the true white is a union of all colours. Sadly, a new age is not yet manifest - 21$^{st}$ century Wales leads the charge of modernity with countryside issues, wildlife and forestry all now subsumed under the departmental title of Natural Resources!

I make this spectral digression because whenever more than one conservationist is gathered together in the name of the wild, there will be a spectrum. And we – in whatever role as academics, practitioners, enablers or philosophers of a potentially revolutionary movement, should acknowledge this. Everyone will have an agenda.

**Rewilding as a social movement**

The nature of conservation as a 20$^{th}$ century social phenomenon is not hard to sketch out in relation to the funding environment of scientific and econometric government policies. Further limitations of the niche are imposed by religious hangovers in relation to wildwoods, witches and pagan mystery rites. As an evolving animal, conservation is now well-adapted to the purely rational and 'scientific' paradigm of resource management and of ecosystems as a service to the economy. What then is *conserved*? Not *wild*life if current trends continue. Certainly - not the *wild*. Most nature as defined is now confined to *reservations*. And it becomes a *spectacle* on the eco-tourist route, with pathways, hides and interpretation boards, together with car parks and glossy tour guides.

Conservation mentality is a reflection of other mentalities. Within national priorities, it loses time and again to the economic imperative of roads, ports – both air and sea, railways, housing, population growth, funiculars, golf courses, jet-skis, fisheries, logging, mining, dams, turbines, biofuels.... all of these conflicts can still be found even in a small and highly developed country such as Britain and they all still act as a *model* for global growth.[8]

In this wider world, wildlife conservation becomes a colluding cousin to devastation of community, cultural degradation and alienation, mass migration to cities and the growth of wage-slave labour in a globalised economy. All of which Britain pioneered. It is a package is now sold world-wide. The ways-and-means for exploitation of natural resources gets covered under the rubric of biodiversity offsets and natural asset banking (note the recent appointment of Professor David Hill, a specialist in such econometrics, as deputy Chair of Natural England).[9]

In the British homeland, until recently, some kind of balance had been reached. Green belt restrictions stood against the tide. National Parks held the line against inappropriate housing, industry and tourism. Areas of Outstanding Natural Beauty presented a unified planning obstacle to ill-advised expansion of industrial structures into the landscape. But within that overall canopy agrochemical farming continued its inexorable re-shaping of the biodiversity profile. The latter system is then legitimised by the 'preservation' logic of subsidies that effectively lock-in biodiversity objectives to traditional farming practices (i.e. holding back natural processes such as succession). Even these subsidised schemes act only as a small niche in a widely destructive production system. The alternative would have been a general more ecological set of standards for all – such as conservation grade for arable crops and organic certification for dairy and beef herds, coupled with a mosaic of truly wild margins, streamside, woodland and wetland under naturalistic grazing.


The deeper reason why these standards were not implemented lies, in my view, with farming as an *industrial* sector within a business mentality. Farmers' magazines communicate a macho fascination with big machinery, are replete with military metaphors of war against pests and managerial targets for efficiency and profit. Farming has failed to meet its social obligation to protect let alone enhance wildlife on farmed land.

As long as these attitudes prevail, the more aggressive stance of the large-scale rewilders may gain public support at the expense of the subsidised farming community, particular the dependent regimes in the uplands. Many of us at grassroots level wish it were not so, but currently, where farming is concerned the Young Turks of the rewilding movement have a justified grievance.

The Forestry Sector, at least over the last two decades, has proven more enlightened. There have been major efforts at reforming the plantation landscape and forestry came to redefine itself as multi-purpose – that is, forests for the common good. However, those forest gains had to be defended recently by public campaign against a sell-off (and sell-out) of common assets to private enterprise. But away from the public eye, the personnel that developed and cared for those community assets, are being sold-off anyway, under a fierce job-cutting programme. This success of British forestry could have been trumpeted as an example to the rest of global forestry – particular to those newly liberalising states of eastern Europe lacking in the democratic practices necessary to safeguard communal interest.

**The impact of industrial scale renewable energy supplies**

The Green political faction, ably supported by Orange, Blue and Red alike, believes that in a time of man-made climate change economic growth and civil culture can only be safeguarded by massive relocation of industrial-scale technology into rural areas. In order to power itself from the dispersed energy of the wider countryside – wind, solar and biomass, the Megapolis must deploy machinery on a huge scale with uncharted impacts both on wildlife and community. The environmental impact of these green energy strategies has been wilfully ignored.

No strategic studies were performed in advance of the extensive lobbying for legally binding EU and national targets. Only after a decade of successful lobbying did many of the NGOs begin to realise the scale of those impacts both at home and overseas. Moreover, the technology for these renewable energy strategies involves large corporations, hugely profitable subsidies, and excessive payments to a few rich landowners. Whereas 'demand reduction' strategies at source, which are not so profitable and would engage legions of small-scale community-based artisans such as fitters, plumbers, insulators and roofers, attract little in the way of campaign support and are allotted miniscule government funds.

The battle against 'climate change' has reached such levels of political and scientific 'consensus' that critics of climate science or policies to address climate change based upon that science, are labelled, denigrated and marginalised. It is then notable that Monbiot's *Feral* contains no reference to the widespread industrial threats to wild nature, preferring instead the easy target of farming subsidies – whilst with other work he advocates a zero-carbon Britain. Rewilding Europe turns the same blind-eye. I am aware of no detailed academic critique within the UK of climate science and the effectiveness of its policy targets (ie whether they can in fact deliver significant amelioration of changes and on what timescale), nor any strategic assessment of the collective damage to other sustainability objectives.[10]

**The Future**

We have heard talk of 'The End of Nature' and of the reality of a modern 'Anthropocene' – where nothing on the planet remains untouched by the hand-of-man. Some of the more recent advocates of rewilding do seem to believe that a Pleistocene Park could recreate former realities, but again wilfully ignore the practicalities of recreating straight-tusked European elephants and their sabre-toothed predators.[11]

Much of this co-opting of the concepts and language of rewilding has its roots in American eco-philosophy and in out-dated conceptions of pristine wilderness and ecosystems in harmonic balance. Ecosystems are not stable but constantly changing. And we would have to go back to the last inter-glacial (125,000 years) before we could find an ecosystem unshaped by the hands and mind of

186

*Homo sapiens.* The late Pleistocene post-glacial pristine wilderness is an enduring myth. Humans had already vastly reshaped the continental fauna and flora of North and South America, Eurasia and Australasia – less so Africa.[12]

Was such anthropogenic influence natural or un-natural change? The answer depends not on science, but the quasi-religious definition of nature. Science colluded politically by separating the human mind from nature (the word itself is derived from Latin *sciere* - to separate). Had science been true to the communality, it would not have disguised itself in Latin mumbo as some kind of ultimate truth, and called itself what it is, *Separatism*. The methodology clearly has benefits, but it also has its downside.

If we are at the end of an era, as many people feel, the 21st century may mark the end of conservation mentality. If it is time for an end to the old collusions, rewilding has the potential for a new social movement. In its end-times, conservation - colonised as it is by corporate managers and target mentality, may even cast itself as the enemy of rewilding – as opposition to letting nature do its thing in the name of management objectives, priority species, biodiversity action plans, and things that volunteers can safely do – like cutting 'scrub' or uprooting 'aliens'. Some conservation organisations have become the wildlife equivalent of travel agents, theme park and gift-shop merchants, encamping on the doorstep of the Nature Reserves they develop. In many localities, such developments can be valuable *additions* to wild space, but often they invade that space – and as the corporate mentality creeps into the mission, more remote localities become targets for growth of the portfolio.

A balance is therefore required, where land can be purchased, preferably by smaller and more local initiatives, and such eco-developments minimalized. For every vociferous rewilding purist with visions stretching across the Pennines, Lake District and Cambrian wildwood, oblivious to SSSIs , ericaceous heath and acid grasslands alike, there are dozens of real-world practitioners willing to cooperate and create a mosaic of wildland sanctuaries of natural process *alongside* the communities of wildlife nature-gardeners and the few more responsible farmers. It is this vision that we must safeguard as a truly transformative relation for human and animal communities.

# References

1) Burns F., Eaton MA, Gregory RD, et al. (2013) *State of Nature Report.* The State of Nature Partnership.

2) Hefferman, Margaret (2012) *Wilful Blindness.* Simon & Schuster, New York & London.

3) See: Deinet, S., Ieronymidou, C., McRae, L., Burfield, I.J., Foppen, R.P., Collen, B. and Böhm, M. (2013) *Wildlife comeback in Europe: The recovery of selected mammal and bird species.* Final report to Rewilding Europe by ZSL, BirdLife International and the European Bird Census Council. London, UK: ZSL
www. rewildingeurope.com and especially: www.europeanrewildingnetwork.com

4) Monbiot G. (2013) *Feral: searching for enchantment on the frontiers of rewilding.* Penguin, London.

5) Lorimer J & Driessen C. (2014) *Wild experiments at the Oostvaardersplassen: rethinking environmentalism in the Anthropocene.* Transactions of the Institute of British Geographers. Citation: 2014 39 169–181 doi: 10.1111/tran.12030

6) Recent discussions in the project management group, in which the Wildland Research Institute takes part, revolve around the community compromises entailed when sheep numbers are reduced and domestic but hardy breeds of cattle graze the woodland under Higher Levels Schemes of agricultural income support.

7) The issues surrounding 'wild' herbivore re-introductions have been extensively discussed in the BANC journal ECOS by specialists from Natural England, the National Trust and the Forestry Commission: see in particular the contributions of Keith Kirby, Matthew Oates, Neil Harris and debates between Peter Taylor, Mark Fisher and James Fenton in *Rewilding: ECOS writing on wildland and conservation values.* Ed. Peter Taylor, Ethos (2011).

8) I discussed this recently following the 10th World Wilderness Congress in Salamanca, Spain (October, 2013), where delegations of indigenous people made presentations of their stewardship of 'natural resources' and 'biodiversity'; but were largely ignored when making a plea for changes in 'western' consciousness (see The Road to Salamanca, *ECOS* 34 (3/4) 2013).

9) David Hill heads up the Environment Bank and the Environmental Market Exchange. The rest of the Board of Natural England show strong representation of farming interests and involvement in agri-environment schemes.
http://www.environmentbank.com/environmental-markets-exchange.php

10) See Taylor, *Chill: a reassessment of global warming theory* (2009) Clairview, Forest Row, England.

11) The practicalities are discussed in Taylor, *Beyond Conservation* (2005) Routledge. The work was sponsored by BANC and deals in particular, with available species for breeding, hardiness, migration and dispersal, contagious diseases, etc.

12) See Flannery *The Future Eaters* (2002) and *The Eternal Frontier: An Ecological History of North America and Its Peoples* (Grove, 2008).

# Environmental Economics and Social Justice: Greens in Cloud Cuckoo Land

*A critical review of recent books and not-so-recent thinking on Green Economics, the 'end of growth', 'peak oil' and climate change – with some material drawn from book reviews in ECOS, journal of the British Association of Nature Conservationists.*

*Paper submitted two years ago for review at the Centre for Green Economics, in Oxford on issues of environment and social justice – with sadly, no response to date!*

**Abstract***: This paper is from an ecologist with a concern for environmental and social justice rather than an economist.. It is submitted now in the spirit of critical review and to provoke a discussion that many working ecologists feel is long overdue.*

Cloud Cuckoo Land is a big country and well-populated. Idealists get consigned there when they lose touch with political realities. But the original meaning had subtleties long since lost to a world of economists and environmental science. This celestial realm originated as a shamanic metaphor from a time when artistry within the city walls could still call on an intimate knowledge of the natural world - the land in question was a city built in the sky by birds – not for the birds themselves, but as a favour to their master-magus shape-shifter, an exiled politician turned forest Hoopoe (the fabulous *Upapa epops*) allied with two disaffected politicians from Athens. It stems from a play, a piece of satirical theatre, perhaps the very first political satire, from the pen of Aristophanes in 400BC Greece. Simply called 'The Birds', it is a story of how the two politicians enlist the magus and the birds to build an interceptory walled city in the sky, through which all of humanity's discourse with The Gods would have to pass. They then get to programme the downloads.

The play was an uproarious success, lampooning serving politicians in their spurious appeal to authority through the developing alliance of interlocutory priests and nascent state religion. I read the play through, including a detailed commentary on the original Greek, for some clues as to the real nature of the place, after realising that many of my former allies and some of my friends were living there!

In 2010, I had a stack of books for review. Some dated back an embarrassingly long time – like Jonathan Porrit's 2005 *Capitalism as if the World Matters* where he argued for a reformed system based not on the exchange-value inherent in accumulation of capital, but for a return to healthy use of profits to sustain useful goods and services. He focused upon the unfettered and scandalous excesses of the corporate world well before it got seriously worse. One book is more recent and widely celebrated – Tim Jackson's 2009

189

*Economics without Growth* – subtitled, 'Economics for a Finite Planet'. Standard perpetual-growth economics, as we all know, has no respect for planetary limits or ecological realities – hence the birth of 'new economics' and the New Economics Foundation (NEF), where David Boyle and Andrew Simms pen a manifesto: *The New Economics: a bigger picture,* also from 2009. Sharing my new economics' review shelf is a weighty ecological tome sponsored by the UN's Environmental Programme (UNEP) on *The Economics of Ecosystems and Biodiversity.*

I realised these particular books all had one thing in common when I received the latest - from Earthscan, appropriately titled *Enough is Enough* and subtitled *building a sustainable economy in a world of finite resources.* All of these titles stem from the Earthscan stable, to which I, as one of their authors with *Beyond Conservation,* often sign-on as reviewer. I wish I could write a 'Beyond Economics' and get to the bottom of why there is such a disjunction between the Greens and the classicists when it comes to the 'finite' resources concept – but to do so, I would have to penetrate the obscurantist world of the *economist* – and as a scientist, I am constrained by the need for evidence and predictability, which does not seem to constrain them at all. And I am condemned to understand better than they, the *ecological* dimension of the ecological economy they passionately proselytise. I have to assume they better understand the political dimension of economics – but all the evidence tells me they do not.

**Economics, not ecology, rules.**

The evidence that economics lords it over ecology is plain to see in the business pages of every major daily newspaper – whether right, left or liberal. As Liam Fox, a former Tory Cabinet member, wrote recently in the Times – 'Economic Policy is the Compass by which all other policies are set'. It should be an obvious fact, a reality of reality politics – Economics is King, not Ecology. Reading Hamish McRae in the Independent of 14th March 2015, he asks 'How can we get back on the long road to growth' – and not a single reference to physical limits, planetary ecology or The New Economics Foundation, and this from an avowedly left-liberal-green quality newspaper.

So, what my friends in the Green Movement are trying (and failing) to do is reverse a very profound directive in human consciousness. Every intellectual move they make appears immediately subsumed by the oxymoronic imperative of 'sustainable' economic growth that hi-jacked the world of Agenda 21 at Rio. At this second 'earth summit' the newly ecologically conscious economist managers perpetrated the seductive myth that economic growth could be decoupled from material growth. Sure, there was some evidence for this – but not of the kind that would pass scientific muster. Economist evidence *never* has to pass scientific standards – that is part of its appeal and power. All of these green reformers of capitalism make these two assumptions – that study of the economy and generation of theory is an entirely rational sort-of science, and that growth in the economy *can* persist and be decoupled from the demand on resources. On this basic assumption, the reformers then seek mechanisms – ways of turning, or rather tuning, the system. There is always a wish-list. There are always case-studies as examples of best practice – little islands of ecological sanity that nevertheless work economically, and if only....

**Green is no longer a radical colour**

Earthscan is a stable. I know this because I have talked to them about a radical book on climate change. After all, they published my radical book on nature conservation. But all stables have a policy (to win!). In the case of climate, the winners are all orthodox – the Earthscan market is primarily academic and bureaucratic (they publish many missives from the UN's work on this issue), and I know from personal experience that both these 'markets' are also camps in a very nastily divided ideological field. In the left-liberal-green camp, climate change science must not be questioned, even, as their most famous cheer-leader, Al Gore, intoned - the science might be wrong. On the right, free-marketeering conservative blue corner of the field, climate change science is a scam – a scurrilous attempt by the funding-hungry computerised ecological modelers of the world to gain a seat on the management board. Egged-on by the sceptic-blogosphere, such as the influential meteorologist Anthony Watts in *Watts Up With That*, the scientists are seen as in cahoots, darkly, with closet 'water-melons' – green on the outside, but red as old on the inside. The right-wing fear a weaseling command economy is on the horizon, with carbon accounting, control, surveillance, and a huge army of bureaucrats ordering daily life as well as directing the money flow.

The Earthscan stable is left-liberal green, of course. Interestingly, their last line of defence against publishing a critique of the UN's climate assessment, was that I should first get past the scientific review process in a reputable journal! The left-liberal green is now very scientific. There was no such pre-requisite for the conservation book!

So, we have to turn elsewhere for a more radical perspective. We can try the academic world – Cambridge University Press recently published *Smart Solutions to Climate Change: comparing costs and benefits*, edited by the arch-enemy of green climate alarmism, Bjorn Lomborg, whose seminal *The Skeptical Environmentalist* offered much apparent ecological succor to growth economistry. Lomborg is a bone-fide political economist and professor in the Department of Management, Politics and Philosophy at Copenhagen Business School – and not an ecologist, as I quickly discovered when I reviewed his work for *Ecos* way back when. Just one example will suffice, where he shows that contrary to the popular myth, global forest cover is *increasing* - he made no distinction between plantation-forestry and the real ecological thing.

### The skeptical environmentalist?

Lomborg's work is a classic example of how to choose the index to suit your argument. Ironically, he accepts the science of global warming and the *Smart Solutions* volume is dedicated to assessing costs and benefits of the strategies proposed for mitigating it. It would make salutary reading for all those campaigners who fought for Kyoto targets of emission reduction, only to be further and predictably outsmarted by cap-and-trade schematics. Lomborg prefers a global carbon tax to finance renewables – a techno-fix that gets us 'half-way'. He only considers the monetary aspects of the technology, not the impact on landscape, community and biodiversity; nor does he address what happens next with a half-way house economy.

Climate Change, incidentally, features as a key driver in *all* of modern green economic solution books. Climate change science may be good or bad science, that is not the only argument – it is what is done with it that concerns us here. So far, all other ecological limits-to-growth imperatives have failed to loosen the hold of classical economics – whether forest loss, biodiversity decline, denuded soils, unsustainable water abstraction…..*none* make it into the business pages, not even under the new guise of ecosystem services, however priced and valued by academicians. But *climate* gets there – usually under carbon trading, carbon pricing, taxes and subsidies for renewables and nuclear technology. Carbon policy is big business - entailing massive flows of both real money and its derivatives, with hundreds of billions now passing through the soiled hands of bankers and brokers. Indeed, there are *trillions* on the global horizon of this global problem, requiring some form of global governance – and of course, global taxes with a new global bureaucracy to administer and account, decide and direct. *This* is the Green Deal and I don't think the Greens can see just how profoundly unattractive it is to a world grown weary of bureaucratic and financial corruption.

The conspiracist may see all this as a classic political manoeuvre – first create the problem, then deliver the solution, which, of course, delivers a role for the politician-manager-expert-consultant whatever. Others may just see a greasy opportunism at work. But who sees the cloud cuckoo?

### Power and control

To look beneath the surface ideology we must turn to the radical stables. I offer two books – David Harvey's *The Enigma of Capital – and the crisis of capitalism*, recommended to me by one of my sons in a valiant attempt to place economic theory within his studies of international law and governance. And Richard Heinberg's *The End of Growth: adapting to Our New Economic Reality.*

Like me, my son struggles with economic theory, despite a very political and academic education compared to my simple science. I am convinced economists (and bankers) protect themselves by obfuscating language.

However, we have one thing in a common and that is a perspective on power. Economists like McRae write as if the dynamics they study exist within a fixed social structure, and its power relations are never exposed or commented upon.

Harvey is a Marxist geographer and the book was described by the Financial Times as 'A well-timed call for the overthrow of capitalism'! On the geographical *principles of capital*, he writes:

> "Principle number one is that all geographical limits to capital accumulation have to be overcome. Capital, Marx wrote in the *Grundrise* must 'strive to tear down every spatial barrier to intercourse, i.e. to exchange, and conquer the whole earth for its market'. It must also 'perpetually strive to 'annihilate this space with time'. .....Early on, urban-based merchants and traders learned that their power to survive with a land-based feudal or imperial power lay in cultivating a superior ability to manoeuvre in space. Merchant and trading capital (along with a nascent banking capital) circumvented and eventually subverted the feudal order in large part by spatial strategies....To this day the capitalist class and its agents maintain much of their power of domination by virtue of superior command over and mobility in space....fundamental, as every general knows to the maintenance of military superiority...thus emerges, a joint imperative within the state-corporate nexus constituted within capitalism, to fund the technologies and organisational forms that assure the continued dominance of space and spatial movement of capital"

Either the Greens do not understand this at all, or like the economist ranks they seek to join, they turn a blind eye. In short, capital will use the Greens and bend their technologies to its purpose. Thus, appropriately scaled 'green' solutions like community wind, biomass, hydro and solar as part of a decentralised grid and low demand structure, get transformed into giant aerospace turbines that wreck landscapes; biomass schemes uproot tropical forests and annihilate indigenous cultures; big-hydro invades once pristine wilderness and huge solar arrays on private farms are subsidised to the detriment of poor households who face ever increasing bills to pay for the subsidies. The technologies are taken over by BP, Siemens, AMEC and GEC – huge corporations with little feeling for local democratic, let alone, ecological concerns.

Harvey contends there is always a crisis for capitalism when growth dips below a critical threshold of 3%. I cannot follow the reasoning entirely, but observationally I watch for that percentage. According to Harvey, capital *must* grow – as an internal law, and like a population, to expand it must create new space. It is obvious from the press that current global growth has only been achieved by capital colonising the available space of China, India and the likes of Brazil and Indonesia. Eventually, it must run out of space. But for me, the key element in the analysis is Marxism's now perhaps long-forgotten concern with *power*. As a sociologist, Marx had one eye for symbol and structure and another eye firmly watching those elites striving to control the structure. Of course, such is no longer in fashion.


### The tipping point: peak everything?

Much more fashionable is Heinberg, of whom the Green MP, Caroline Lucas says: 'Read this and have the light switched on!' Growth is at an end already, says Heinberg, because of resource depletion, environmental impacts (climate change!) and crucially, crushing levels of debt. His other works – *The Party's Over, Power Down, The Depletion Protocol, Peak Everything* and *Blackout* have all been published by Clairview – which also happens to be the publisher of my own climate unorthodoxy, *Chill*. But whereas no Green would be seen dead with my tome, Heinberg is endorsed by Lester Brown, Herman Daly, Hazel Henderson and Bill McKibben. All Greens want to believe in the End of Growth, as much as they want to believe that there is a Climate Crisis. He argues the end of growth is with us now, and the reason is to be found in the depletion profile of fossil fuels. It is too readily forgotten that the *growth* of modern capital and industrial society has been built upon a supply of *cheap* fuel.

However, when Heinberg comes to the *what* of what will replace the fuel and the system, he wanders into the same land as the cloud cuckoo – renewable and sustainable technologies will fix it. He needs to read Lomborg on costs. How can an ailing system at the end of growth pay for expensive fuel technology? Many press commentators have pointed out that oil prices in excess of $100 a barrel were responsible for western growth performances below 2%.

Heinberg is right, I suspect, about indebtedness and the end of growth, though perhaps a little premature – the current demise is largely an indebted *western* phenomenon, capital having been exported to the expanded space of China, India, Brazil and Russia – all still growing and keeping the global average above 3%. They can pay for expensive fuel because they are running massive trade surpluses and accumulating huge sovereign reserves as opposed to sovereign debt. On a private level too, Asian billionaires now outnumber Americans, with Russia not far behind – there are about 1500 in global total. Vast wealth and the power it brings is being concentrated in very few hands.

China's new premier recently announced that the future of the country lay in the expansion of *consumerism* at home. China already accounts for 30% of global oil and gas demand, is the world's top emitter of carbon, and is building coal power stations at a rate that dwarfs the rest of the world's renewables investment. All this was driven by global capital flows from Taiwan, Japan, Europe and the USA. Manufacturing relocated on a massive scale. China was not party to the Kyoto Protocol – nor were the other BRICS, and the western parties that reached their 12% reduction targets would not have done so without that relocation of capital. Kyoto was an out-sourcing of carbon emissions and an outsmarting of the Green Movement by capital – so smart that it managed to get the Greens to campaign on its behalf, under the leadership of Al Gore.

## Where are the real Greens?

So – what is going on? What can be drawn from this confusing picture that actually relates to the real green concerns of humane community: food, water, fuel, security, social justice, resource depletion and pollution, as well as a caring for all the other species we share the planet with? The one thing I conclude is that Greens do not yet understand key aspects of economics and science. Both disciplines have an historical relationship to power in that they generate *theory*. Economic theory is treated as if it were science, when clearly it is not, and science is treated as some value-free fount of planetary wisdom, despite a track record that shows exactly the opposite. Just as Harvey tracks the alliances of banking with the merchants and the empire and hence also the industrialists and military, so also science became allied with the same merchants and their empires of business – not with the commune and the indigenous, not with sustainable community and cultural integrity, and far too lately did conservation *science* emerge, already too compromised by the alliance to be effective.

In NEF's manifesto book, Boyle and Simms see a 'cuckoo in the nest' – that of financial services replacing trade in goods – where 'only 5% of the titanic daily money flows has anything to do with the facilitation of goods or services'. They bemoan that 'the money market offers returns that no natural system could ever provide' and they do provide what appears a very sound critique of the system and what could be done. But are they aware that many of their green colleagues are fully prepared to play the derivatives game with carbon credits and trades?

This is what the naïve Green economism cannot see – it tries to play the same game, already conditioned not so much by the rules it tries to break, but by the concepts behind those rules – it is stuck in the same box. Economic theory is a cover for those in power. It is not science but spell-binding. Science itself barely exists – it has been taken over by the needs of capital and an enslaved technocracy and hence works for the ends determined by power – it too casts spells, hoping to net more funding and influence at the highest tables. The great majority of scientists are directed in their work by the imperatives of the market: in industrial agriculture and food processing, in the 'defence' industry, in pharmaceuticals, biotechnology, and genetic engineering, as well as in the advanced engineering of cars, ships, roads, airports. These are all the avenues of 'development' and are marketable. The Greens seem unable to see that their climate modelling allies are from the same cadres as the developers of GMOs and nuclear power – the modelers talk the same language and frequent the same clubs (and lodges). And they cannot see that they themselves now compete for

195

access to the same elite boardrooms, learning the lingo, wearing the cloned clothes and donning the same conceptual frameworks.

The last of these requires the greatest of scrutiny. In science and politics it was what is omitted that is hardest to 'see'. Green economists talk of 'externalities' as if all can be measured and compared within a single index – that is *exactly* the same methodology that 'we' (meaning the early 'greens' in the 1970s) criticised within the nuclear industry, where a childhood death from leukaemia was assessed as 'years lost' on the same index as a miner with lung cancer – the former entirely innocent and ignorant of the risks, the latter paid and protected by Unions and more or less cognisant of those risks. Further, the nuclear industry continually ignored *locus of control* issues in risk assessment, as well as the displacement of risks and benefits. Opponents were dismissed as emotionally or politically motivated, whilst their managers acted as if all their decisions were arrived at by scientific logic alone. Thus, today I witness the *absence* of strategic impact assessments of global biofuel demand, hydro-development and turbine expansion – in particular upon indigenous peoples. For example, European biofuel targets are aided by significant investment in oil-palm in Colombia, with 400,000 acres cleared not of forest, but subsistence peasants (the indigenous and their forests are protected by UN treaty), leading to one of the most serious migrant problems in the developing world. How is this to be indexed as an externality and would it make it into Lord Stern's next book on the costs of climate change inaction?

**Biochar to solve climate crisis**

The climate alarm has brought forth a plethora of 'mad science' schemes, all competing for pilot project funding – ranging from giant kites tapping the jetstream at 10km altitude, fertilising the ocean carbon removal plankton with iron, to spraying reflective barium into the stratosphere – none of which could be classed as economic propositions. Biochar is not so mad. The recently formed International Biochar Initiative offers Biochar as the latest and most plausible solution – and Earthscan have published the findings of 50 scientific teams in a 400-page volume *Biochar for Environmental Management*. I present this as an example of green econometric thinking – the following brief critique was written in 2010 and published in the BANC journal ECOS.

Basically, if plant material is burned in a low-oxygen incinerator, just as with traditional charcoal, black carbon is produced. If this is done on a large scale and the carbon buried in surface soils, then models show that it remains there and adds other benefits to the soil condition, such as nutrient retention, and the whole cycle can take out sufficient carbon dioxide from the atmosphere to make a difference. The Earthscan volume is long on details relating to yields and benefits, with 48 papers, but short on costs (2 papers) and availability of land – no detailed evaluation, with just one graph drawn from a study that showed state of the art carbon capture technologies could bring atmospheric

CO2 levels down to 300ppm by 2040. That graph applied to *all* carbon capture technologies and did not evaluate costs.

As any ecologist and rural sociologist would expect, a global biochar project would be a massive undertaking with large-scale impacts on agricultural, forestry and other cultural practices. The proposal is that normal agricultural and forestry 'wastes' are used and only a few special carbon sequestering crops in order to minimise the impact on food production. The feedstock is gathered, transported and pyrolised to produce a mix of gas for electricity generation and biochar for carbon sequestration and soil conditioning. To some extent, pilot plants that make use of biological wastes already exist for the production of electricity and heat and a little tweaking can produce charcoal as well as gas but with a loss of conversion efficiency.

This all looks very ecological but there are two crucial questions to answer relating to costs and whether there is enough material out there to make a difference (not that I believe halving emissions by 2040 will make much difference as in my own analysis, the *main* driver of current change is not carbon dioxide but natural oceanic cycles). On cost, the analysis presented shows that a plant processing wastes from 20,000 ha with a haulage distance averaging 14 km would on current values make a loss of $40/t of feedstock processed in fast pyrolysis where more electricity is generated (with less valuable biochar) and $70/t for the slower pyrolysis used primarily for biochar. The future economics depend upon competing electricity prices – in the US data provided, prices would have to rise by 45% for the fast pyrolysis to break even and by 400% for slow pyrolysis (where little electricity can be sold). This explains why even ordinary biomass burning for electricity has not penetrated the market. Biochar itself would have to be worth $250/t (as sold to the agricultural sector) to make the slow process profitable. However, credits for GHG reduction under emission trading schemes could potentially make it profitable – the data show that at $70/t of CO2 equivalent the slow process becomes profitable.

One can quickly see that as fossil fuel and hence electricity prices rise and with a higher CO2 equivalent price in the cap-and-trade systems, biochar becomes profitable, but its economic feasibility will also rest upon the *scale* of the subsidy required. The question then remains - is there enough charcoal? (and also – is there enough money!). The crop residue yields used in the analysis amount to 3.75tC/ha, which seems rather high, especially as it allows for wastes left on the land to control erosion. This is the same order as can be expected from dedicated Short Rotation Coppice energy crops in a temperate climate, and thus might be optimistic. From this feedstock, the net carbon dioxide offset is calculated at 0.2t CO2/t of feedstock or 0.75tCO2/ha.

From this data we can do a few gross calculations that the biochar strategists do not. The total area of UK crop land runs to roughly 10 million hectares, which would then sequester 7.5 million tonnes/annum of CO2 out of roughly 500 million tonnes annual emissions – or 1.5%. The subsidy cost to make it profitable would be $70 x 7.5m, or $500 million *per annum*. Of course, the UK is a highly populated industrial country, and there are very large areas of sparsely populated productive cropland elsewhere – in the USA, Russia and eastern Europe, Argentina and Australia - approaching perhaps 2 billion hectares. If all of this were utilised to provide feedstock (with mineral-rich biochar returned), then about 7% of global carbon dioxide emissions could be offset at a cost (to the taxpayer) of $100 billion per annum. Forest wastes might add another 3% for a similar price. The cost might be lower given that savings could be made where labour and land costs are lower.

### The military model of a command economy

One can readily see why dozens of agronomists, foresters, biofuel technologists, bankers, brokers and carbon credit specialists would set up an international biochar group and favour an international carbon sequestration market. It is the same system that would drive an expanded wind turbine programme, biofuels for transport, tidal barrages and, of course, a rejuvenated carbon-friendly nuclear industry. All of these programmes are currently uneconomic in a free market, but become so in a regulated carbon economy based upon taxation (effectively a *military* model, which is perhaps why so many campaigners unconsciously adopt military metaphors). It is also, of course, sailing very close to a *command* economy, which is why there is so much opposition from right-wing middle-America.

If it is all put together, I can believe that sucking carbon out of the air and using renewable sources, and using energy more efficiently can *technically* reduce emissions by 80% by, say, 2050. But is it politically or economically feasible? Other energy and offset options will require even higher subsidy, but if costs were close to biochar then an eventual $1 trillion/annum would be the cost (or investment) for an 80% reduction.

An effective socially sensitive and ecologically managed biochar programme could potentially, at some vast 'cost' or 'investment' have a small impact on carbon dioxide levels *and* contribute to social justice – but this presupposes that the current capital system and its derivatives markets can actually adapt to local circumstance, local democracy and community well-being.

### An economist offers a blueprint for a safer planet

On the latter question, we have a new book by Lord Stern that tells me I am wrong to be sceptical. *A Blueprint for a Safer Planet* follows on from his world-leading Stern Report on the economics of climate change commissioned by Tony Blair, which found, by cost-benefit analysis, that the costs of not mitigating climate change far outweighed the costs of mitigation at 1-2% of global GDP/annum to 2050. As practical ecologists at BANC, we are perhaps a little less enamoured of cost-benefit analysis, having learned that economists have little compunction in choosing parameters that suit their intended conclusions. And where no monetary value can be attributed, some factors can simply be left out. It has always been easier to calculate the costs of action rather than the impact of non-action. In Stern's case, the rule-book was rewritten and inaction, with all the complexity of future uncertainty and valuations of environmental and social costs, comes out more expensive than action.

The *blueprint* offers little more than the original report, which was widely slated by fellow economists –hitherto wedded to discounting future costs, which Stern eschewed, but feted by governments and environmentalists (who now, it would appear, embrace such cost-benefit projections, despite all past experience of how the figures get loaded to produce the politically desired economic outcome). One trillion dollars per year might well only amount to 1 or 2% of global GDP by 2050, but that does not mean it would be readily available. Governments have indeed found (or printed) that kind of money to bail out the banks and motor industries, but that has been a 'one-off' hit and we can see the difficulties that causes. Otherwise, many developed (and bankrupt) economies struggle to maintain anything like 1-2% growth.

At the time (2010) of this review of Stern the global economy as measured by GDP had contracted by about 2% over one year. Carbon emissions were down as a result. Everyone talked of increasing efficiency and green investment as the future, but then governments throw huge sums into a process aimed at kick-starting the same machine that not only created the slump, but also the so-called 'climate crisis'. My conclusion is that the modern growth-centred economy cannot cope with either a 2% contraction (or cost, or added investment) even for one year, let alone the next 50. I also think this slump (in confidence) was a direct result of the oil-price rise in 2009 to $140 a barrel and that this is a harbinger of the future.

## Wishful thinking and sloppy arithmetic

In a couple of pages of the only real examples in Stern's book and from which we are meant to gain confidence in his projections, he tells us that Germany has 23 GW of installed windpower, providing 7% of the country's electricity. He tells us that this has been achieved by the use of feed-in tariffs which guarantee a price for the carbon-free electricity. Stern quotes the detail of €9.2 cents/kWh for onshore and 13 cents for offshore but not the standard tariff, so we don't know the differential nor the scale or cost of the subsidy. He tells us that Germany intends to more than double its wind capacity to 55 GW by 2020 – and then quotes figures that expect a *fourfold* increase in TWh generated (delivered energy). This 400% leap in efficiency per GW installed comes from 'repowering' with bigger turbines, to give Germany 25% of electricity from wind. But the 'power' is already in the capacity figure, so the increase must come from some unexplained and hitherto unreported leap in efficiency (most

199

reports are of *less*) This then translates to 'Germany is a clear example of how government policy can support a transition towards close-to-zero-emissions electricity generation'.

Germany was the only example given. The leap from 7% to 25% I then regarded as unproven at least, and the remaining 75% of transition unexplored. Further, we could not work out from Stern how much it was costing the German taxpayer. This kind of reckoning apparently supports the 1% of GDP figure and the original Stern Report was full of such generalisations and great leaps forward. In the blueprint he now moves from 25% to near-zero (i.e. 100%) in one sentence without any supporting argument and no indication that all other renewables are 200-500% more 'costly' than wind. In the event, Germany had reached about 10% of electricity consumption from wind by 2013, and about the same amount for all fuel consumptions from renewables – but with the Finance Ministry warning that the high costs of the transition could not be borne further. This for one of the richest countries and most successful export economies in the world.

Had Stern turned to Denmark or Spain for his examples, he would have been more than unsupported. Unable to redefine their economies by exporting industrial capital to China, both invested heavily in renewable energy supplies – and became world leaders. Spain experienced *rising* carbon dioxide emissions - by 30% in ten years, despite the investment in renewables. Danish consumers pay 200% over UK electricity charges, all of that in a special tax, and though government sources laud emission reductions, these are complicated by export and import of electricity to Norway and Germany – Earthscan's *Atlas of Climate Change* recorded 5% *rising* emissions for Denmark to the year 2004.

And there is absolutely no time-related analysis of the actual impact on climate from the reduced emissions. Yet this level of thinking was going to be the basis for a new climate treaty in December 2009 (now rescheduled for December 2015)! In *any* analysis of climate change, it should be admitted that *dangerous* vulnerability is here *now.* Whether warming or cooling, adaptation is necessary to save real lives in the real decades immediately ahead. Stern points to a figure of $279 million that was then (2010) being spent on adaptation globally - not in special funds, but in an identifiable portion of the $100 billion of Overseas Development Aid. This was one third of one-percent of an ODA budget that goes to accelerating growth and energy demand in the standard model economy – as does, of course, the whole of the international capital investment flow – which dwarfs ODA, and upon which the phenomenon that is 'China Inc.' was created and exempted from the Kyoto Protocol.

**Chill: a reassessment of global warming theory (and action)**

In my book I take the environmental movement to task for accepting this low level of analysis. The impacts of mitigation technologies upon the social, cultural and wild environment will be immense but are not assessed by them, nor by Stern. The 'costs' of mitigation, despite what Stern believes, will pre-empt many other environmental strategies. Yet, none of the environmental groups has taken a critical look at the *science* of climate change itself - the complex modelling, the relation of atmospheric carbon dioxide to temperature, the time-lags, the role of natural cycles, and the ultimate question of whether emission controls can deliver *any* climatic effects before the end of the century.

There are clear issues of social justice that 'green' targets have been blind to – the high costs of renewables are ultimately reflected in fuel prices and impact those already living in fuel poverty. How does a concerted campaign that naively hands over technological solutions to big multinational corporations reflect a commitment to social justice?

As an ecologist, I have always been open to being convinced that at some future date, humanity could be endangered by carbon dioxide induced runaway global warming – but the IPCC models do not convince, and Stern and all the others simply build on that UN assessment without question. I was concerned with what is absent from the models – the play of natural cycles, and the fact that temperatures higher than present are recorded throughout the Arctic (in ice-core proxies) for the time of the Viking colonisation of Greenland. These are the same environmentally concerned  modeling UN minds that brought us 'dilute and disperse' for toxic wastes and now see nuclear power and GMOs as a future salvation. Environmentalists now seem to accept without question (or analysis) the authority structures and banking practises that will have to be put in place to make a low-carbon economy work.

As Mike Hulme points out in *Why we disagree about climate change*, that is because it is not in their interests to question. On the other side of the fence, an increasing number of conservative or right-wing voters, with their antipathy to taxation, increased regulatory control and interference in free markets, will oppose this new carbon economy and also, of course, question and disagree with the IPCC assessment. Meanwhile, in the heat of growing disagreement nobody pays much attention to *adapting* to inevitable changes, whatever the cause.

If the environmental campaign groups with whom I have had a long history of collaboration are to separate themselves from the backlash that is building, then I would suggest they slowly opt out of the carbon emissions, low carbon economy, and renewable energy arguments, and focus upon actually protecting the environment and the vulnerable communities that live there by refocusing on creating *resilience* to change.


**Getting real: there is no solution!**

In order to get out of the box, let us suppose that *there is no solution:* that renewable energy cannot replace fossil fuels; that the economic system cannot survive 'peak oil' and that mass indebtedness spells the end of growth. Population will grow by another billion at least, before natural processes of stress and disease begin the cull. Climate change is as real as it always has been, is largely natural and cannot be mitigated – crops will fail and famine is inevitable. I would say there is a 50:50 chance of this being a correct political, ecological and scientific assessment and hence a valid basis for policy formulation - but this tack cannot be allowed by the Greens, and that is why they are in cloud cuckoo land. They *have* to *believe* the system can adapt and the technologies can deliver. And they cannot question the structure of power – because, of course, they want to *join* it!

The Greens need to read Aristophanes – part shaman and a long way from the realms of modern science and economics, he chose the *cuckoo* for good reason. It is a master of ruthless deception, by which it ensures that its offspring get fed. At the end of *Prosperity without Growth*, having rehearsed all the standard wishes for a sustainable, ecological and equitable life, Tim Jackson states 'structural change is essential at the societal level' – and argues for three things: we have to establish ecological bounds on human activity, fix the illiterate economics of relentless growth and transform the damaging social logic of consumerism. But like all the other books, he assumes it *can* be done, carried by the force of rational argument and reform, with the main tool in his box the trump card of a carbon currency courtesy of Mr Gore. This is the Green's city in the sky – an interlocution where the Gods are still economists. I had to smile when I saw Tim recently described as 'the economist' – his PhD was in Physics! As professor of Sustainable Development at Surrey University, he is busy developing a more appropriate index that reflects well-being rather than wealth, and the grail of a steady state economy. But if Harvey is right, capitalist structures cannot cope with the steady state. Already, this year sees China Inc reducing its prices and bent upon stimulating a wave of *consumerism* at home!

It seems that in all this green economics, belief is more apparent than science. And just as I have argued over climate change – adaptation to inevitable change makes more sense than misconceived, ineffective and hugely expensive mitigation strategies, I think the same might be applicable to the economy. It is going to crash. What then constitutes an ecological adaptation strategy? Everything these green economists suggest, including all technical and social innovations, is predicated on a *stable* economy (with all the elites firmly in place, but carefully advised) – and that, truly, appears to come straight out of the cuckoo land clouds.

**Books reviewed:**

**SMART SOLUTIONS TO CLIMATE CHANGE** Bjorn Lomborg ed. Cambridge University Press, 2010, 413 pages Ppk £19.99 ISBN 978-0-521-13856-7

**THE ECONOMICS OF ECOSYSTEMS AND BIODIVERSITY IN NATIONAL AND INTERNATIONAL DECISION MAKING** Ed. Patrick ten Brink. Earthscan, London. , 2011 494 pages Hbk., £60.00 ISBN 978-1-84971-250-7

**THE NEW ECONOMICS** David Boyle and Andrew Simms. Earthscan, London, 2009. 192 pages. Hbk, £13.49 ISBN 978-1-84407-675-8

**CAPITALISM AS IF THE WORLD MATTERS** Jonathan Porritt. Earthscan, London, 2005, 336 pages. Hbk £22.99 ISBN 1-84407-192-8,

**THE ENIGMA OF CAPITAL** David Harvey. Profile Books, London, 2010, Hbk 296 pages, £14.99, ISBN 978-1846683084

**PROSPERITY WITHOUT GROWTH** Tim Jackson. Earthscan, London, 2009. 264 pages, Ppk £9.99 ISBN 978-1-84407-894-3

**THE END OF GROWTH** Richard Heinberg. Clairview, Forest Row, 2011, 320 pages Paperback £14.99, ISBN 978-1-905570-33-1

**ENOUGH IS ENOUGH** Rob Dietz and Dan O'Neill. Earthscan, London, 2013.240 pages. Ppb £12.99. ISBN 978-0-415-82095-0

**WHY WE DISAGREE ABOUT CLIMATE CHANGE** Mike Hulme, Cambridge University Press 2009, 392 pages, paperback £15.99. ISBN 9780521727327 (Hardback £45 ISBN 9780521898690)

**BIOCHAR for ENVIRONMENTAL MANAGEMENT** Ed. Joannes Lehmann and Stephen Joseph. Earthscan 2009, 416 pages, hardback, £49.95 ISBN 9781844076581

**CHILL: a reassessment of global warming theory** Peter Taylor, Clairview 2009, 404 pages, paperback £14.99. ISBN 9781905570195

**A BLUEPRINT FOR A SAFER PLANET** Nicholas Stern, Bodley Head 2009, 246 pages, hardback £16.99. ISBN 9781847920379

# UK wildlife and climate change: Nature's disaster or dynamics?

*This essay was first published in ECOS, 28 (3/4) 33-39, 2007, as a critique of one of the first major reports on the potential impact of climate change on the British fauna and flora.*

How to assess the impact of climate change on UK wildlife? There are perhaps two approaches: one would be to ask experienced naturalists to assess what they have seen over past decades and project this into future decades assuming the same progression of climate changes. That would be fraught with difficulty – they would have to make selections to reflect the changes, and how would they isolate other factors, such as the intensification of agriculture? The other approach would be to build a computer model using more 'objective' indices.

As far as I know, significant government resources have only been put behind the computer model approach – and the MONARCH project[1] is the most extensive review of the potential impact of climate change on Britain's fauna and flora – taking seven years, involving four major research bodies and consultancies (ADAS, CABI, BTO and ERM) and funded by a partnership of just about all the relevant government departments and agencies from the Forestry Commission, the JNCC, SNH, CCW, NE, Defra, and voluntary bodies such as the National Trust, the Woodland Trust, WWF and RSPB, plus the UK Climate Impacts Programme at Oxford.

Having read the conclusions of phase 1 of MONARCH and as a practising ecologist with some responsibilities in advising on land management and climate change strategies, I have to say that it is next to useless. But, as an independent consultant, how to say this to just about every hand that might ever feed me? And why do so when the recommendations for action support the goals of the more creative approaches to biodiversity that many of us have been advocating over the last decade? My only answer is my belief that we need an awareness of the limitations of our methodologies. Otherwise these studies could backfire and endanger the goals of landscape-scale conservation that everyone acknowledges is required to make our wildlife more robust to change.

To be fair, the MONARCH study states some of the important limitations of the methodology it has chosen – selecting a relatively small number of species not for their particular susceptibility to climate change, but because good data existed across Europe that could be used with the model chosen to calculate an index called 'climate space'. This index determines how much room a particular species has in Britain to 'move'. But only in so far as climate factors are concerned – it does not address actual habitat or a species' ability to physically move across or through any biological barriers it might encounter. The only biology used is a measure of climate adaptability drawn from knowledge of the species' range in Europe.

But there are greater problems than the ones acknowledged and which would challenge any methodology. The first relates to the degree of confidence in largely computerised and hence un-validated predictions of future climate regimes; the second involves the way in which UK biodiversity is measured and valued; and the third to the timescales for the effects of any policy initiatives such as adaptation might direct. The fourth is the horseman of mitigation strategies and their impact on the very biodiversity they are meant to protect. Unfortunately, MONARCH assumes an unjustified progression in future climate regimes, accepts UK BAP targets and definitions with little reflection on their wider bioregional significance, and fails completely to model the interaction of mitigation responses with adaptation strategies.

### Uncertain climate futures

Despite the prevalence of 'best guess' projections – as advanced by the UK Climate Impacts Programme with its use of regional computer models (either based at University of East Anglia's Tyndall Centre or the Met Office's Hadley Centre in Exeter), there is considerable scientific uncertainty as to the future unfolding of UK climate in a 'warming' world.

This is the case even without any major critique of the 'global warming' model driven by carbon dioxide. The translation of the so-called consensus model to regional levels is still very uncertain. Accelerating warming in the Arctic could potentially lead to a cooling of the NE Atlantic region as the Gulf Stream is slowed by freshwater inputs to the northern end of the 'conveyor' system. Other models of the main climate driver, not favoured by the IPCC, are based on giving greater weight to solar cycle changes and their link to cloud cover. Some solar scientists expect a rapid downturn in northern hemisphere temperatures in coming years. Despite the opinion of the UN and the majority of science institutions, including, it would seem, all the funders of this study, it is a *political* decision to exclude this model, not a scientific one. It is based upon the needs of the policy makers for a single answer.

Thus, any reviewer is faced with choices:

1) provide projections for change in either direction,

2  provide projections for the 'best guess'

3)  provide timescales based upon various global emission scenarios

4 provide timescales based on solar cycle projections.


In practice, there are forces militating against exploring the first and last of these scientifically valid choices. Funding bodies do not like uncertainty and policy makers likewise – so exclusions are made. Thus, the only major study of climate impacts on UK biodiversity provides only UKCIP's 'consensus' model with three timescales (2020, 2050 and 2080) and two global emission scenarios and all the other non-specialist bodies on climate in the MONARCH consortium collude with this.

## UK Biodiversity indices and values

There has been a long running debate within *ECOS* on the values inherent in the UK Biodiversity index and its Action Programme, but despite such intelligent critique the BAP remains as the central plank of UK policy. Its limitations are doubly highlighted when used as a basis for climate impact studies.

Firstly, the UK BAP, despite the provision for habitat plans, is species focussed and most importantly, relates to species that are already *threatened* – that is to say, in decline or in vulnerable small populations. The list of BAP priorities is also strongly representative of professional scientific conservation interest – wherein there has been little self-reflection on the *value* of species, not only in relation to ecosystem function, but to the wider public psyche. As I have argued in *Beyond Conservation*, a scientistic approach to nature conservation has probably contributed to its ghetto status, especially with respect to governmental priorities.[2] There has been a failure to translate the public affection for nature and wildlife into effective indices and actions.

When climate change is considered, the species focus compounds these problems. Many 'rare' species are limited in their UK distribution because they are already on the edge of their range. They are not necessarily threatened with respect to their wider distribution. That wider distribution is also likely to have a climatic component to its limits. The British Isles is a maritime climate province bordering the wider continent, thus, in the north and west of the island, there are habitats and species that are restricted to this maritime border, with some smattering of endemic species or subspecies and some very important major populations – some of which are abundant and not particularly threatened (e.g. seabirds, coastal heath flora). However, the south and eastern parts of the island touch the range of continental species adapted to drier environments; whereas the northern provinces may capture the southernmost populations of essentially northern and often circumpolar species.

Within this context, each species also faces threats in the modern era from other dynamics – especially agricultural intensification and loss of habitat, plantation forestry, water extraction, disturbance, persecution and invasive introductions. This compounds attempts at identifying climate change as causative in any past changes in distribution, and hence predicting future responses.

On a biological level, it is hardly ever recognised by conservation programmes that species are always 'threatened' with extinction or under pressure, some more than others at any particular time. Species are the sacrificial front-line troops of the evolutionary process and like the generals in the rear, it is the

*Genus* that usually persists and hence evolves. Species come and go as the environment, including the climate, changes, or new competitors come along. For example, there are several Fritillary species in the genus, all hardly distinguishable by lay observers – the same for leaf warblers of the *Philloscopus* genus, but whatever happens to the climate and niches they occupy, some of them will likely make it and the genus will survive and potentially radiate another supply of species. What is nature conservation doing when it interferes with this process? I am not saying here that conservationists should do nothing, only that they make their interventions transparent, especially to the public that pay the salaries and put up the research funds

### The nature of the 'threat'

Thus, any map of rare and threatened species of Britain and Ireland will not necessarily reflect that species' global status nor its vulnerability to climate change. When it comes to evaluating species' response to change, there seems little awareness of the way in which 'rarity', 'charisma' and 'nationalistic' values come into play. In some sense *all* species are going to be affected by climate change, and obviously not all species from nematodes to fritillaries are equal, whether to the conservation scientist or the public mind. In this respect, the bluebell is of observably higher value than the cudweed. But it is the cudweed that features in the shortlist for MONARCH.

### Timescales for adaptation and mitigation

In the orthodox scenario, the UK climate warms to 2080 by as much as 2 C. But what will this mean for habitats and species? The projection is for drier and hotter summers and warmer and wetter winters – but as the summer of 2007 demonstrated, the average can be punctuated by extremes – in this case of flooding. There is also a potential for late frosts and gale damage. These are not easily factored into the model. Sea temperature changes and resultant food chain effects may also be marked. It is not clear that these kinds of uncertainties are reflected in the simple index drawn from a species' wider distribution.

Some changes are already evident. Spring has advanced by two weeks and the growing season is longer. Winters are warmer and wetter (though some have been very dry) and summers drier with a marked drying out of upland habitats and eastern agricultural land. Larger insects have noticeably declined in abundance. But isolating effects upon fauna and flora is not easy: the past two decades of warming (previously the globe cooled from 1945-1980) have also coincided with major agricultural change – in particular the winter sowing of wheat, early cutting for silage, grass monoculture and loss of species-rich meadows; new and powerful veterinary biocides have been introduced that affect dung-fauna and have wide-reaching knock-on effects. There may also have been major habitat changes in the winter range of summer visitors such as warblers.

These changes make it difficult to ascribe current declines to climate change. Conversely, some 'gains' are clearly climate related – such as the colonisation by little egrets of the southern and western estuaries and marshes.

It is not an easy matter therefore to identify potential changes in a warmer or cooler Britain as individual species' responses are not well understood – but certain generalisations on habitat (using the orthodox warming model) could be made:

- there is likely to be further loss of wet pastures, particular in river valleys in the south and east; and upland (and coastal) heath and grassland will be drier and more susceptible to fire damage;

- there will be a gradual retreat of the sub-alpine zone on northern hills, with some habitat being replaced by scrub.

One does not need a computer model to draw these conclusions – any competent naturalist could do so. And equally, most naturalists would be able to estimate 'climate space' and then add on the crucial element of how much real habitat exists within that space. But computer modelling is a modern necessity if studies are to bear weight.

And actually, naturalists with a feel for their particular birds, bats or butterfly ecotype distributions usually know enough genetics to be cautious in the assumption that just because a species occurs in Caledonian and Balkan pine forests the former will have genetic access to the latter's climatic adaptation – this seems to be a fundamental flaw in the concept of 'climate space' upon which the MONARCH study depends.

However, there is one further factor mentioned at the outset – the widespread impact upon habitats that mitigation policies may bring. The recently announced EU biofuel targets will likely lead to widespread intensification of agriculture and forestry in the UK; wind turbines already threaten raptor populations, such as the sea eagles in the Hebrides and kites in Wales; and estuarine barrages will impact upon waterfowl habitats. Which mitigation strategies are going to save *our* redshanks and lapwings that have been so recently decimated by agricultural intensification is far from obvious, but the growing global demand for woodchip to burn is certain to suck in habitat as far away as Latvia; likewise biodiesel and ethanol targets will affect Brazil and Indonesia.

In its final analysis of 32 species the MONARCH report identifies, as one might expect, a proportion of losses (8), gains (15), and no change (9), though it warns the proportion is not representative so no conclusion can be drawn. Despite this, the report then concludes that *"loss or shift in climate space for British and Irish wildlife will be more severe unless greenhouse gases are cut"*. It recommends more conservation effort, better habitat management, and the creation of a more resilient and permeable landscape. The study purports to have identified the potential consequences of *"failing to reduce emissions and strengthens the case for action"* such as the *"need for the conservation sector to advocate the development and implementation of a robust mitigation policy"*.

The latter conclusion is dangerous political and ideological polemic dressed up in the guise of a scientific and objective study. It goes way beyond the science and in particular the very limited science of MONARCH's methodology. At the outset the study talks neutrally of impacts – but by the end it drops into the ideology of 'threats'. How have they evaluated the gain of a little egret in the Somerset Levels – which I watched with great pleasure today, against the loss of an obscure bat that I and 99.9% of the public are never likely to be able to distinguish from any other bat? The same argument will apply to all the families and orders affected.

And what business is it of the likes of WWF, RSPB, Woodland Trust, Natural England, SNH, CCW and the National Trust to call for mitigation strategies when they provide no study of the likely impacts of these (which are huge!), and no analysis of the timescales for mitigating actual climate change (at least 50 and probably 100 years before emissions can be stabilised at *current* levels which are apparently already driving the changes).


**More rigour, less collusion...**

Of course we need action to address human welfare needs and environmental stability in case climate change becomes more severe. But in my view there has been an unacknowledged collusion of government agencies, NGOs and other parties in assuming climate change is strictly bad news for the UK's fauna and flora in all situations. This is a grossly simplistic outlook. They make an *a priori* assumption that the balance of impacts can only be a net *loss*, despite there being little solid evidence in their analysis to support this. They seek to justify the targets of emission reduction in order to mitigate such losses but with not even a reflection upon the impact of those mitigation strategies on the biodiversity it sets out to protect.

Even though there is an equally forceful call for adaptation strategies such as larger scale habitat creation, this collusion does not serve the wider public campaign for nature. The report is transparently weak and as such unlikely to influence policy makers engaged in what is perceived as a battle to save the planet. At a time when Friends of the Earth and other environmental NGOs argue for major sacrifices of Britain's few remaining wild areas to wind turbines, I doubt we are going to convince anyone that *biodiversity* matters with these kind of studies. There is a complete absence of treatment of recent and high profile gains, especially to the nation's much loved avian fauna – such as little egret, Purple heron, and great egret, and spoonbill may follow (the great bustard and sea eagle have come from re-introductions and enhanced management).

I would argue that the main drivers for enhanced biodiversity are habitat creation, agricultural extensification and raised public awareness and willingness to pay for these programmes – climate change is in my opinion virtually irrelevant. By joining on the climate bandwagon and ignoring the scientific uncertainties and inherent problems of indices and value, more support may be gained for habitat creation, but there is a real danger of backlash once all of this becomes transparent, and more particularly if the carbon dioxide model has been overplayed. A little more circumspection and critical appraisal of modelling would not go amiss.

## References

1. MONARCH – Modelling Natural Resource Responses to Climate Change - *A synthesis for biodiversity conservation.* www.ukcip.org.uk

2. Taylor, P. (2005) *Beyond Conservation* Earthscan, London

## Abbreviations

ADAS: Agricultural Development and Advisory Service consultants

BTO: British Trust for Ornithology

CABI: Commonwealth Agricultural Bureaux International

CCW: Countryside Council for Wales

Defra: Department for the Environment, Food and Rural Affairs

ERM: Environmental Resource Management

JNCC: Joint Nature Conservation Council

NE: Natural England

RSPB: Royal Society for the Protection of Birds

SNH: Scottish Natural Heritage

WWF: World Wide Fund for Nature

*A response to key points in this article has been made by representatives of the MONARCH consortium. This can be viewed on the Blog section of BANC's web site at www.banc.org.uk*

# Rewilding the political landscape

*Rewilding has been branded a political gimmick by some. In fact it represents a grass-roots shift in thinking towards creative landscape-scale conservation with multiple benefits. This essay was published in the BANC journal, ECOS 30 (3/4), 2009.*

Whilst rewilding has seemed too daring for some NGOs and agencies to embrace, politicians have not been so cautious. David Milliband flagged it first in a speech when he was environment secretary, and Hilary Benn, his successor, endorsed the concept as a new way forward in conservation at Labour's 2009 party conference (Jonathan Leake, *Sunday Times*, 27 September 2009). Some journalists dismiss the notion as a political gimmick demonstrating a lack of appreciation of the real issues in the countryside (Terence Blacker, *The Independent*, 30 September).

Over the past five years, the Wildland Network has initiated a series of regional seminars and exchanges to promote the initiatives of the National Trust (e.g. at Ennerdale[1] and Wicken Fen[2]), the Forestry Commission (Ennerdale and Glen Affric), the Woodland Trust, RSPB, the Wildlife Trusts and the public subscription projects of Trees for Life[3] and Carrifran[4,5] as well as individual landowning developments in Alladale[6,7] and at Knepp Castle Estate.[8] Additionally the Network has focussed attention upon the restoration of key species, such as wild grazers and their predators.[9,10,11,12,13] Thus the 'rewilding' wave is not a new political gimmick but a response by government to this new wave. A Wildland Research Institute has been launched at Leeds University and there are ongoing studies at Aberdeen University on the potential for wolf re-introduction in Scotland. (wolvesandhumans.org and see also Paul Eccleston, *Daily Telegraph*, 29 November).

## In the agricultural wilderness

In eastern Britain, fenland and coastal marsh restoration projects co-exist with high production wildlife-free zones, creating a potential mosaic. The recent recolonisation of the region by the common crane, a large bird that requires disturbance-free nesting zones more readily associated with Scandinavia and Eastern Europe, is an indication of major progress toward wilder land.

The trends toward intensive agricultural production and the concomitant loss of wildlife on both arable and pasture land can be partly addressed by smaller scale mosaic approaches that make use of wild headland, margins, coastal strips, streamside and corridors, using extensive grazing by special breeds and targeted subsidy. In this strategy, even the wildlife-deserts of the grain-belt can be improved without significant loss of production, employment and changes in rural life. No one is advocating wolves in East Anglia, Dartmoor or Exmoor, but with the Forestry Commission now officially admitting they have feral panthers in the Forest of Dean,[14, 15] and lynx being regularly sighted across Britain, including in the Mendips[16], there must be a case for official return of Eurasian lynx, especially in regions afflicted by an over-abundance of roe and muntjac.[17]

Progress in this area would be made much easier if land-owners could get payments for any acreage taken out of production and given over to this kind of 'neural network' of connectivity.[18, 19] Where such networks acted as corridors between core reserves, the latter might contain wild grazers such as free-ranging cattle, deer, ponies and boar.[20] We would encounter issues of road-safety, disease control, pedestrian safety and public rights of way[21], as well as crop damage and given the over-developed Health & Safety culture, prospects are perhaps not so good, but then rewilding also has to be extended to the human psyche.[22] In Romania in the mixed landscape of the Carpathians, I was struck by the absence of fences and warning signs – even in the towns where road-works presented dangerous holes to the unwary – the whole culture was wilder in the sense of not so incredibly uptight about risks. If you have bears in the woods, the best protection comes from a cultural knowledge (and acceptance) of the risks, not fences with warning signs to the uninitiated.

But again, in the English *farmed* landscape, wolves and bears are not a prospect, and though lynx might be, the main concern is with bird species, flowers, insects, rodents, amphibians and reptiles. The sea eagle in East Anglia might pose more of a challenge given its (undeserved) reputation for taking lambs – but this is (again) more of an issue of education and responsible media-coverage.

These issues are topical. A recent seminar by the British Ecological Society and Flora Locale tackled the theme: would it be better to have separate land for wildlife, or have more wildlife-friendly farming methods? The event took a closer look at the prospects for rewilding agriculture but positing the false dichotomy of reform versus separation. An eclectic mix of speakers attempted to come to some conclusion. It was clear to me that farmers, an example being Robert Sutcliffe near Winchester, who leave large field margins, cut hedges at the right time, eschew silage for hay and who farm for quality – whilst also supplying TESCO, can achieve a great balance. His operations are clearly economic yet he maintains the biodiversity of farmland typical of three decades ago. He works with satellite-based precision drilling and fertiliser techniques and has reduced nitrogen dressing fourfold.

Tim Benton, presented the million Euro results of his models at Leeds University showing that organic production would not necessarily benefit wildlife – contrary to every expectation drawn from previous studies, and this encapsulates the problem. Defra and the EU fritter ever more funds away on computerised assessments (with dubious methodology) at academic institutions, rather than the footwork of networking best-practice followed by communication at a grass-roots level. What is clearly required is a cultural shift – and neither they nor the academics are capable of leading such or nurturing it.

Equally, a cultural shift in diet and purchasing habits would cause huge differences to the analysis of conflicting land-use for food and biofuels. With world population set to add another billion mouths to the nearly seven billion of today within the next 10 or 15 years, and the EU pressing biofuel targets upon the same cultivation area, the prospects for wildlife on farms and even marginal land, do not look good. However, the degree of intensification required also depends upon the market for meat products – which consumes seven times the land directly needed for vegetable protein. Simon Fairlie presented some intriguing, if rough, calculations on organic/chemical and meat/vegetarian/vegan alternatives. As livestock pastures are lost to arable there are gains for woodland and hence the potential for wildland. Patrick Whitefield showed how highly productive permaculture units as small-holdings could repopulate the land and also create small-scale havens for wildlife.

Climate-change reared its all-pervasive head, with Defra concerned for food security as well as low-carbon farming and ecosystem services such as carbon sequestration and flood alleviation, but there was no detailed assessment of how biofuel or woodchip targets would be met and what impacts are expected – largely because the targets have been set without any such assessment. Agriculture in general aims to reduce its carbon footprint by 30% by 2020, but apart from the advantages of restoring soil carbon and organic/permaculture systems that have less reliance of fossil fuels, mainstream farming is fossil-fuel intensive though mechanisation, fertilisers and pesticides and it is hard to see how production can be maintained as systems revert to less intensive energy use.

The question uppermost in my mind remained unresolved: is it better to separate wildland (and biodiversity issues) from agricultural land – including within the same farm? This boils down to answering how effective have agri-environment schemes been at halting the loss of biodiversity, and from the limited analyses on offer, I could not discern an answer. The higher-level schemes of subsidy are voluntary and still a small proportion of farming operations, whereas the more pervasive entry-level schemes offer little that is convincing. Nothing at this meeting convinced me that separation was not the best way forward – and that this would work either as part of the farm's own zoning, or as a targeted purchase strategy on the part of wildlife groups.


**Rewilding and conservation: are they at loggerheads?**

In my own neck of the woods in the South West there is a good example of the opportunities for wildlife groups to purchase strategic agricultural land. On the

Somerset Levels just west of Glastonbury lies the Avalon Marshes project. In this area of flooded peat workings, the RSPB, Natural England and the Somerset Wildlife Trust own several contiguous patches of land covering several thousand acres. The project has created a nationally significant amount of reed-bed interspersed with open pools, alder woodland and adjacent wet pasture with ditch boundaries. Recently the Hawk and Owl Trust purchased over 100 acres of former arable land adjacent to the National Nature Reserve at Shapwick toward the western end of the marshes.

## Is conservation wild enough?

This purchase well illustrates the forces at work that counter wildland initiatives. First, several kilometres of new barbed wire fences were erected and the culverts repaired. A small car-park was created, with new gates and information boards. The arable land was to be grazed by sheep and cattle – domestic, of course. On my last walk down the long and now wired-in drove I was led right up to an ancient oak with a large gabled box conspicuously hammered to the trunk. It sported a neat little perch. All that was missing was a sign saying 'Owl's House'.

The Levels are nationally important for their Barn Owl populations, hence the interest of the Hawk and Owl trust in buying land, with the aid of numerous charitable foundations. A good proportion of the population is maintained by such nest-boxes. I was interested, therefore, to attend a talk given by the naturalist Chris Sperring, conservation officer for the Trust, entitled 'Is conservation wild enough?' In his soul, Sperring clearly didn't think so, but he outlined the advantages of HLS payments per acre of land as long as it was grazed in an environmentally friendly way. The Trust gets an income stream. He felt that this also made scientific sense in that nutrient rich arable land would gradually be depleted and returned to herb-rich pasture. Currently, there are no specific schemes whereby land such as this could be turned over to non-agricultural use or wild-grazers. It would require NE to bend the rules – which we know it sometimes can, but more, for landowners like the Trust to know what is feasible. For example, Charlie Burrell managed to do a great deal on 3000 acres of the Knepp Estate in Sussex with English Longhorns, Exmoor ponies and Tamworth pigs.

How far could we go in an environment such as the Levels? Or elsewhere in England such as in the Great Fen project. How far is the Knepp estate a useful pilot? What projects might succeed on Dartmoor, Exmoor or the North Pennines, with greater potential for landscape-scale projects? And in Wales, in the Cambrians or Snowdonia? Or in Scotland – with much larger contiguous land-holdings in Glen Affric, Alladale and the Cairngorms, where there are some very significant private sector initiatives.[23]

## Wildland values extend beyond biodiversity

The pitfalls of biodiversity indices and targets have been well rehearsed in *ECOS*. Yet, in many discussions I witness there is little appreciation of the limited meaning of the numbers and the operation of species and specialist bias. Thus, the same old arguments resurface about rewilding compromising biodiversity targets. The theme lay unacknowledged in Tim Benton's study which compared organic farms with the same land category, region and farming mix as non-organic – which was probably scientifically accurate, but if the starting base is in the middle of an East Anglian prairie then a farm with lower inputs into such an artificial and wildlife-poor environment could well register less biodiversity. The study aimed at correcting a bias created by most organic farms being in the west and most conventional equivalents being in the east of the country – all very academic, but of little help in deciding whether an organic policy would have overall benefits for biodiversity.

The key issue so often not addressed by groups focussing upon biodiversity and established 'conservation' concerns, is that defining wildlife is a cultural issue as much as a scientific one, and even the science contains often unacknowledged cultural bias. The value of wilder cultural landscapes (as in Ennerdale), rural crafts, traditional farming and forestry, eco-tourism and the health and educational benefits that accrue to people's welfare are as important as the conservation of individual species or habitats. At the other end of the spectrum, there are large holdings of 'wildland' with very little of the original flora and fauna remaining, yet they have strong appeal in the absence of obvious human artefacts - as the John Muir Trust demonstrates. These large wilderness areas are candidates for interventionist rewilding with the return of seed-trees and eradicated species – as in the Trees for Life vision for Glen Affric.

Other large area initiatives demonstrate techniques of wildlife-friendly land use more appropriate to buffer zones and corridors: for example the extensive farming and forestry in Ennerdale, where stands of exotic conifers have been removed and fell-sheep replaced with cattle breeds capable of roaming both forest and moor. This joint National Trust and Forestry Commission plan does not have a fixed end-point. It starts from where the land and the people are now and moves at the community's pace in a generally wilder direction, but it is adjacent to other FC and NT holdings and the prospects are there for a very wild core area to be developed if funds could be made available for a transition from traditional practices to wild grazers and perhaps even the lynx as predator.

There is a recurrent theme in discussions on these potential core areas – a tendency to think *either/or* as if any new idea or pilot implies a complete rethink (and funding scheme) across all sites. It doesn't of course. There is a great deal of sense in targeted grant schemes available for selected areas, such that they do not compromise or interfere with other areas where practices might

216

have other objectives – for example, in the maintenance of heathland by domestic grazing.

**Rewilding conservation**

So, what are the prospects for a rewilded conservation sector being given a better political environment? People are more questioning of scientific authority when they see it led so often by corporate goals and managerial convenience coupled to specialist interests they cannot comprehend. There is greater popular defence of the grey squirrel than would have been anticipated, as also with Sika deer and other aliens that are well suited to cultural landscapes. As conservation groups have reached out and won broader public subscription they are, perhaps, having to take on public rather than specialist values. This can be a double-edged sword, however, and as with the eradication schemes for hedgehogs in the Hebrides, the balance can be awkwardly tipped by lack of ecological understanding.

The problem with conservation is not just a matter of getting the right subsidy regime – it lies with the mentality of management, goals, corporate structures, econometric minds and the whole language of ecosystem services and the 'customer' paradigm that goes with these times. Bill Adams[23] picked up on this in last edition of *ECOS* and it is heartening to see academia taking a stand, but the conservation sector is now big business, accounting for £500m of expenditure in the countryside (about five times the whole upland subsidy for Wales), and whilst that presents a tremendous opportunity, it also constitutes a major constraint. If we are going to move beyond the pilot projects we have monitored for the past 10 years, conservationists are going to have to go wild themselves! Someone has to start taking risks, and pursue the prompts from Labour Environment Ministers.

**References**

1. G. Browning & R. Yanik (2004) *Wild Ennerdale – letting nature loose* ECOS 25 (3/4) 34-38

2. A. Colston (2004) *Wicken Fen – realising the vision* ECOS 25 (3/4) 42-45

3. A. Watson Featherstone (2004) *Rewilding in the north-central Highlands – an update* ECOS 25 (3/4) 4-10

4. P. Ashmole & H. Chalmers (2004) *The Carrifran Wildwood Project*

ECOS 25 (3/4) 11-19

5. H. Chalmers (2007) *Ecological restoration without all the pieces – early news from Carrifran* ECOS 28 (3/4) 89-95

6. R. Sidaway (2006) *Alladale's fenced wilderness – making a breakthrough?* ECOS 27 (3/4) 30-35

7. P. Taylor (2008) *Alladale's wilderness – seeing through the fence.* ECOS 29 (3/4) 18-24

8. P. Taylor (2006) *Home counties wildland: the new nature at Knepp.* ECOS 27 (3/4) 44-51

9. N. Harris (2006) *Ecosystem effects of wild herbivores – lessons from Holland* ECOS 27 (3/4) 58-60

10. M Oates (2006) *Grazing systems and animal welfare – matters of life and death* ECOS 27 (3/4) 52-57

11. D. Blake (2007) *Deer in Britain: the challenges for nature conservation* ECOS 28 (2) 41-49

12. P. Hadfield (2009) *Too hard to bear? People and large carnivores in Slovakia* ECOS 30 (2) 76-84

13. D. Hetherington (2006) *The Lynx in Britain's past, present and future* ECOS 27 (1) 66-74.

14 J. McGowan (2007) *Big cats in Dorset: the evidence and the implications* ECOS 28 (1) 73-78

15. P.Taylor (2002 *Big cats in Britain: restoration ecology or imaginations run wild?* ECOS 23 (3/4) 30-64

16. Moiser C. (2002) *On the prowl, Lynx in the British Countryside*, ECOS 23 (2) 9-13

17. D. Hetherington (2009) *The history of the Eurasian lynx in Britain and the potential for its re-introduction.* British Wildlife 20: 77-86

18. A.Parfitt (2006) *New nature in Holland – attitudes and achievements* ECOS 27 (3/4) 65-69

19. S. Carver (2006) *Connectivity of nature in the Dutch landscape* ECOS 27 (3/4) 61-64

N. Harris (2006) *Ecosystem effects of wild herbivores – lessons from Holland* ECOS 27 (3/4) 58-60

21. M Oates (2006) *Grazing systems and animal welfare – matters of life and death* ECOS 27 (3/4) 52-57

22. P.Taylor (2005) *Beyond Conservation.* Earthscan.

23. Adams, B (2009) *Conservation and consumption.* ECOS 30(2) 2-10

218

# Re-wilding the grazers – obstacles to the wild in wildlife management.

*This essay was published in:*

*British Wildlife Vol 20 No 5 (Special Supplement: Naturalistic Grazing and Re-wilding in Britain), pp50-55, June 2009*

*I specifically wanted to provoke ecosystem managers into reflection on their own role in keeping the wild at bay.*

British wildlife habitats have a multi-dimensional quality that can easily be overlooked – the most obvious dimension of physical ecology might appear to the less enquiring eye as a mosaic of woodland, heath, dry and wet grassland, reedbed, salt-marsh and mudflats with associated communities of plants and animals, but the professional eye sees another layer of activity required to maintain these habitats in some kind of optimal condition according to a set of management objectives or targets; and then there is another dimension that contains the processes whereby these objectives are set. It is with regard to this latter dimension related to the role of grazing animals and wildlife that I would like to contribute some discussion.

I was recently asked to present a radical view, based upon my book *Beyond Conservation* and the work of the Wildland Network to a special meeting of PONT (the equivalent in Wales to GAP – the English Grazing Animals Project), after which there followed a day of discussions on the theme of 'How wild should Wales be?' I was arguing for a radical system of core areas and corridors of *wildland* that would go beyond the current paradigm of small and increasingly beleaguered 'nature reserves' surrounded by agricultural or forestry land where, in recent times, a huge, costly and largely failing effort has been aimed at managing these essentially industrial and economic systems to become more 'wildlife friendly'.

Most participants – drawn from a range of practical land management professionals in government agencies, farming, forestry, and the voluntary sector, had recognised a wave of interest in 'rewilding' and in particular, the return of the larger and more charismatic of the exterminated mammals, as now practised in some of the nature reserves in Holland. However, as the day progressed, I became increasingly doubtful that anything really wild was likely to emerge from the meeting. As with all paradigm shifts – it takes time for old ways of thinking to change, and as in so many areas of human endeavour, the most resistant force in the face of new thinking is bureaucratic.

219

The dimension of the desk interpenetrates all aspects of British wildlife, and for the most part its aspects are hidden from ordinary view. It is at the desk that objectives and targets are set – and it would be a worthy exercise on any field excursion if whenever a species is being observed, a backdrop of a desk and a manager is projected onto the habitat behind it, because in this bureaucratic dimension there are forces at work at least as potent as climate or geology at shaping habitats, but far less studied and understood.

If we examine the case of grazing animals in the context of landscape scale rewilding projects, the following dimensions unfold:

*The need for grazers.*

There is a general acceptance of the need for grazing animals to maintain a diversity of habitats and species in virtually all Britain's nature reserves – and with a marked decline in the economics of grazing, this is proving problematic. The Grazing Animals Project and PONT have thus had plenty to do in brokering grazing agreements and we have seen an increased use of hardy breeds of pony such as Koniks and Exmoors, and of cattle such as Highland, Belted Galloway, Old Gloucester and Longhorns in wildlife reserves. Debates have emerged about 'naturalistic' grazing and the re-instigation of natural processes, an essential element of large-scale rewilding schemes, but there is wide spectrum of understanding regarding what these terms might mean.

A natural grazing regime could not be natural unless it operated over a sufficiently large area for effective dispersal and utilisation by grazing animals of a range of habitats, particularly during harsh weather in the uplands, or flooding in lowlands; it would not be natural if there were no predator-prey interactions affecting dispersal patterns, mortality and fitness selection if not actual population sizes (which tend to be controlled more by available food supplies); and there also needs to be a *guild* of grazers and browsers – a range of large mammals occupying different niches. In the latter respect, the mega-herbivores that have co-evolved with north temperate forest structure, such as the straight-tusked elephant, forest rhinoceros, and northern hippo were exterminated about 30,000 BP. These animals create clearings and maintain riparian meadows which are then grazed and browsed by wood bison, moose, forest cattle, tarpan, boar and beaver – all four of which are now found only in wilder areas of eastern Europe. In their natural dynamic state, this herbivore guild would have had European lion, sabre-tooth cat, leopard, hyena, bear, wolf and lynx to predate adults and young. It is seldom appreciated that previous inter-glacials were only marginally warmer than today and that north-adapted equivalents of modern African or Asiatic fauna roamed the Atlantic oak forests and riparian meadows.

*The original herbivore guild of Atlantic oak forest habitats: dark shading identifies the remnants in the British reserves.*

It is clear, therefore, that the term natural can be of little guidance – even if qualified as 'near' natural, or naturalistic. A line can be drawn anywhere with regard to biological era or the degree of naturalness envisaged. And it is at this point that the bureaucratic mind can make decisions which may conceal all manner of reasoning related to processes within its ministry. If nothing can be entirely natural, then compromises are easier to make – and this will very much depend upon the strength of other forces represented at the desk, such as farming, forestry, tourism, recreation, access, veterinary security, public safety, accountability, land tenure, and cultural identities, in addition to any interests on the part of wildlife enthusiasts.

*Wild grazers or hardy domestic breeds?*

How much easier then for land managers and planners to opt for safer and perhaps more economically proven options!

As I listened to plans for a large-area scheme in the North Cambrians, headed by Montgomeryshire Wildlife Trust, and seeking to model the collaboration of

*Konik ponies grazing in a National Trust fenland reserve (National Trust)*

voluntary bodies with government and the water industry (such as the National Trust-Forestry Commission-Water Company project in Ennerdale), I could see the radical vision of a true core area beginning to fade into the compromise zone of SSSI targets for grazed heath and Tir Gofal type Single Farm Payments forming a co-ordinated landscape-scale buffer zone, with the Forestry Commission restructuring its plantations to incorporate grazed zones and more native woodland.

The grazers could range from the current hardy breeds of sheep, through Highland or Galloway or Welsh Black and the various breeds of Welsh pony. Every economic interest would be appeased in some way as unprecedented new levels of finance were accessed. Undoubtedly, BAP targets and SSSI favourable conditions would be met. In ten years or more, there may be more plovers, grouse, ring ouzel, kite and stonechat, as well as fritillaries and orchids. Eco-tourism might prosper under a branded regional identity. And upland organic meat could be marketed as wildlife-friendly.

*Exmoor ponies living wild in Exmoor National Park (Toby Hickman)*

There is no doubt that such a model – as now being developed in Ennerdale, would reverse some of the decline of species in our uplands, and may help to solve the decline in farming and give more meaning to what is on many sites an entirely uneconomic forest enterprise. Water companies might also benefit from reduced costs in maintaining water quality and silting. Flood control in lowland areas might also benefit.

But what about the *wild* in the wildlife of Britain? This model is management oriented. It *maintains* a bureaucracy, and although each member rightly sees themselves as pursuing a worthy objective on behalf of nature conservation, it is important that each reflect upon their own interests and how this affects the final managerial outcomes. If every interest has to be appeased in the final outcome, then we end up with a situation where a large and extensive public movement toward rewilding is thwarted by narrow self-interest and an unimaginative bureaucracy – as happened with the blocked project to re-introduce the beaver to Scotland.

There is no doubt that truly wild grazing animals present major problems for the bureaucracy. The list would include:

- the absence of any developed grant structure for non-economic grazing animals;

- issues of veterinary safety (foot and mouth disease, for example) and of domestic water safety (cryptosporidium);

- issues of animal welfare in non-intervention regimes during harsh winters, or in fighting and general disability with cattle, and more especially horses;

- public safety for walkers and open access;

- the introduction of predators such as lynx (and wolf in the Highlands) would raise issues of compensation for livestock kills;

- new populations of red deer or re-introduction of roe deer raises issues of forest damage to plantations;

- wild boar can be destructive of croplands;

- beaver interfere with drainage.

In the light of these problems and of the acknowledged low-risk, try-to-please-all -stakeholders manual of bureaucracy, what chance then of a truly wild zone experiment in England or Wales? There is a much better chance in Scotland – especially now that the pioneering Trees For Life group are purchasing a 10,000 acre estate contiguous to the Forest Enterprise and National Trust for Scotland land in Glen Affric, an area that has been the subject of a prize-winning programme of Caledonian Forest regeneration. This zone extends to a possible 1500 sq km collaborative enterprise with other estates and public land – large enough for a wider herbivore guild to include boar, beaver, wild horse and wild cattle, perhaps moose and wood bison, as well as lynx, wolf and possibly also bear.

In England we have several developing smaller scale schemes that are nevertheless revolutionary in their potential. At Knepp in Sussex, an area of 3000 acres is mooted for wild or hardy breeds to graze freely, and in the fens, the Natural Trust is targeted 10,000 acres for purchase next to its reserves at Wicken Fen, where it already grazes the almost wild-type Polish Konik horse. Ennerdale has pioneered cooperative management between forestry, agricultural and water interests over a large upland area. Such schemes could be developed in Wales if ways can be found to integrate common grazing interests on the moor, uneconomic forestry plantations that could be restructured and water industry interests and their potentially available finance. But the chances are that the current bureaucratic paradigm will prevent anything truly wild happening for some time yet. It is not that the land is not available – there are suitable sites where these interests could be integrated; nor is it an absence of finance – funds can be found within the current structures with a little bending of rules. The obstacles are largely cultural: farmers want to continue within a small-business semi-industrial production model – with deference to environmental objectives for which they are paid extra, and the land managers of voluntary bodies and conservation agencies, together with the wildlife scientists themselves, are still locked into an old set of BAP targets and managerial practices that have already been subject to the compromises fought for in relation to these other economic interests. Many of the target species depend upon a stasis of secondary habitat that can only be maintained by intensive management – and letting things go wild could have uncertain impacts.

The one potential agent for more radical change is the growing realisation that upland farming has deluded itself about the business-economic paradigm – very few farmers are free agents economically – they are maintained by state subsidy, and hence subject to political forces beyond their control. Rural decline is a fact of life in the hills, despite the raft of schemes to keep it going. It is doubtful whether unimaginative environmental schemes will sufficiently appease a growing public unease at farming subsidies. The future in the uplands may lie in integrated large area land management schemes for water, forestry, carbon sequestration, and wildlife enhancement where traditional farming has a role mainly in buffer zones.

I believe that the wildlife enhancement component now needs to take a leap of imagination – more connected to the *meaning* of wildlife than to esoteric biodiversity targets. There is a huge groundswell of public concern for wild places that now includes a global consciousness relating to biodiversity loss, climate change and the place of nature in our lives. This represents both an opportunity and a crisis. The world is faced not just with the loss of iconic species such as tiger and polar bear – but a future of degraded ecology including our own life support systems, and yet it continues to follow a development model and set of material values has signally failed to grapple with these issues in an effective way. We in the western industrial nations have promulgated this model and from the pioneering work of the last ten years, we know the model is amenable to change if the values change. The Dutch government has demonstrated this with extended reserves, re-introduced species, core areas, corridors and even wildlife bridges over motor-ways. Wild areas are not incompatible with industrially advanced society, even in the most populated of countries – the secret is connectivity and an inclusive mosaic of habitats.

*Reconstituted 'Aurochs' in Dutch nature reserve (Hans Kampf)*

This, I would argue, is the true value and meaning of *wild* grazers. They signify and represent this shift in paradigm, They *communicate* through their iconic status – the *wild* in wildlife means something – there is an element of risk, of potential loss, and perhaps most importantly, a statement that we, the managers, are not in total control. In this there is a potential renewed reverence for nature and natural processes – and it is this that has the greatest chance to 'save the planet'. And no one is talking of turning *all* farmland or forestry into wildland, not even all grouse-moors, wild heath or reedbed – rather that we select a few large core areas and make room, in this crowded land, for the spirit of wildness itself – and nothing symbolises this more than a herd of wild grazers, with the chance perhaps, of sighting a stalking lynx or hearing the howl of a wolf.

The return of potentially dangerous predators to a crowded island is not necessarily fanciful. Within a half-hour drive of San Francisco there are well visited country-parks, such as Point Reyes, where puma raise their kits, and deer and ranch cattle maintain the coastal heath. Not a few ecologists, farmers and foresters could show us similar breeding territories for our own feral big cats that now regularly appear on the policeman's country beat. I would argue for a more relaxed attitude to risk – indeed, that such is a moral imperative if we are to entreat Indian villagers to tolerate tigers on their boundary, or Africans the lion and leopard. It is time for our local wildlife organisations to move to a wider stage – what we do here could have global resonance, if we are bold enough.

226

# Conservation on its last legs – the prospect for rejuvenation

*As a provocative on 'refreshing conservation' this article argues for a change of paradigm – to let die what no longer is vital in the world of nature conservation, and look to the seeds of new life. (published in ECOS 36.2 pp22. 2015)*

## Deathly secrets

Is UK nature conservation effectively a dead parrot? Of course it is still alive on the ground in our beleaguered land and marine nature reserves and agri-environment schemes. But we have to face the facts of life: organisms and organisations have a useful life-span and Nature herself organises the end of such things. They grow old, decay and die. In our less wild cultural and conceptual landscapes, we don't like to face death. Conservation is no different. There is much talk of rejuvenation, but I don't think fresh approaches in nature conservation will be easy. There are too many old forces inherent in the structure and too many employees dependent upon the industry that Conservation has become.

However, I would argue that 'rejuvenation' in the sense of something new and positive, is already happening – but not necessarily under the name of Conservation. Rewilding, for example, has grown from a fairly narrow focus upon restoring ecosystem dynamics, to a broader inclusion of wilder farming and forestry, educational and health-oriented projects, river restoration, wildlife corridors in cities and programmes for the deeper psychology of relationship to the land, wildness and nature. And many other strands of activity also embrace these wider links between nature and wellbeing. BANC has been in the forefront of this paradigm shift – organising regional networks and seminars, taking a cross-sectoral approach, and publishing the discourse, and all this despite a shrinking membership base and no outside funding. This is more than re-branding. It represents a more holistic and creative movement, solidly based in community, and with a holistic outlook on nature.

## Creative agendas are out there

Thus, despite being weighed down by professional obligation, there are many signs of innovation amongst some groups. For example, with the John Muir Trust taking a more positive look at ecological restoration of the landscapes it has purchased and protected; the National Trust and Forestry Commission have embraced wilder themes such as naturalistic grazing in Ennerdale and Wicken Fen; the RSPB and Wildlife Trusts, along with the National Trust, are taking a lead with landscape-scale management projects; the Woodland Trust is also experimenting with woodland grazing regimes in Scotland. Many of the above have collaborated with the Soil Association on a progressive 2014 report *Square Meal* relating food to health, agriculture and wildlife.[1] But generally, the larger organisations are only able to tinker, to slightly adjust their practices and modestly embrace a new sensibility – nobody is taking risks and dreaming of a strong grass-roots revolution in how we engage more holistically with nature.

It should be clear that tinkering is not enough. The general climate is one of losing resources and political influence at a time when new forces of degradation are arising, such as industrial structures for renewable energy in the countryside; and some old enemies seemingly resurgent, such as intensification of farming, the sale of public forests, housing pressures, port and other infrastructure developments. In such an adverse climate, the tendency is to stick to what you know best: to protect past gains, but with a pilot scheme or two to test the waters. There is some value in this caution. The forces ranged against conservation would exploit any lessening of focus on the protection of what has been gained over the past 50 years, but we do have to look closely at the dynamics of a failure to make the required impact on government policy and consumer behaviour.

Political commentators suggest there are no votes from prioritising environmental issues. Yet, there is evidence that the environment and wildlife are dear to the British psyche. The large memberships of the National Trust, the RSPB and the campaigning NGOs are testament to that engagement. So why is it that five million voters and a £500m per annum sector make no waves on the political scene?

**The structural failures**

The first prerequisite for effective change is to recognise the depth of failure. In the Conservation sector, loosely defined to include all wildlife organisations and landscape protection bodies, after 10 years of pilots in which different organisations have combined to produce landscape-scale projects, with the National Trust, Forestry Commission and Water Companies to the fore, the main wildlife organisations are only now coming together to consider joint projects. But the difficulties encountered are both structural and conceptual. For example the remit of the RSPB, with an annual budget of £130m, is naturally focussed upon birds and bird reserves, the Wildlife Trusts on relatively small but numerous nature reserves, the National Trust on cultural landscapes as well as wilder land, and the FC only just manages to maintain its multi-purpose remit. There would be great power in all of these organisations working more closely together, combining resources, embracing new concepts that would engage a broader public and operating on a landscape scale that included other sectors – such as health, food and education. For that, there needs to be a more holistic ideology that goes beyond the conservation paradigm. Once united, a more coherent force would make its presence felt in the political world.

At county level, Local Nature Partnerships may be part of the way forward, but in their early years they have struggled to make waves, although examples such as Devon have embraced the health agenda well. Overall amongst the LNPs, a

228

lack of resources may be holding them back, and they have had to play second fiddle to business and economic voices gingering the same range of public bodies.

Back at the national scale, there is a model for this kind of cooperative endeavour – it is in the Climate Coalition, where the wildlife bodies, most notably the RSPB and WWF, have taken a lead role, and now work together with aid organisations such as Oxfam. It is with great irony that I mention the Climate Coalition, given my own stance on the poor science of climate change, but it is a useful example of how an organised campaign with a simple message can get through to the political world. This 'green' lobby has actually unlocked *billions* of government subsidy for the environmental cause. The irony for me is that no member of the Coalition has the remotest sense of the impact on wildlife, community and indigenous peoples that achieving their campaign goals will trigger, and indeed, already has triggered. I give one example, that of the Blue Heart of Europe Campaign concerning Balkan wild rivers and the rash of hydro-projects they face, including major proposals in National Parks. In 'normal' circumstances, none of these projects would gain finance, but there are vast funds available in European banks to fund private operators who are paid over the odds for carbon-free electricity. As with industrial wind turbines, returns on capital of 12% are guaranteed for 25 years.

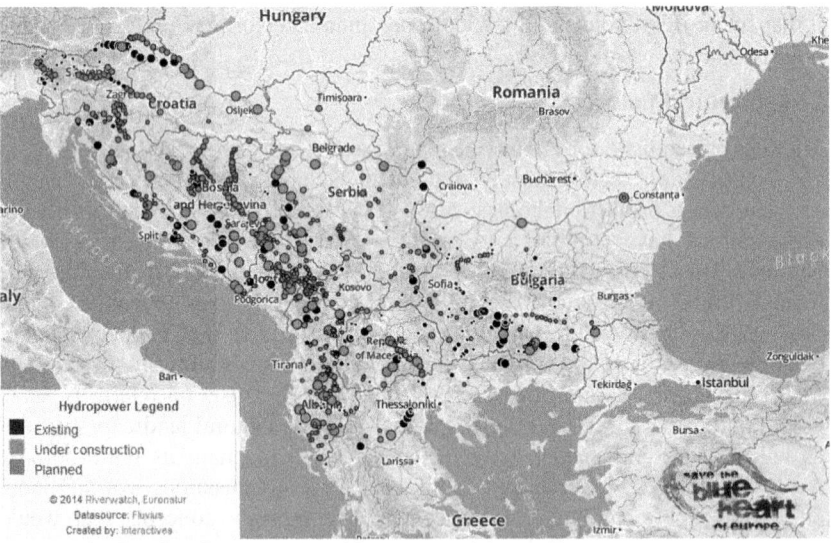

*'Green' hydro-development in wild regions of the Balkans*

**Note: in converting to b/w the four sites 'under construction' do not stand out, the rest are in planning.**

http://www.balkanrivers.net/en/content/about-us

229

Whatever new coalitions are forged, thought must be given to the pitfalls of the media, simple messages, and the way campaign goals are evaluated. It is irresponsible to lobby for a goal and then walk away leaving banks, the private sector and beleaguered governments such as in Albania, Macedonia and Montenegro, to sort out policy on the ground.

The dark side of campaigning organisations shows itself when, having unleashed such destructive forces, they then gain more membership traction by *opposing* the consequences of their actions – as in the ongoing fight by the RSPB to protect Hebridean landscape and its eagles from extensive wind turbine proposals. I believe the strongest safeguard is to focus upon real community and change at grass-roots level first, and let this change speak to the political world. This is where the goals need to be set – on reducing consumptive demand at home.


**Political prospects**

A stronger local base does not mean less influence on government. A well-developed communications and lobbying network that was closely in-touch with proposed government legislation, as well as technical change and strategic thinking, could martial its members for internet lobbying, letters to MPs and major demonstrations. Rather than big organisations like the National Trust or RSPB having their own lobbying units, I would prefer a developed communication system with their members where each member then acts individually.

Necessary as it is, this system is still *reactive*, rather than creative. Thus, there needs to be an effective movement *from* the creative grass-roots outward. Trees for Life, in Scotland, is a wonderful example of what can be achieved by practical and cooperative endeavour (with the National Trust and Forestry Commission) coupled to excellent media material. This example is specific to wildlife and wild land, but the methods can be applied to practical examples closer to the centres of populations which lead much of the political agenda.

We need some new strategic and creative thinking that is more directly relevant to the political and economic agenda. For example, imagine that instead of new cities, we restructure the 'green' belt – in place of wild-lifeless fields of rape, corrugated barns, pylons and projected giant aerospace turbines, each city would have a 'hinterland' of landscaped eco-dwellings, passive solar, turf roofed, log-cabin construction, with short-rotation coppice, new woodlands, ponds, wilder river margins, buried pylons, localised organic food production, good public transport links coupled to community vehicle rentals...where people can choose to leave the centres of cities for a less stressful, less consumerist life on lower incomes. There are over one million unemployed, several million poverty-stricken pensioners, hundreds of thousands of disaffected young people who if they could afford it, would live for their art or music or writing or computer graphics – but in low-cost communities, which could readily exist on the edge of the city.

To generate support for such a major change there would need to be pilot projects and good communication – that is, visualisation, in order not to engender mindless protectionism. In this way, a new wave is created – one that brings people closer to the nature that birthed them and can nurture them. Only then will they vote for it!

Instead of this – here is what the current Coalition for policy action will bring to the table – another ten thousand giant aerospace turbines, two hundred wood-chip power stations, five tidal pools with all the quarried rock it takes, and biofuels from Borneo, Kenya, Colombia and all the world's other biodiversity hotspots.[2,3]


## Climate resilience – time for a policy grounded in reality

As I predicted in my book *Chill* there has been a major 'pause' in global warming. Contrary to some media reports, the heat is not hiding in the oceans – it is being dissipated both there and in the upper atmosphere. I further predict that within five years, the flat-line will be a slight decline in temperatures. At that stage, the pause or hiatus in temperatures will be a similar extent to the period of warming experienced from the 1970s to the late 1990s. This may be enough to more fully question the main climate models which dictate so much of the current focus on the topic. What then happens to the reputation of those who have claimed so much certainty in the science, especially many science institutions? And then to the bodies in the Climate Coalition that espoused this cause so strongly? There is a real danger that a right-leaning body politic will ride triumphant over the corpse of environmentalism, and never listen to any more 'scare stories' from the green-corner.

Peer-reviewed papers in solar science are warning of the potential for a new Maunder Minimum where the sun's energy declines and northern hemisphere temperatures drop significantly – as happened between 1400 and 1700 AD. The Meteorological Office is studying this behind the scenes. These realities of uncertainty require an *adaptive* response. If the conservation sector can get so heavily involved with broader policy issues such as energy supply, consumer demand and even climate science – then it is not beyond its remit to get involved with a real model for our future – one that integrates all the objectives of what used to be called sustainability.

We need to develop policy beyond a hopeless and vastly expensive mitigation via emission reduction. The concept of *adaptation* to inevitable change, whether warming or cooling, is one that the Climate Coalition could embrace, whilst reviewing the science properly, instead of promulgating what is a supply option, not a demand-reduction scenario (which never would make a media message). Barrages, biofuels and wind turbines affect landscape and undeveloped wild landscape that is not renewable. Community, once destroyed, is also not renewable – especially not indigenous community now affected by massive hydro development as well as biofuel plantations. The focus needs to shift from the global to the local, where the issues are real and the players are accountable.

Current 'renewables' stand at about 4% of national energy demand. The EU has a 30% target by 2030 (and the UK a target of 80% by 2050). What would be the impact on wildlife and landscape of such a huge increase? We don't know because nobody wants to. This is a wilful blindness. It is a consequence of simple-minded single-message lobbyists leading the agenda. Nobody wants to challenge the development model, especially not the conservative conservation sector that has persuaded itself the model is alright, it just needs better regulation.

**Restructuring**

For most political parties, the priority is to sustain this development model, not to move toward a truly sustainable lifestyle. The ideology of plundering ecosystems to get wealth, and then repair them with the profits, is still current across the globe – most especially, of course, in China. All that is now happening is that 'renewable' energy technologies are being harnessed to the old development model – the world is following our example, cutting down the remaining forests, industrialising agriculture, moving people to cities, eradicating most of the large herbivores and all of their predators, powered not by fossil fuels but wind and palm oil. And all we have to offer is an econometric 'ecosystems services' accounting system for Natural Capital. That is not going to do it.

If *all* of the environment and wildlife groups came together with a major initiative that addressed the broader concerns of the centres of population – in particular, housing and the cost of living, healthy locally sourced food, and less mentally stressful work – this would act as a creative critique of the development model.

We need a common ideology that addresses the global model of development. The current model will destroy what we value even in a stable climate. We must argue *for* Nature....*human* nature as well as animal and plant nature, where the true human being inherits a soul-enhancing and tranquil landscape, rich in wildlife; where most food is organic; water is recycled; consumption is reduced and with it energy demand. And we need *new* models of development around the world that safeguard these values. We need recognisable social programmes to reconnect people with Nature. The pilots already exist – we need to study them, communicate and lobby for them.

We need to do this not to balance our carbon budget but for the good of our own human nature and its *resilience* to the changes ahead. The globalised economy is vulnerable to financial collapse.

## References

1. Soil Association et al (2014) *Square Meal: why we need a new recipe for farming, wildlife, food and public health* Soil Associaton, Bristol.

2.War on Want, 2008 *Fuelling Fear: the human cost of biofuels in Colombia.* www.waronwant.org

3. Taylor, P (2009) *Chill: a reassessment of global warming theory* Clairview.

# PART 4

## RECOVERY PROGRAMMES

*It has been obvious to even the very first 'therapists' that the structures of modern society damage the human system in pervasive ways. Freud and Jung first began the explorations of the inner world of psychological damage – with Freud concluding controversially that almost all had sexual dysfunction at their root. With the later bio-energetic work of Wilhelm Reich, western psychotherapy began to embrace 'bodywork' – deep tissue massage with energetic release; and explore the inter-relations of thought patterns, vestiges of physical and mental trauma, with physical diseases and mental 'disorders'. Much of this later work parallels eastern knowledge of yoga and tantra, the life-force that is kundalini or Chi, and the concepts of balancing forces of yin and yang, negative and positive polarities, dark and light energies.*

*Intact indigenous cultures do not share these problems of inherent damage. Thus, when a tribal trance dance is instigated, each dancer can draw freely on balanced energies, with no barriers to the life currents as they reach the 'dream' centre in the brow. Trance dance is the ultimate form of yogic, tantric or shamanic practice – but in the western world of modernity, few dancers have a clear undamaged body-mind, and there thus needs to be training, therapeutic practice and long-term commitment.*

*It is my personal 'belief' that the dreaming power of the trance dance is one of the most powerful tools we can use for world change – whether it is for a more sustainable environment, a more heartful relation to nature, or a more peaceful co-existence among nations. All change has first to be dreamed.*

*It is also my supposition, born of many slight glimpses, that there exists a cadre of magicians who maintain by force of will and inner sight the all-pervasive American Dream. This dream purports to be about 'freedom' yet has been built upon slavery and genocidal land-grabs. It is heavily disguised but at its core it dreams the consumer-society wherein the human soul loses its free will and creative power, to be consumed by an elite for purposes of their own privileged position. It may be that this American Dream is quite simply a fortuitous evolution, with no intent other than basic manipulation and control – that is, there are no magicians behind the scene! The evidence, however, points to magician-dreamers who practice secretly among us – cadres who care little for the wild, for nature, or for freedom to express the creative power that lies within all human beings. I would argue that it is this aspect of our education, knowledge and freedoms that must be liberated if we are to approach a more balanced and ecologically sustainable future,.*

# The End of the World: shamanic and scientific perspectives on a world in crisis.

*Background paper to a presentation at a panel on 'Invisible Cultures' at the World Anthropological Congress, British Museum, London, 2012.*

**Abstract:**

*After leaving an academic path in anthropology, the author joined the environmental revolution of the late 1970s and 1980s as a scientist-activist, advocate and lawyer, whilst at the same time undergoing intensive training in yogic and shamanic practice - the latter to better understand the nature of perception, risk and threat. This paper charts a course through environmental issues and human values, commenting on the sadly limited role of anthropology in the unfolding environmental debates. The author still operates as a respected conservation ecologist yet also leads an international shamanic dance troupe in its seventh year of ritual trance dance. Here, he offers an insight into New Age tribal consciousness - as reportage rather than academic analysis at a time when Anthropology is just beginning to integrate the insights of those few academics who have entered the shaman's realm.*

## Introduction

As a brief student of social anthropology (I undertook a Diploma course at Oxford University), I learned that its realm encompassed a spectrum leaning toward scientific methodology at one end and something approaching the poetic at the other, where the former sought to 'explain' cultural phenomena the latter more to interpret. After a watching period trying to decide how valuable the discipline could be for my environmental work, I offered the observation that a third pole existed but could only be seen if anthropologists looked at themselves with the same critical faculty they looked at other 'tribes' – anthropology had its rituals of field work, presentation of papers, critiques and defence of positions and the above all, a *need* to develop theory that related as much to its own status as to the science it espoused (1). At that time, sociological studies of scientists at work had barely begun and I have sadly had little time to explore what has been done since (2).

I supposed then that the scientific pole represented the professional and academic anthropologists' role within the culture that supported them financially, but I could find nothing on how anthropologists saw themselves as an influence, in particular on how their casting of theory might affect a broader politic. I saw anthropology as metaphorically striving for a kind of *Merlin* position in relation to the 'King' of modern government and political economy– and it is a strange feeling, three decades later during what the shaman's world calls the 'end-times' to observe a banker not a sociologist occupying that key position and not only bearing the name Mervyn King, but naming his redemption strategy the 'Merlin' project! (Mervyn is Welsh for Merlin!).

At the time of my studies, Claude Levi-Strauss was the most successful caster of theoretical spells – at least in book sales, and Durkheim the ancestral model. However, I was rapidly coming to the conclusion that modern academics might feel they were explaining the world, but I could not see much evidence of them *changing* it. After many years since of environmental policy work at all levels – from small communities, through government and up to the UN, I have seen very little to convince me otherwise. The discipline certainly sharpened my own awareness of what was happening around me – particularly on a linguistic and symbolic level, but if social anthropology has changed the world more directly, I have not observed it. This is in rather stark contrast to the competition from 'ecologists' – who were then also flirting with political theory and who now occupy key positions within the financial world and the UN in particular, despite a rather small power base in political institutions (3).

**Ecologists occupying the soothsayer's position**

Much of the success of the 'green' movement was laid down in the anti-nuclear campaigns of the 1970s, consolidated in the 80s by action on pollutants, and then from the 1990s, through the energy and climate debate. Riding on this wave of concern, 'ecologists' now sit on the bridge with the captains of industry and finance, and on the back of the climate campaign, at all levels of governance (4).

Currently, there are proposals that would see trillions of dollars flowing to eco-finance and development committees within the IMF and UN system – with minimal elected oversight, and engendering a great deal of political opposition to what is seen by adherents of liberalised and deregulated markets, as movement toward a command and control economy.

What tends to be missed by those engaged on either wide of the political divide is the role of the hidden technocrat – mostly scientific professionals who also represent an agenda of the science institutions. The current debate between 'greens' and 'free-marketeers' is almost entirely within the technocratic paradigm and 'community' values – particularly *indigenous* community, hardly feature in any of their development proposals (5).

Way back in the nuclear-alternatives debate, when the nuclear side seemed to be losing public support, a team of Dutch social psychologists, under contract to the International Atomic Energy Agency, warned the Agency that the expansion of nuclear power could 'undermine the very creativity of youth'.

They also chided the IAEA in its expectation that providing more factual information would ameliorate the opposition – they reported that people could be divided into two types in the way they evaluated information, those whose main focus for evaluation of 'progress' was 'community oriented' and those for whom it was 'technological'. There was a division of internal and external values and it was roughly equal throughout the general population. Those leaning toward evaluating human progress in terms of the quality of community relations tended to reject the nuclear option (6).

It took some effort to discover these reports, which the IAEA had buried, and I tried at several points in the policy process to use this information. For example, in 1977 , acting as an intervener for national NGOs during the Windscale Inquiry on the impact of spent-fuel reprocessing – an essential component for plutonium-fuelled reactors (7). The Inquiry inspector simply stated that he could make no use of the information in relation to government energy policy. Again, in 1985, not as a litigant, but as an assessor on a government commission into nuclear waste dumping at sea, I sought to convince the other scientists on the panel that sociological evidence on the 'meaning' of the ocean environment, for example to Spanish fishermen, was as important as apparently scientific radiation dose calculations (8).

In both these circumstances I learned that the policy process found it difficult to encompass what my opponents regarded as 'soft science' (no 'hard' facts). The scientific world view dominated the psyche at all levels of policy making, with little appreciation of its limitations, and certainly, of past errors in scientific assessment and prediction. It was clear to me that the technocratic value system identified in the Dutch work operated throughout the bureaucratic environment in national government, the EU and the UN, and to the detriment of more internal community values.

**Staying within the science paradigm**

However, in terms of my work direction, I abandoned social sciences in favour of a hard-edged scientific and legal critique, though I continued to observe the gulf in value systems and more particularly, its disposition in relation to the structures of power and decision making.

It was relatively easy for technocrats to control the regulatory process with regard to the risks they themselves deemed worthwhile - by emphasising the factual 'science' and demoting the sociological and psychological impacts to the realm of subjectivity and emotion. For example, an average person might find any level of contamination by man-made radiation unacceptable – no matter what the 'scientific' assessment of risk, but to the bureaucrat there would always be a scientifically definable level of low but 'acceptable' risk (9). And whilst it was the case that some prominent sociologists of science warned about such technocratic definitions of risk with regard to comparability, locus-of-control and the disposition of benefits in relation to acceptability, they were largely ignored (10).

I could add many similar examples from my later work in nature conservation – where scientific values have predominated over the popular, and professional assessments have decreed the course of action without the least reflection of how those professional assessments contain hidden values as well as strategies that ensure a future role for the professionals concerned (11). For example, reduced management or intervention in rewilding programmes can lead to a readily quantifiable 'loss' of biodiversity, whilst the benefits are not so easily quantifiable in terms of common values relating to beauty, wildness, scale, abundance and the dominance of natural processes (12).Managers in key positions to influence policy are hardly likely to support a policy that recommends less management!

That environmental science has hidden values – from pollution and risk control to conservation strategies, is hardly acknowledged in the policy process. And likewise hardly within the working lives of scientists – for example, social, political and even gender influences in the construction of hypotheses and the resources devoted to exploring them. I have written extensively on these issues and have to say, my criticisms are largely ignored, and what successes I have had have come from persistent work *within* the dominant paradigm.

In my recent work on a re-assessment of climate change theory, I limited any reference to sociological and psychological analysis, again in order to prevail within the dominant paradigm -the predictive models are open to serious criticism with a large literature on their uncertainty that is not reflected in policy documents. I had not bargained however on a complete refusal of those defending UN, government and NGO policy positions based on this science to engage in rational scientific argument! A clear vested interest had developed around the model predictions.

There remain some interesting linguistic and psychological observations that beg for a social anthropological inquiry – for example, the models almost entirely fail to incorporate natural *cycles* (13). Indeed some climate scientists refuse to acknowledge such cycles even exist – much to the consternation of the community of paleo-ecologists!. Most model-builders are mathematically trained physicists with little experience of the world outside of their virtual realities.

When I turn my attention to my former environmental allies who now insist that man-made pollution is wholly responsible for potentially catastrophic global warming, I note that they use the same class of fear tactics that our former opponents used in the nuclear debate. They also resort to the same kind of apparently predictive but unverifiable computer models that the nuclear industry relied upon. They form the same kind of alliances with industrial and banking organisations. And they denigrate their opposition as emotionally or politically motivated and unscientific.

Despite anthropology's apparent lack of impact on any of these environmental issues, I feel an allegiance to the discipline and remain hopeful of its potential.

But I want to speak now not as a scientist (I still hold a professional practice as a conservation ecologist), nor as an environmental activist – but as a 'member' of an invisible culture – that of the modern 'urban tribal'. Throughout my scientific and political work, I have maintained a foot in another camp.

## The New Age 'tribal community'

My own community, has been investigated and 'explained'. The broader 'New Age' community in Glastonbury was subject to a monograph in 2001 by Ruth Prince and David Riches (14). In their desire to explain what they perceived as a New Age 'religion' the anthropologists seemed to lose sight of the effects of their own allegiance to theory. At one point they admit that New Age communities are loose and incoherent, and at the next they are comparing them as a category alongside other categories of organised religion. The need to categorise has forced the data into a preconceived notion – a necessary prerequisite to fulfil some theoretical ambition to explain cultural change.

Most 'tribals' I know would not consider themselves as either a social movement, a religion or even a part of the New Age culture so apparent on Glastonbury High Street with its profusion of crystal shops, pagan boutiques and centres for alternative therapy. The tribal culture is largely in retreat from the mainstream and visible only on market days when local produce comes to town. People gather socially and shop socially. Many live in various temporary structures such as benders and yurts in the surrounding woods (that some also own or which have a friendly owner). In some cases planning permission has been given for a small settlement. Of late, several of the 30+ generation with small children and some inheritance have bought farmhouses with land and enabled their friends to settle in temporary structures on their land. There are dreams of eco-dwellings and eco-villages for the more settled whilst others live a nomadic existence working the summer festivals and spending the winter in Glastonbury, or as often as not India or central America.

This counter-culture most certainly reacts against the mainstream – where most see an empty, rampant materialist and ecologically unsustainable society well on the way to its own destruction and seemingly unable to change course. They want to live more closely to the Earth, in respect of Nature, grow their own food and educate their children outside of the State system. There is naturally a real problem earning enough money without compromising their values – but many have jobs looking after the elderly or handicapped, working with wood, making tipis and yurts, jewellery or clothes, and some have set up small businesses employing their friends – for example, importing 'tribal' clothes, which in Glastonbury can be very stylish and expensive.

In my view the anthropologists missed the essence of the New Age tribal because they were so intent on constructing a model for all 'religious movements'. Modern tribal consciousness is the antipathy of religion and I cannot see how one can fully describe something wholly in terms of its relationship to other things which it is not. In particular, the shamanic element of modern tribalism cannot be compared to most aspects of religion. A shaman may be a 'priest' but only in rudimentary functions of choreography or interpretation. In modern shamanism, anyone can access the training and a connection to one's own source of knowledge is encouraged. and there is a growing fusion of eastern yoga-tantra and Buddhist knowledge with North American and Amerindian. I cannot see how this can be 'understood' outside of a real experience of shamanic consciousness.

Not everyone within the tribal community is schooled in shamanic ways, but most are familiar with the basics of a 'shamanic journey' and many have taken such plant-spirit-medicine as Ayahuasca, Peyote and San Pedro, mostly in ceremony with visiting Amerindian shamans. There is a modern tradition of sweat lodge, following the lunar calendar and the old Celtic cross-quarter days, equinoxes and solstices, dance gatherings (Breton music is popular) and playing music or drumming at music festivals

I have no ethnography, no notes or interviews – any such objectification and distance would seem almost a betrayal of the community to which I belong. As one of my tribal shaman-brothers remarked when I told him I would present a paper... 'anthropologists are the enemy – the very worst of the scientists – they work for the Empire, they gathered the data for the extinction of indigenous peoples'. I don't agree with this perception because I know a little of recent efforts to interpret, help and protect indigenous cultures – such as by Jeremy Narby's work in the Amazon, for example (15). But science *is* in itself the White Man's medicine and anthropology does seem to lean in that direction in its efforts to 'explain' culture and develop theory

Thus, within this loose agglomeration of tribal community there is no membership and no inaugural initiation – though plenty of initiatory experiences (sweat-lodge, fire-walk, power animal journey, trance-dance and 'plant medicines' are all readily available). The one thing that unites this loose 'tribe' is identified by the anthropologist readily enough – reaction to modern supposed civilised life, or 'Babylon', which they see as destroying the soul of humanity as well as its ecological support systems. They turn to other cultures to recover lost knowledge of another way of living. I am part of the recovery team. I have helped to organise teaching camps, bring over indigenous elders, shamans and teachers, adapt other more eastern cultural sources, such as yoga and Tibetan tantra, and also work with neo-Druids engaged on a similar task (16).

Without a deeper experiential understanding of shamanic perception and the nature of 'inner' vision, researchers such as Riches and Prince have no insight as to the reality of what they are seeking to 'explain' - they outline the circumstances for the reaction as counter-cultural, but really have no idea of what it constitutes. This was also the response of ethnographers to the Ghost Dance 'religion' of the American plains tribes between 1870-1890. A people faced genocidal war and as a consequence, the tribes came together. A unifying 'religion' arose that sought some kind of accommodation with the dominant Christian invaders. The last Ghost Dance shaman, Wovoka, of the Paiute, dressed as a missionary man in western garb and told the ethnographers

' Jesus and our message....alla same'. (16)

There is a problem though, and one well-understood by modern tribals who have worked with Native American teachers – shamans such as Wovoka sought a common language for things that the Christian religion had no comprehension of. And they also sought to conceal the meaning of their own actions. Those tribal dancers were in a state of shamanic consciousness and I have yet to see whether modern anthropology understands this now any more than it did in those times. In our dance work in Glastonbury we have spent over six years working to rebuild this form of consciousness, one which our Celtic ancestors would have held in its undamaged state.

## A modern Ghost Dance

In 2004, I finally gave up trying to influence policy on energy, planning and risk (17), and limited my work to the rewilding of nature conservation – with a significant part of the latter project directed toward rewilding the human and working to introduce shamanic perspectives to scientific ecologists (18). However, during an impromptu vision quest on Native American territory in Nevada in October 2005, I was 'asked' (by a disembodied ancestral voice), to start the 'Ghost Dance' and to follow this through to 2012.

Up until that point, my 'spiritual' life was largely oriented toward the neo-Druid revival and deepening my knowledge of yoga tantra (19). It took some time to agree the quest and to fully understand the mission. This dance is now in its seventh year. It is from the perspective of the Ghost Dance 'shaman' that I now look back at the past decades, evaluate the meaning of 2012, assess the reality of the scientific quest for both knowledge and understanding of Earth's ecological processes, and look to the future hoping to find some allies among social anthropology!

My hopes are not high. In the limited reading I have had time for, I came across this statement in *2012: decoding the countercultural apocalypse* edited by Joseph Gelfer and containing this preface by Michael D. Coe, a Mayan specialist at Yale and Professor of Anthropology, Emeritus:

*'The Maya were adept at many things, including mathematics and rudimentary, naked-eye astronomy, but their mystic take on the end of the world is trumped any day by what modern science has to tell us about these matters'* (20)

This shows a rather typical naive perception of modern solar science as well as the usual 'mystic' appellation for any knowledge outside of the scientific method. Firstly, modern science as it applies to the Sun is in a state of disarray. Having for decades taught that solar output (visible light spectrum) was *constant,* the satellite era soon showed that it varied in clear cycles. Further, only in 1999 did papers begin to appear on the cycles of the solar magnetic field and their correlation to periods of warmth and cold on Earth. From 1900 to 1990 the Sun's magnetic field steadily increased by 200%, after which it declined and global temperatures levelled off. There has been no statistically significant extra surface 'warming' since 1995 (21).

NASA has spent billions of dollars on models to predict the magnetic cycle – largely because of the major implications for satellite technology when impacted by the coronal mass ejections that tend to occur at the peak of the cycle. In 2006 NASA confidently predicted that the coming cycle would peak in 2012 and would be the biggest yet. That cycle did not meet the computer expectation - it started two years late and is much smaller than the previous. NASA has now revised all of its predictions and states that there is a possibility the Sun's magnetic field will go into a Grand Minimum, a form of magnetic hibernation. The last time it did this between 1600-1650, the northern hemisphere cooled dramatically and affected the global mean temperature. This effect is thought by some to be on a roughly 800 year cycle from trough to trough. (I argued in my own work that this natural cycle can explain 80% of the observed 20$^{th}$ century warming).

And with regard to the mystic non-science of the Maya.....how could the world possibly end in 2012? Well, firstly, what the Mayans meant is not that clear. I have friends who are Mayan specialists and their interpretation varies according to the meaning attributed to the 'glyphs' at the end of the calendar . There is little debate that the calendar is accurate and that the Mayans tracked the rising of the winter-solstice Sun through its 26,000 year precession cycle (22). That cycle ends in 2012 according to Mayan time-keeping (and they are the only people who have tracked this cycle). From an urban tribal perspective, they are the tribal 'timekeepers'.

I don't read the 'end-of-the-world' as in some planetary collision or earth-upheaval – rather the end of an era and a shift in consciousness - a period of some kind that had meaning within Mayan cosmology. How much physical disturbance might be expected varies from those modern Mayans who expect some kind of subtle shift in consciousness to those who warn of major catastrophe. I am more concerned with aspects of consciousness than physical realities, but we *can* certainly talk of the 'end of the world as we know it' – and scientifically.

Most people have no idea that since 2008 - when the US National Academy of Sciences reported on the issue, that very large magnetic pulses arrive on Earth from the Sun at irregular but periodic intervals of about 200 years – the last was in 1859. The NAS reported that should such a 'Carrington event' (named after the British astronomer who observed it) happen today, it would likely irreparably disable the global electricity grid. America could not then feed 95% of its population. Immediately, all cities would be without light, water, transport and modern communications. In my estimation, such an event would qualify as changing the world as we know it and with catastrophic consequences. There would be a significant shift in consciousness – much as has been recently reported from Japan in relation to their technological dependence following the tsunami and nuclear meltdowns.

The UK and most other countries were slow to pick up on the NAS report, but recently it has made the press when government instigated a select committee (under defence) to which I made a small contribution (23). I have since been in conversation with specialists at IBM, one of a number of multinationals now making emergency plans which may include relocating their headquarters. This is what Coe eulogises as 'modern' science, yet a whole technological civilisation has been built upon a solar constancy that never existed – and which science itself kept quiet about! Modern civilisation could be brought to its knees by a natural solar event that occurs on a regular basis!

This places Mayan prophecies in proper context. But the scientific potential for such upheavals misses my point – which relates to their 'mystic take'. The Mayan culture was essentially *shamanic*. Their top-deity was the Jaguar. This is of some note considering their level of architectural, mathematical and agricultural knowledge in what was a settled, artistic and civil culture. But the shamanic nature of Mayan culture is hardly acknowledged by archaeologists, historians and anthropologists – in a rather similar way in which Egyptian shamanic culture of animal-headed 'gods' is also largely ignored (24). The reason, I would suppose, is that none of these disciplines contains any kind of shamanic training and thus, the shamanic element is not appreciated or understood and cannot be represented as anything other than 'mystic'.

I would personally expect that the Mayan did not have, as often regarded by historians, a 'Jaguar-God', and for the same reason the Egyptians had no animal-headed 'gods' – the deity was not a *god*, but a shamanic *power* (referred to as a *neter* by the Egyptians). And I would argue that unless the observer has experienced what in shamanic training is termed a *power animal journey*, there can be no understanding of the difference between a 'god' that is 'worshipped' and an animal power that is invoked.

*Black Jaguar : 4'x4' painting (oil on board) for invocations at the altar of the Ghost Dance*

As it happens, in 2012, the Mayan glyphs predict the return of the '*ultimate Jaguar*' which is a cosmic power. Historians and archaeologists would translate this as an expectation that some great Jaguar 'King' from hitherto is expected to re-incarnate and rule again. But again, this is to completely fail to penetrate the shamanic reality – where the Jaguar *represents* the ultimate predator and *ruler*. These realms of understanding are as inaccessible to modern Mayan specialists such as Yale professors of anthropology, as they are to modern Egyptologists attempting an understanding of the lion-headed 'goddesses'.

In this vein, the popular writer Graham Hancock has argued that paleolithic cave paintings cannot be understood from outside of the shamanic perspective within which they were painted. (25) He thinks that the painters were in trance states induced by hallucinogens or by trance-dance and bemoans the response of the anthropologist specialists in this field who refuse to experiment with their own perceptive ability – either by taking the hallucinogens or by dancing! I sympathise and would apply the same argument to the Mayan or Egyptian artefacts. The inner journey, so readily dismissed as 'mystic' can be a source of knowledge – and it is from this source that the Mayans drew.

In shamanic practice, the trance ability is an ability to enter the 'dreamworld' and has to be honed and strengthened much as a mathematician might train his or her logical faculty. Real shamanic knowledge is thus out of the reach of the

244

ordinary person (as well as the ordinary anthropologist). A few exceptions have undergone the journey (with Ayahuasca) in the spirit of humble inquiry and have been deeply struck by the beauty of the insights they have gained. Francis Crick, the discoverer of the structure of DNA admitted in his autobiography that his insights first came during a 'trip' on LSD.

Indeed, any biography of the truly great insights of science would reveal the role of 'dreaming' in the revelation of scientific truths (Newton, Galileo, Tesla, Mendeleyev and even Darwin). Yet, dreaming is not encouraged let alone an integral part of the training readily available in scientific institutions. I will return to what training might exist but is not be so readily available.


## The dreamworld and other dimensions of knowledge

The ultimate shamanic journey takes the form of an initiatory journey to the centre of the galaxy. This is beyond the comprehension of anyone limited by normal modes of thought and perception. The end of the Mayan calendar happens to coincide with an alignment of the winter solstice Sun with the dark rift of the Milky Way and is within a few degrees of the astronomical Galactic Centre. For the Mayan, this point, referred to as Hunab Ku, was the cosmological mother of the Universe. The Egyptians are held by some to have had the same knowledge (26). Modern science only identified galactic centre with the birth of radio-astronomy as it is a powerful radio-source.

Despite ample documentation of altered states of consciousness the majority of the scientifically trained have never had an out-of-body experience and the few who have will not have embarked on any kind of training to move the locus or focal point of their conscious awareness. The commonest western experience comes from martial artists who are taught to shift that locus from the head to the *hara* – just below the navel. Thus, the notion that a disembodied point of individual consciousness can 'travel' such a great distance seems absurd to the scientific mind – but most such minds are actually scientifically illiterate. Ecologists, for example, seldom comprehend the advances in modern physics where mathematicians invoke and construct eleven dimensions of reality in order to reconcile the laws of gravity with the other cosmic forces. In the shamanic dream-world dimension, the journey takes no time because it is made in a dimension that has no time. Hence, there is no distance. Is this dream-world any less real than the world of quantum dynamics where electrons 'communicate' instantaneously over apparently great distance? In actuality, I would argue, the dream-world is infinitely more interesting because it has *content* and thus meaning!

On this 'galactic journey' human consciousness is obliterated momentarily by the experience – and it is an initiation, an experience of the void. On return, the shaman has undergone a transformation that is beyond description in terms of ordinary reality. I have no doubt that shamans far more adept than I would stay conscious for longer and gain more insight and that when Mayan shamans danced their own Ghost Dance (in the skins of black jaguars) they would gain knowledge of value and meaning for the disintegration of the times they faced.

The problem now is that modern science only *describes* alternative dimensions where time does not operate - the modern physicist is not trained to *enter* them! Paradoxically, the founding fathers of modern physics and hence western science, all *practised* entering these inner dimensions of the dream state! The Royal Society was founded by a small group of *alchemical* freemasons led by the renowned astrologer Elias Ashmole. (27) At the outset, modern science was practised by magicians – as in *magii* or magus, and curiously, few modern scientists are even curious as to why this was and what subsequently happened. There is hardly any appreciation in scientific circles of precisely what alchemy constituted, Instead there remains the popular misconception that it was a fool's errand to create gold from base metal. There is no remnant knowledge of the strength of the inquisition in 1600 AD and the need to codify and keep secret all activities that trained the inner perception of reality.

European Alchemy was an inheritance of the Greek *hermetic* tradition of inner 'work' on the self – what would in New Age parlance be called the 'dreambody'. This hermetic tradition (after Hermes, the interlocutor God between Man and the Underworld) directly followed instruction of the Greeks by the Egyptians – whose inner knowledge was gained from Thoth, half-man, half-bird (the Ibis-headed 'god'). Any study of this inner path to knowledge will immediately throw up parallels with yogic training, knowledge of kundalini and tantra that derives from the ancient Vedas and may well precede Egyptian 'tantra' (28).

One can deduce from the biography of Ashmole that the alchemical freemasons had previously practised a form of tantra known as the alchemical or 'inner' marriage, for which a knowledgeable sexual partner was essential. This inner journey sought to balance the male and female components of consciousness. Essentially, this is also the central teaching of yoga-tantra. Ashmole finally gave up because of problems with his wives – a woman of such knowledge was hard to find after several hundred years of ritual torture and execution. In freemasonry, the male mind finally found its answer to the problematic female mind – that part that eschews logic, favours intuition, dwells so often in emotion, and is forever changeable and unpredictable. More potently, the collective 'divine' feminine tends to destroy things in fits of cyclic frenzy – not something a New World Order would find endearing! In the New Age, 'she' is revered, at least in Glastonbury, as the 'dark Goddess', but there is nothing new here – the Greeks called her Chaos and the Indians, Kali. It is hard to appreciate just how far patriarchal culture and its systems of knowledge has moved from any kind of balanced perspective. I am also of the opinion that hermetic knowledge is still very much alive within modern secret societies of magical freemasonry – but, of course, well hidden.

All this is mythic mumbo-jumbo to the average technocrat behind a desk in Brussels, or the funding committees of the Research Councils (unless, of course they have progressed beyond their particular local Lodge).

And if there is a social anthropology of the origins of modern science and its claim to objective knowledge then I would hope to find it in the panel discussions of this conference, but my interest is not just a question of academic study or retrieval of an historical perspective – the modern scientific mind is, in my view, an *amputee*, deprived of a whole hemispheric experience and more importantly, a *training*. The roads within the right hemisphere or 'female' mind of intuition, feeling and dream, lead also to rhythms of creation and destruction – very dark places for the modern male mind to explore and not risk madness. Thus, I would argue that in our clearly patriarchal culture, the amputation has been a deliberate avoidance of these darker realms of reality.


### Science and the repression of holistic knowledge

I would not want to project my limited experience of indigenous communities – but I have found some very happy and blissful people, grounded and connected to the Earth and in community, not afflicted by existential fears of survival or competition, with balanced sexuality, centred in their personal power, full of heart, free with their voice to sing and to dance, and with many in the tribe who can 'see' with their inner eye and a few who have been highly trained since birth to do so. This, in my estimation is the true heritage of what it is to be human. It is found well-articulated in yoga-tantra, the hermetic tradition and in the Egyptian teachings of Thoth. It is not far removed from Druid knowledge and is paralleled in Native American and Amerindian concepts of energy and consciousness centres in the body.

I look around at modern civilised men and women and I find that all of the six 'centres' of consciousness – the *chakra* system in yoga-tantra, representing security and the experience of unity, duality and sexuality, power, heart, voice and vision, have been systematically damaged. Most people I meet and work with experience a base-level insecurity. They have no real supporting community and feel at the mercy of competitive forces. This existential fear closes off the base chakra and prevents the full flow of life energy, the *kundalini*, into the body's energy centres.

This subtle energy flow – symbolised in many cultures as a serpent-power, has a tendency to flow upwards to the second level – that of the sexual organs, but here it is essentially linked to the experience of duality and separation (where the base is linked to the consciousness of unity). Yoga-tantra meditations seek to remedy this perception and balance the male and female polarities that drive desires. Where sexuality is severely damaged – repressed, abused or misdirected the flow of energy is further constricted or most commonly in males, simply discharged.

247

There is thus little flow left into the belly, the *hara* - the centre of gravity and personal *power*. Most modern humans in their urban hierarchical environment hold little personal power or creativity and have virtually no free 'will' in the sense that they are doing what they *want* to do. They are ever subject to a higher authority. There is thus very little energy left for the fourth level of the *heart*. They do love, but it is personal and not very persistent – their love lacks power. which can only be derived from the flow of energy from the lower chakras. They may profess abiding love as taught by great redeemers of the human condition – but when threatened, they retaliate, often with overwhelming force and animosity. The modern civilised human experiences little voice (5$^{th}$ chakra) in their own affairs and very limited vision (6$^{th}$ chakra). {These issues are dealt with more fully in the following article on bio-energetics}

These are my damaged people – the remnant tribes. If they try to dance a 'long-dance' – the Native American Ghost Dance was over four days and nights, the results are very predictable – it turns into a shake-out. There may be visions but they have little power. Modern youth needs alcohol and drugs to get 'off its face' and their attempts at 'tribal trance dances' are far from inspiring (with the exception of workshops and rituals sun my friend and Ghost Dance ally, Zelia Pye). Only the urban-shamanic Five Rhythms of Gabrielle Roth approaches the repair-job on the required global scale.

This matters to me in my task as the Ghost Dance shaman (29). All of my dancers are damaged and requiring repair – including myself. Indeed, it is only through my own therapeutic journey that I can know how to approach their limitations. Our goal is to free the 'energy' body such that the dreaming faculty can be empowered. This work can only be understood by those who have either some *hermetic* knowledge, a background in *kundalini* yoga, or deep levels of shamanic training in places where it is available - such as in the Amazon and Mexico. The final 'seventh level' is that of a *surrender* to the higher power or that which is already dreaming this existence – and this is the ultimate purpose of the Ghost Dance ritual. Perhaps only in Glastonbury could one hope to pull together a team of modern dancers already schooled in kundalini practices and the shamanic journey.

When the rising serpent-power is directed to the sixth level – the 'third eye' of New Age parlance, then it empowers the dreamer and the dream. The Ghost Dance is a collectively empowered dream-dance. Most people do not consciously power their dreams and hence most dreams do not manifest. In collective terms, the dominant dream is that which is most empowered by all the social dreamers – and this is largely unconscious and fearful or illusory. Fear is a powerful energy for the manifestation of dreams – that is, that which is most greatly feared, eventually manifests. The most powerful dream manifesting in modern times is not one of sustainable, equitable and ecological development, but the American Dream of *individual* liberation. Even when held strongly, few manifest this dream because they are too fearful, and merely continue to exist as the base-level of a pyramid of power within someone else's dream. Some would argue that the pyramid maintains its power through illusion, poor education, disempowerment and where necessary, violent and conspiratorial repression. It has its own shadow, of course, wherein the most powerful nation on Earth, is also the least secure and is currently engaged on the manifestation of its greatest terror (ironically, Al Quaida means 'The Base' in Arabic!).

Finally, there is the question of what lies at the end of the inner journey – the rebalancing, the alchemical marriage and the highest yoga tantra? This is the goal of the Ghost Dance. The shaman and yogi *knows* of an underlying presence, variously articulated as a loving 'great spirit' that posseses the qualities of both father and mother. In yoga-tantra, which represents in my view a more mature knowledge, this love is sovereign – it resides in the human heart, and the human heart is seen as a fractal of cosmic consciousness. This is an experiential state of unity, of the truth that there is only one being – one universal consciousness, and it *has* to be experienced to be known. Once experienced, it places the individual human consciousness in perspective as a persistent illusion.

The original Ghost Dance of the plains tribes – as taught to them by the mountain Paiute, sought to reconcile the spirits of the Red Man and the White Man and to dream a time when the children of the soldiers would come to respect the ways of the 'true human'. The tipi fields at our festivals and the burgeoning tribal and shamanic consciousness are tribute to the power of that dreaming. The modern Ghost Dance seeks to reconcile the still errant soul of the White Man with the indigenous soul of humanity, and to dream that restoration. This has to be done not on the mental level, but in the morphic field of the holistic and restored human being. Its dreaming power rests in the heart, the voice and the Ghost Dance songs. For the individual dancer, the journey is equivalent to a yogic training or shamanic 'death', where the survival strategies of the ego are surrendered – there is no turning back, and the whole of life then become the dance.

The consequence of *knowing* this fully human being (Gnosis in the ancient texts of the early Christian era)– or rather practising it, because it takes a conscious effort and training to breathe and align consciousness in this way, is to experience a state of bliss and complete security. The human individual is no longer identified with the vulnerable physical state, but with an eternal anchor. Anthropologists might well suppose this a mental state of illusion, almost as a mirror to the mystic who sees science as equally illusory – but the deeper question is, who gains from the illusion of insecurity maintained by a culture of individuality and an education founded in the scientific method of separation? I think that would be a suitable quest for an anthropology of invisible cultures.

*The 'Stonehenge Skull' – carved by Steve Mitchell from a piece of original sarsen stone discarded during renovations and dedicated to the Ghost Dance.*

**Notes and references**

1) As a mature student at the Institute of Social Anthropology I already had an involvement in environmental issues as an activist and scientist.

2) I was deeply impressed by Barry Barnes' 'Interests and the Growth of Knowledge'.

3) I would be interested to hear of any studies on the rise of ecological 'theory' in politics and in particular the role of the technocrat in policy making.

4) For example, the ecological issue of climate change is entirely defined by bureaucratic scientists with a now global influence on development policy. Global carbon trading reached $176 billion in 2011, rising from $5 billion in 2005, and working largely through the Clean Development Mechanism.

5) This is important because 'clean' energy developments, particularly in the form of biofuels, tend to industrialise agricultural production in otherwise subsistence economies – destroying community and accelerating migration to overcrowded cities; as well as developing remote mountain regions for hydro-power and cutting down primary forests for wood-fuel or biofuel plantations. In developed economies, wind turbine deployment on a large scale has divided communities and impacted the quality of rural life.

6) I discussed these works by Pahner and Novotny in 'Nuclear Power in Central Europe', *The Ecologist* Vol 7 No 6 pp216-222. (1977) and the text of this paper was used in the Open University's 'Control of Technology' course.

7) See *The Nuclear Controversy* (with Martin Stott) Town and Country Planning Association, London (1980) for a summary of the issues at the Windscale Inquiry.

8) See 'The Interpretation of Monitoring Results' in *Radiation & Health*, ed. Southwood & Russell-Jones, Wiley. Pp19-45. 1987

9) I discuss this issue in 'The Precautionary Principle and the Prevention of Marine Pollution' (with T. Jackson). *Chemistry & Ecology*, 7: (1-4), pp123-134. 1993.

10) Brian Wynne's work at the Centre for Science Policy at Lancaster University was a notable effort to make these points within the EU bureaucracy.

11) See 'Rewildng the grazers – obstacles to the 'wild' in wildlife management' *British Wildlife* Vol20 No5, Special issue: Naturalistic grazing and re-wilding in Britain. 2009

12) There is a compendium of articles on these issues from the journal of the British Association of Nature Conservationists in 'Rewilding' ed. P. Taylor, Ethos, Oxford. 2011.

13) See my book 'Chill: a reassessment of global warming theory' Chapter 16, 'Reflections from Anthropology'. Clairview, 2009.

14) The New Age in Glastonbury: the construction of religious movements. Ruth Prince and David Riches, Begrhahn Books, Oxford (2000).

15) Jeremy Narby (1999) The Cosmic Serpent: DNA and the origins of knowledge, Putnam, London.

16) see Michael Hittman, 'Wovoka and the Ghost Dance'. University of Nebraska Press, 1990.

17) My last work with government agencies (The Countryside Agency and the Department of Trade and Industry) sought to visualise change in the landscape and in communities through the use of computer virtual reality – see ) *Visualising Renewable Energy in the Landscape of 2050.* Multi-media Project for the Countryside Agency, Cheltenham. (2001) and accessible at www.ethos-uk.com

18) see Chapter 9, 'The healing Forest' in my book, Beyond Conservation, Earthscan, 2005.

19) I have written about the struggle to maintain yoga and the spiritual path within environmental work in 'Shiva's Rainbow: an autobiography', Ethos, Oxford, 2004.

20) Joseph Gelfer ed. '2012: decoding the countercultural apocalypse'. Equinox, Sheffield, England.

21) I discuss solar science at length in 'Chill' where I present evidence that recurrent natural climate cycles peaked in the late 20th century, are caused by magnetic cycles on the Sun, and are currently turning downward.

22) See John Major Jenkins 'Galactic Alignment: The transformation of consciousness according to Mayan, Egyptian and Vedic traditions', Bear & Co. Rochester, Vermont (2002) And also: Geoff Stray, 'Beyond 2012: catastrophe or ecstasy' Vital Signs Publishing, Lewes, England, 2005.

23) see the UK Parliament Defence Committee report: Developing Threats: Electro-Magnetic Pulses (EMP), Feb 2012.

http://www.publications.parliament.uk/pa/cm201012/cmselect/cmdfence/1552/155203.htm

and also the June 2012 issue of National Geographic Magazine, which has an article explaining recent solar science and outlines the potential for a global catastrophe

24) see: Jeremy Naydler's 'Shamanic wisdom in the pyramid texts: the mystical tradition of ancient Egypt. Inner Traditions, Rochester, Vermont, (2005).

25) Graham Hancock, 'Supernatural: meetings with the ancient teachers of mankind'. The Disinformation Company. Ltd., New York. 2006.

26) see Paul LaViolette's 'Earth under Fire: humanity's survival of the ice-age' Bear & Co. Rochester, Vermont (2005) and 'Genesis of the Cosmos: ancient science of continuous creation', Bear & Co. (2004)

27) see Tobias Churton's 'The Magus of Freemasonry: the mysterious life of Elias Ashmole – scientist, alchemist and founder of the Royal Society, Inner Traditions, Rochester, Vermont, 2006.

28) see 'The Hermetica: lost wisdom of the Pharaohs' by Timothy Freke and Peter Gandy. Tarcher, London, 2008.

29) For a more detailed account of the modern Ghost Dance see 'The Ghost Dance in Avalon: countdown to 2012' *Caduceus* Vol 80, pp14-17, 2011.

*Epilogue*

*In 2013, NASA published a scientific report on a super-flare that had occurred on the 'far side' of the Sun on July 23rd 2012. The report calculates that the power of this flare was many times that of the Carrington event, and had it been 9 days (of solar rotation) later, its full force would have impacted the Earth. Thus, by grace or fortune, humanity was reprieved – at least from a more sudden descent into Chaos!*

# Bio-energetics and the recovery of the indigenous soul

*Paper as background to an invited presentation at the 17ᵗʰ International Convention on Research in Parapsychology and Bio-energetics. Rimini, Italy, 2011.*

The recovery from centuries of cultural damage began with the founding fathers of modern psychology – Freud and Jung, and was advanced by Wilhelm Reich in the science and practices of bio-energetics. In many ways, their work parallels the practices of yoga and ancient arts of sexual union, except that the ancients did not have to deal with the level of damage that exists in the 'western psyche'. This damage is 'energetic' – both mental, psychological and physical, because of course, as bodyworkers we know these worlds are not separate.

### Boundaries and Instruments

The boundaries of modern science are created by the instrument-makers and indirectly the bounded imaginations that create the instruments. Now that quantum physics has reached the level of instrumentation where matter – in the form of electrons, is seen to arise from the 'nothing' that is sub-quantum, the age-old boundary prompts the question – what lies in the fields beyond?

And physicists tell us that out of this dark field, our modern reality, at its most basic level of the smallest particle, is born as if out of another dimension. Indeed, some particles are able to come in and out of existence – that is to say, in and out of the physical dimension to which science applies itself. If we look further into the greatest unsolved mystery of science – the nature of gravity, we find physicists resorting to as many as *eleven* dimensions in order to connect the known forces of the material world to the mysterious force of gravity. Science, therefore, has no boundaries other than the limit of its imagination and the ability to measure things, and it knows that powerful elements of creation lie beyond that limited realm.

So why should parapsychologists and bio-energetics have such a hard time with the world of science? I work in that science world – on ecological systems, energy strategies and climate change and in all but the last, I have a solid reputation with several papers to my name and endorsements by top professors in my field. In the latter – climate change, I have experienced a barrage of criticism and personal attack, though not yet answers to the science questions I raised (the details of which are in my book *Chill: a reassessment of global warming theory*). The world of science often attacks its critics – and in the case of climate science, that world has a lot to lose from any revisions of the theory. But in Parapyschology and Bio-energetics, where is the threat?

Although I have a background in science and policy analysis, I have also spent at least half my time working with the yogic 'sciences' and how they apply to breath- and body-work. There is a yogic science of the energy body, with which I am sure this conference is familiar. I have read little of modern bio-energetics but have great respect for the works and insight of Wilhelm Reich. Up until very recently, my two worlds of ecological science and yogic science were kept separate, although I did approach the unseen worlds of energy from an anthropology of medicine and causation, which I studied for a while when I thought the academic realm might offer a way forward. It did not, and I have practised my science and environmental activism in the realms of policy. In those realms, you learn to keep the 'weird' side of things quiet. The institutions of science are no less repressive than in Reich's day, and their mentors only marginally more progressive than in Galileo's time.

Fortunately, the penalties are not as severe, but they are nevertheless a strong deterrent to wandering from the orthodoxy – reputations are attacked and careers and funding at risk. And although I have less concerns on that level than most, as I work independently and live closer to my yogic science than any other, I am concerned to have some influence on policy and in that respect, enemies can and do make a great deal of any untoward leanings.

In this latter respect, I thought, way back in 2004, that I would be leaving science and policy to become more of a writer and a yogi – and thus, published an autobiography, *Shiva's Rainbow* that laid bare not just my somewhat naive and disjointed psyche (the story is set in 1984) and the political worlds of science and environmental policy – I was chief advocate for Greenpeace at UN conventions, it also went into my contact with Himalayan masters, Freemasons, astral or remote surveillance, homeopathy, astrology and my struggle to make sense of the divine feminine. Things were okay for a few years – I published a leading book in *rewilding* which aimed to create a bridge between the world of ecological science and shamanic realities. *Beyond Conservation* was published in 2005, and I also set up a professional network of land management practitioners – The Wildland Network. I worked primarily with foresters, ecologists and park rangers, as well as government agencies. But sadly, they did not really want a bridge, despite my many pleas that 'conservation' would never reach the really wild part of the human psyche. I argued that our work was very much a *soul retrieval*. But they were locked into the paradigm of scientific ecology – often more by their institutions than their hearts. Still, that work is ongoing.

The problem arose when, as a result of needing to know much more about the dynamics of climate change, I investigated the science in detail. I needed to know just how much time we had because the urgent remedies that were proposed – river and tidal barrages, hydro-schemes, biofuel plantations, turbine arrays, nuclear power stations and genetically modified plants, threatened to undo all of my work. I needed to know whether the sacrifice was necessary and whether the timing might allow a more integrated approach.

I discovered rather quickly that the climate science was not only very poor, but very wrong in its assessment of urgency – and that many other scientists thought so too, including several with the UN framework. I published my views in 2009 and that is when, for the first time in my career (and having gone up against a lot of powerful industrial interests), I suffered from personal attacks aimed at denting my credibility as a scientist. One 'green' activist professor read my autobiography and wrote the most scurrilous attack, mining the book for anything that would discredit me in the prejudiced halls of science'....whilst at the same time, stating that I had a sound reputation in the fields of nature conservation.

I don't aim now to go into details – the purpose for this talk is to note that the institutions of science attack their critics and even more so if those persons have leanings toward anything beyond the 'fringe' of their reality. In Britain recently, the Royal Society has regularly launched attacks on homeopathy, chiropractic and astrology, as well as upon critical scientists challenging, for example, the epidemiology of immunisation programmes and safety of vaccines, medicines and pesticides. The Society regular espouses the benefits of GMOs and nuclear power. It is most vehement against climate science 'deniers' or 'contrarians' and justifies the War on Climate in the same terms as or even more important than the War on Terror.

**Attack and defence, camouflage and manipulation – through history**

So – as a practitioner of alternative 'medicine', and someone working in the realms of both shamanism and science, I am an easy target for this level of deliberate attack. It does not limit my work, however – I am still engaged in the science of climate change, as well as rewilding the nature conservation paradigm. It does actually have a positive side – it gives me insights into the insecure scientific mind and perhaps also to something a bit darker.

Why would such powerful institutions bother to attack homeopaths or astrologers? And why did it so powerfully attack Reich? One answer would be that it does so unconsciously. I am not aware that there is much of a literature on the social psychology or anthropology of scientists as a sect or a tribe within the modern social order. Another answer would be that it does so deliberately, as part of a concerted programme of media control and maintenance of its influences in education, medicine, the industrial and military complex and the production of material goods. In which case, more of an historical analysis is required. And perhaps the truth is that *both* answers are true.

I will start with the historical.

We can usefully begin with the founding of the first 'western' science institution The Royal Society in 1655 in London. Most other science academies were derived from this initiative. It is a good place to start not only because of its influence within science, but also because we have some good historical data on the people who founded the Society and their social world at the time. I will draw on a recent biography of Elias Ashmole entitled, *The Magus of Freemasonry* by the Masonic scholar Tobias Churton.

Ashmole was in the founding group, despite having little experience of 'science' itself – he was more interested in museums and collections on one level, and alchemy on another. Indeed, most of the founding fathers of the Royal Society were practising alchemists, as later were some of its great luminaries, such as Isaac Newton. He and Ashmole were also practising astrologers, with Ashmole giving astrological advice to both government and royalty. All of these alchemist-astrologers were also freemasons. Indeed, a case can be made that the Royal Society was born out of a marriage between alchemists and freemasons – the alchemists *became* freemasons and then developed their new rules of science – known the world over now as the scientific method.

Few lay people actually know much about the methodology of science – and indeed, most people leave school without ever really understanding or practising it despite studying science subjects. Only at more advanced University level, do would-be scientists actually have to apply their techniques and generate useful data in a particularly thorough and realistic scientific way. Many of the tricks of the trade are only learnt at a doctoral level. And the vast majority of doctoral research projects are compartmentalised, often inane and make insignificant contributions to knowledge. Thereafter, the great majority of 'scientists' work as technicians with a very narrow focus – either in commercial agriculture, the food and drink industry, medicine and defence. Very few ever reflect up the process of science. And very few outsiders in the form of sociologists and social psychologists delve into the realm of science itself, and more especially not - its relation to medical, educational, engineering, defence and financial institutions.

These institutional levels are very far removed from the pioneering work of the early scientists on the physics and chemistry of matter, or indeed, from the modern frontier of particle physics and astronomy. The vast majority of 'scientists' have a limited knowledge base and are simply technicians within an empire of material goods, especially electronics, weaponry, pharmaceuticals, agri-business, brewing, the food industry and the 'educational' worlds that train people for these positions. Yet, on an institutional level, the image is deceptively projected of a pure and objective humanitarian quest for knowledge.

We will return to the issue of deception on a modern political level – after examining deception historically. Freemasonry and alchemical practice were always secret. Freemasonry had less of a problem in that it managed to camouflage its relation to God – their deity was overtly symbolised as an architectural power by the use of the *dividers* that a mason would use for measurements. The secret society could purport to consist of under-employed monument and temple builders with an esoteric interest in sacred geometry. As such they were no threat. They kept their relation to other 'Gods' secret because this would draw down the full and potentially fatal repression of the Church – which was in 1650 still a global power greater than royalty and military or the nascent merchant banks. Masonic societies drew their growing membership not from science, but from these bankers, brokers and accountants, together with lawyers, the judiciary and the police. Eventually, royalty and the military were recruited. Membership was only by invitation and all ritual kept secret – on pain of exclusion and in severe cases of betrayal – the threat of an unpleasant death.

**Alchemical marriage on the rocks**

In the case of Elias Ashmole, we are given a clue as to the appeal of Freemasonry through his difficult marital relations. This is central to the secret practice of alchemy – which is deceptively coated in chemistry and the transmutation of metals, when in fact, as I am sure many of you will know, it is a practice for the raising of consciousness. In particular, as Churton points out though not in these words, it is a tantric practice with the *alchemical marriage* fundamental to success (*al chem* meaning 'out of Egypt' in the sense that 'chem' was a multivalent term for the black soil of that land, for the land of the Nile itself, and perhaps also for the ultimate darkness of realms such as are symbolised in Hindu symbology as the Goddess *Kali*).

Ashmole was finding things difficult on that level – the women were not entirely cooperative. Perhaps not surprising since there were no schools of tantra staffed by the sort of women who could teach its deepest mysteries and techniques. Whatever had been developed in Egypt over several millennia, had been effectively lost.

We have no access to what these 'magi' got up to in 1650, but from eastern tantric knowledge, now more available in the West, we can reconstruct the scene. For the marriage to work it has to be an internal balancing of 'male' and 'female' forces within the bio-energetic body. This could always be done alone – and indeed, in modern patriarchal India, yogic knowledge is generally packaged as if it is a viable non-sexual path to higher consciousness. Yet, all yogis know that the highest yoga tantra is greatly accelerated through engagement with am adept yogini.

True tantric yoginis are very rare – and most eastern teachers of tantra are male and keep secret what they learn from their consorts. The old alchemists had no easier a task as a modern day tantrika – partners with real knowledge were very

258

hard to find. Hence, I would argue, the historical switch from alchemical tantra to a more attractive and apparently singular male world of Freemasonry – in which they would find some resonance in its use of the Qabbala. The balancing energies were now to be engaged internally - in theory. In actual practice, I suspect rituals often made use of high-class prostitutes as depicted in the film *Eyes Wide Shut,* and in the antics of Silvio Berlusconi – sometime Prime Minister of Italy and one-time member of the P2 Lodge in Rome, who seems to suffer serial scandal in relation to beautiful escorts and strange 'parties'.

The important aspects of this history are two – the gender issue and the secret teachings. The latter are seldom portrayed for what they are – a route to apparently higher consciousness. They involve not only ritual but training of the inner faculties of the mind. Much of the ritual is empty of meaning – that is deliberate. Initiates into higher teaching are chosen and only after initiation, will some rituals be practiced and become meaningful. The point here is not to particularise those teachings but to be aware that they require skills for an *internal* journey, a relationship to the otherworld reality and a training of what we might call paranormal abilities such as inner sight and vision.

Anyone who has trained on any kind of programme of expanding their consciousness knows that abilities such as telepathy, clairvoyance, astral projection and projection of thought are all made more accessible by such training. In eastern Yoga, these *siddhis* are not the goal, but consequences of the inner practices and have to be handled carefully. I will note at this juncture, that the vast majority of the public, including most of my ecological and 'green movement' colleagues, have no direct experience of this internal work and have been taught to deride it.

So – with this historical background we can better understand the evolution of science itself. It is a curious evolution. A group of dedicated magicians (magi) with very good connections to royalty and the newly unfolding banking system decide to found an institution of knowledge that eschews the internal world of consciousness and espouses only an external reality – that which can be measured and quantified. All reference to the inner journey of the initiate is expunged and the outer world has no meaning other than as the work of a cosmic Grand Architect. The task of the scientist is no longer divine, but simply to divine the inherent laws of a mechanistic Universe.

**The rise of the scientific society**

The first and foremost element of scientific method is that of objective observation and measurement. Reality must be divided with the dividers of measurement, however much of a continuum it appears to be. Newton was expert at this – in for example, separating the different wavelengths of white light using a glass prism. This led to the very useful science of optics and its instruments. The physical world thus began to 'give up its secrets' in the form of regular laws and mathematical relationships. The world of fluid dynamics, atomic billiards, and electrical circuits birthed ever finer instruments as well as useful tools in controlling nature and enemies.

Science was on a roll – it created medical understanding (albeit mostly in terms of pumps and valves and skeletal engineering) that was useful in mending bone structures and faulty valves. Eventually, the biological sciences developed anti-biotics and the faith in science leapt in the public mind. Much of the revolution in health that has been put down to such advances in science, actually came from simple engineering of clean water and sewage, with warmer and better ventilated buildings coupled to better nutrition. But biology, engineering and chemistry drove a massive expansion of agriculture – both combining to drive human populations from a few hundred millions, to seven billion, occupying over 40% of available energy niches on land and sea.

This is viewed as one of the greatest successes of science, yet leaving aside the threat of climate change, there is a very real danger of ecosystems collapse under the weight of human demand.

In addition, the complex dependency of modern society on electronic systems means that a perfectly natural and relatively frequent solar tsunami ( a magnetic pulse from a super-flare) could bring the resultant civilisation to its knees within a few months. This was the subject of a high-level report by the US National Academy of Sciences to Congress in the autumn of 2008

Science has been a double-edged sword. But we need to look more closely at its shadow side. It was built-in at the start with the failure to embrace the alchemical woman.

Here I tread warily. Our modern European languages are the imperial product of centuries of invasion, repression of indigenous cultures and severance of connections to the land and to the past. Our cultural ambassadors continue this process of attrition in every corner of South America, Africa, and Australasia. So please bear with me in grasping for words and understanding of truths that are long buried within my own and the general western psyche.

**The original feminine**

Woman, by nature, is opposite in consciousness to man. This is, of course, modern heresy – women are accorded exactly the same education as men. That is part of the problem I will try to address. In the modern world, women are *equal* to men and can do all the things men can do – and they have fought hard for that equality, but important as this political struggle has become, it misses a vital point – which is not about equality, but difference. Things can be equal but different – as in light and dark, or positive and negative charge.

In their long struggle to become equal in *power*, most women have neglected the nurturing of their different nature. Indeed, with the systematic eradication in western culture of women teachers through branding and ritual execution (and in eastern patriarchal traditions by other means of repression) few women have any access to the deeper teaching of female consciousness. Many would simply not know there is any difference between men and women – or though if they really thought about it, they would know, but perhaps be reluctant to accord value to the feminine ways of knowledge.

Female consciousness is rooted in the dark not the light, in the dream not the world of logic and externality, in the body first and the mind second, in the realm of feeling, intuition and the myriad qualities of the emotional heart, rather than in logic and the apparent constancy of science. Furthermore, this consciousness has unpredictable moods and irregular cycles – it challenges prediction and certainty, rule and regulation. As such it is primal and primary, orgasmic and creative and at the same time loving and nurturing, protective and fierce....yet also capable of immense destruction. It is as close to death and decay, water and the earth, as it is to air and fire, growth and life. Female consciousness has no difficulty including male consciousness, if temporarily, and can match it in most realms, whereas male consciousness requires years if not lifetimes of training to even begin an effective move in the opposite direction (at least in my humble experience!). This was the alchemical marriage that foundered and we now live in a mentally unbalanced society.

In my public presentations on climate change science – though not yet in the academic institutions where I have also lectured, I present a picture of this imbalance as it affected the science. Climate science was born of a virtual reality computer model of mathematical constructs – models that either completely ignored or could not incorporate *cycles,* with their irregular periods and in-exactitudes. The premise of *prediction* led to a downplaying and exclusion of the unpredictable. Furthermore, the models were *light-based* – in the sense of dealing with wavelengths of visible or infra-red energies and neglected the *dark* fields of magnetism with their regular but inexact rhythms and their *unknown* mechanics and laws relating to solar-terrestrial effects.

The arch-alarmist, Al Gore, makes a filmed presentation entirely focussed upon carbon dioxide – for which we was awarded both a Nobel Prize and an Oscar. Carbon is the enemy and carbon taxes are the weapons of defence. He did not mention his own investment bank, carbon trading, carbon currencies and the ultimate global governance (of banks) that goes with it. But we will return to that. The archetypal magicians trick is to draw attention to something and away from something that he or she does not wish to be seen.

Thus far is our history. It is either accidental – a simple progression, or a conscious magicians trick. So let us look at what might be gained from the trick.

Legions of young minds, male and female, now receive an education without any formal instruction as to their inner world. They have no training in meditation. They are taught that inner worlds are secondary – imaginary and a lesser reality. The female abilities of *knowing,* often where someone is despite

261

the distance *and* what they feel, are not encouraged and trained. Inner sight is disabled. They are led to 'believe in' the external measurable reality. Many deep contradictions in science are held from the student's initial view.

But more – this state of being is one for masses of people deluded into thinking only the external is real, and coinciding for the most part with having little of no contact with the land. They live a life in an apartment or block of cells, or an urban single family house with no real community, and they are financially trapped by a system wherein they must 'work' like drones in the greater 'economy' in order to pay for rents, food, clothes, water and warmth – all of the *basics*. The *economy* is built upon a fundamental philosophy of individualism, material value and above all *scarcity*. The result is a very basic *insecurity*.

### The bio-energetic body and its seven levels

I want to symbolise this base-level insecurity with reference to the yogic system of knowledge with which I work. The base-chakra or lowest energy centre is both an energetic reality – for those with subtle vision or senses, and a psychic centre. In the latter respect, thought can influence how open and flowing the base chakra can be and any negative thoughts or fears close it down. Thus, most people in modern society, have a very limited flow of energy *into* this centre. We would call this energy flow *kundalini* and in ancient India (and Egypt) this energy is 'symbolised' by the serpent. In their essence early Egypt and also ancient Vedic yoga, were essentially *shamanic* cultures – the snake was not a symbol but a *neter* – a power, and the object of ritual was not to 'worship' but to *embody* that power. The shamanic mind extends its consciousness and the human absorbs the power of the snake – in this case, the power of spiralling energy flow.

This power is something the snake has that the human has little of – the power of rhythmic movement, the wave-form and the spiral dance. And the shamanic mind knows, that the snake on Earth is a representative of a cosmic *neter* - *w*herever we go in the Universe, we are going to find serpent power in some form or even beyond form.

The energy of this wave-form is fundamental to life. It energises all of the higher chakras – and tantra teaches how to awaken and strengthen the flow – as must have the alchemical marriage of the Egyptians. This 'path' is now effectively blocked on a massive social scale. The average person, uninitiated into spiritual matters, lives in basic insecurity with the mind tossed this way and that with worries about mortgage, rent, jobs, food, terrorists, viral plagues and alien invasions.

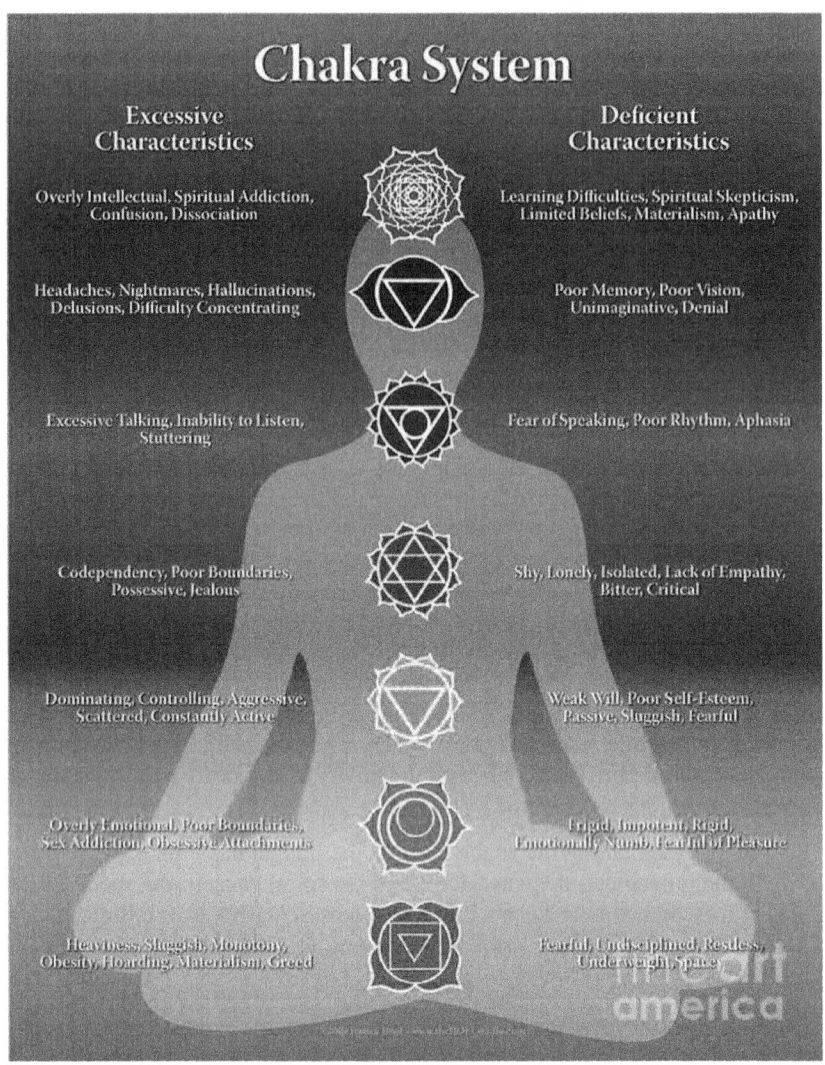

# Chakra System

| Excessive Characteristics | Deficient Characteristics |
|---|---|
| Overly Intellectual, Spiritual Addiction, Confusion, Dissociation | Learning Difficulties, Spiritual Skepticism, Limited Beliefs, Materialism, Apathy |
| Headaches, Nightmares, Hallucinations, Delusions, Difficulty Concentrating | Poor Memory, Poor Vision, Unimaginative, Denial |
| Excessive Talking, Inability to Listen, Stuttering | Fear of Speaking, Poor Rhythm, Aphasia |
| Codependency, Poor Boundaries, Possessive, Jealous | Shy, Lonely, Isolated, Lack of Empathy, Bitter, Critical |
| Dominating, Controlling, Aggressive, Scattered, Constantly Active | Weak Will, Poor Self-Esteem, Passive, Sluggish, Fearful |
| Overly Emotional, Poor Boundaries, Sex Addiction, Obsessive Attachments | Frigid, Impotent, Rigid, Emotionally Numb, Fearful of Pleasure |
| Heaviness, Sluggish, Monotony, Obesity, Hoarding, Materialism, Greed | Fearful, Undisciplined, Restless, Underweight, Spacey |

*From the base to the crown – the kundalini wave and its psychic attributes. Artwork by Jessica Hoel (www.thehoelstudio.com)*

Only when feeling safe and secure, can the psyche allow this energy to rise and energise the second chakra – the sexual centre. Early depictions of the shaman and magician often show an erect phallus. And we know from modern anthropology that we are as closely related to the very sexual and peaceful *Bonobo* as to the 'demonic' and aggressively hierarchical chimpanzee. I borrow the term demonic from Richard Wrangham's book *The Demonic Male* on the two potential evolutionary paths and their dichotomy. In the peaceful ape,

263

females banding together countered male dominance and this ape evolved peaceful means of dealing with invaders – the females had rampant sex with the interlopers!

The human is a highly sexual animal. It has the greatest concentration of pleasure neurons of any ape – particularly at the female organ – concentrated at the clitoris. I would love to spend more time on this topic – but in short, will argue, that this organ evolved to 'stoke the fires' of the serpent journey – the energy having great benefits if it is pulled higher into the third chakra. That does not often happen – all boys and most women are trained in youth, not by teachers, who are largely absent, but by their peers, who know no better than to rapidly disperse this energy.

That deprives the third chakra of power. The third chakra is the centre of gravity, the place of the will and the generator of personal authority. Not only has it a minute amount of help from below, it is hit by constant repression from above. Children are taught to obey authority and seldom express their own creative power. Scientists spend the best years of their young lives learning to cite the authorities.

If the sexual centre is not distracted – at its extreme in the training of celibate fighting monks in the Buddhist Shaolin tradition, the power centre is able to store this serpent power as Chi, and 'extend' it in ways quite beyond scientific understanding in protection again blows or the repelling of attack.

But in modern society, this flow of energy upwards is a trickle and the next destination is the heart. This is a much misunderstood human organ, centre and chakra. In bio-energetics we know it has an emotional intelligence and great depth. We know it has a magnetic structure - a fractal of the Earth field and the solar also. We know more of its symbolic nature – the heart of the lion and the oak and the creative and passionate source of human love. It holds the element of courage and integrity, constancy and love. And it can also be afflicted by doubt, resentment, envy, jealousies and revenge. It has a dark side that I call the basement of the heart.

In my own yogic work, I call the lower entrance to the heart – the channel from the third to the fourth chakra, the doorway to the basement (as did the Druid shaman – it was *derwen,* the oak power and the flowers of the oak were held to have magical healing powers for the heart).

Not many enter this doorway. The flow is very constricted, most especially in those who throw open the upper windows and profess great love. As do, for example, most Christian and Islamic sects. And as soon as they feel threatened, the teachings of their masters and sages go out of that window. Christians have a long history of invasions or crusades, torture of heretics and execution of their perceived enemies as well as systemic genocide of indigenous peoples. They are at the mercy of their heart's shadow. Their heart has no power – no strength from the belly. It is infected by insecurities, sexual repression and lack of personal authority. If an ancient Bishop tells them they can lay aside the deepest teachings of their master Jesus, they do so – in the name of security in the face of an enemy.

Of course, there are also many saints, just as there are Sufis, who have understood the mystery of atonement, but they have failed to alter the course of this history.

Where there is so little heart, the voice suffers disempowerment – the fifth level of consciousness is also readily suppressed. And here the dimensions of the mind begin to take their root. The fifth chakra also holds the power of spoken truth. When energised by an open heart, that truth becomes the unity of all human beings – that is, the truth that we are all one human, evolving through time. It therefore teaches responsibility and the extension of love beyond tribal boundary. In the depth of the human heart everyone is equal in the sight of love.

That truth, as we know, struggles now to manifest. As does a reliable vision – the sixth level. Most people have no inner vision of any constancy or power and their dreams cannot manifest. The Magus knows the rules – dreams must be energised by emotional power from *below.*

Furthermore, most people cannot 'see' beneath surface realities. They have no developed sixth sense – and hence are easily deceived. When what sixth sense they do have tells them to beware, they just feel uneasy but lack the confidence to act.

And so we have it – a majority of human beings with no initiation into power, hence powerless. They populate the lower levels of the pyramid. Somewhere above them, like a mirror of all past Empires, initiates live a privileged life and make all the real decisions. In the modern world, that empire is economic – which is to say, the bankers make most of the decisions about what gets built and where. Governments as well as corporations must all defer to the banks.


The modern Green Movement, iconically led by Al Gore, would have a global carbon bank, paid for by carbon taxes, administered by unelected technocrats and directed by investment bankers. And all of that prospective empire of rather expensive technological solutions, rests upon the science of climate change. Much as the early scientific mind saw Nature as something to conquer, climate has become an another external enemy and the scary climate story another level of inculcated fear and insecurity.

In climate science, the Sun plays a mysterious role. It is known from the ice-cores that solar forces drive climate changes far greater than we have seen in the last one hundred years. Physics once held a notion called 'the solar constant' – that was dispelled as soon as space-based instruments measured the inconstant output of its light. Only later were its magnetic fields measured and extrapolations made back into the past – all periods of low magnetics were cold periods. No one yet knows what the mechanisms are, though there are candidates and dozens of papers exploring the data. But we can look more usefully at the symbols of the Sun in human consciousness. If carbon is the signature of earth-bound *fear,* solar hydrogen is the symbol of eternity and spirit.

Gore plays on our carbon-life-form identification with the external and material body where only death and taxes (his carbon taxes) are certain. The science is logical, linear, computed and predictive. The world of solar – especially its dark side, is mysterious, uncertain, irregular and unpredictable – its elements are simple. It is a symbol not of death or burnt wood, but creative power and love. Small wonder Gore would have us look at something else.

In relation to sleight of hand, it is obvious to me that mitigation of climate change by emission reduction will be ineffective – most of the change stems from a natural cycle. What *is* needed is a massive programme of adaptation and *resilience* to change – at the grassroots community level of soil, water, food and forest. Currently, despite pleas from UN committees, less than 1% of climate funds are spent on these programmes, and less than 10% of all international development aid.

And where does this leave the magicians? Somewhere behind the scenes, they gather for their rituals, but still with the secrecy of old. We are expected to believe the projected image of humanitarian purpose and ignore the commitments to symbolic magic. But it is less *what* they do, as to what is not done in their name. There is no meditation taught in schools and no inner path of the spiritual warrior. Thus are billions of people in modern scientific and 'religious' culture disempowered at the deepest level and easily manipulated into the serving at the base of the pyramid. Conspiracy or coincidence? All I know is that if I was asked, with all my knowledge of yogic science and the shamanic realms, to devise a strategy for world domination, I would devise the scientific method and marry it to religions that already separate ordinary people from their own divinity and inner knowledge. 'Science' in Latin, means 'to separate' – it is either magicians' trick, or a very convenient co-evolution with the capitalist enterprise.

266

# An Epilogue on How to Rewild

I have been asked at various times whether a 'manual' for rewilding could be produced. That is not so easy, because every piece of land and group of people is different and I would recommend reading about the experiences of the projects we have documented at BANC and in process of being updated in the UK by Rewilding Britain, a new umbrella organisation. Here are some reflections.

The first thing – to listen! To sit on the land. And to clear the mind of all its projections and mumblings, prejudices, theories, competing voices....to let go of as much as possible of the personal and the factual, and then *ask* the land itself – 'what does the spirit of this land want?'

And then to listen.

It is important to make a record and not to edit what we hear, however challenging it may be.

Every patch of land has its spirit. I don't mean disembodied entities of any kind – though some may feel such presences, rather that every place is unique and at the same time part of a continuum that is both physical *and* of an invisible dimension that underlies all physical reality. Indigenous peoples, more wild than we, do not differentiate these worlds – they acknowledge them both as interpenetrating time and space, but more, that this dual world has an abiding *consciousness* that is aware of us, the human, and can speak our language. Different cultures ascribe different names to this spirit of nature and the names are less important than the qualities that are *felt.* Such a shamanic consciousness does not seek proof of such reality - it simply listens, sometimes as a child would to a father or mother, sometimes as brother or sister, and sometimes as lover.

However, we don't have to 'believe' in other worlds – we just need to listen to the land and reflect upon what we hear, even we think what we hear is a reflection of our own psyche, or an echo of our own inner thoughts. It is the reflection that is important. What we hear should then be held precious and accorded some respect at all points in the decision processes affecting a rewilding project.

Many such projects start out with an individual looking at a piece of land and thinking simply, 'what if'? What if the forests were brought back, or extinguished species returned? What if we left the land alone? What if we enlarged the areas under protection?

And for sure, there will be more than one person involved or implicated in any vision – there is very little unused land in Britain, and the land may not be owned by the dreamers, and the dreamers may not all receive the same dream! Many of the projects in the UK and elsewhere start out as community programmes – creating tree nurseries, buying land, clearing invasive plants, and the vision is negotiable within the community. Where outside sources of funding are available, the funders may have their own visions and compromises have to be debated. The essential element in all of this is the *communal* relation to the land. A true rewilding project rewilds both the ecology and the human.

In this there will be a wide spectrum of involvement. I have been involved in two examples at the extreme of that spectrum. My friend and colleague, Simon Ayres, helped to found a small community initiative in West Wales which we titled The Welsh Wild Land Foundation. It had particular pieces of land in its vision that were located in the North Cambrian Mountains, some of which were up for sale. The group began a programme of education and outreach, small-scale tree planting and nurseries, and set about fund-raising. Within a few years it had support for a part-time crew of communicators and approaches from funders to buy large tracts of degraded upland pasture (overgrazed acid-grassland). Management plans and overall vision were simple: to regenerate native woodland cover and naturalistic grazing. Funding was forthcoming for a small enclosure and experiment with beaver in one part of the watershed. Each year the group grows in strength and confidence and as rewilding becomes more widely accepted, this one small initiative is attracting the attention of the larger conservation organisations. Given the nature of the Welsh upland farming and forestry communities, re-introducing large wild herbivores, even red deer, let alone wild cattle, bison and beaver,, and even more so, the lynx as predator, though the ecosystem  might support them all, much negotiation and compromise lies ahead.

At this grass-roots level, it is my observation that spiritual values (with even some shamanic practices) are the primary motivation for regenerating wildland. Humans are part of the process, but the overall vision is of a sanctuary that will be visited but not dominated by human use. The practical issues of management, whether of reforesting, re-introductions or visitor numbers, are all very much down-the-line and subject to debate – however, following the Wildland Network initiative, the group have ample contacts and sources of advice.

The other example relates to a much larger tract of land that is already under sympathetic ownership – Ennerdale in the west of the English Lake District National Park. The Forestry Commission own areas of both plantation forestry (alien spruce and larch) and ancient native woodland. The National Trust own adjacent pasture and moorland in the upper reaches of the Dale, and a Water Company – United Utilities, owns the lake. The pastures and moorland are grazed by domestic stock run by tenants of the Trust. These three organisation set up an advisory group to which I was invited, along with colleagues from BANC and later, the Wildland Research Institute at Leeds University. But in essence, the vision was held by two people – Rachel Yannick at the Trust and Gareth Browning of the Forestry Commission, and their task was to gain the cooperation of the farmers and recreational users of the valley in creating a 'wilder' Ennerdale. It is, and always was seen to be a long-term evolving project with no fixed outcome. All of the people who loved, worked or visited the valley were duly respected, their opinions listened to, and a cooperative outcome assured. Progress has been slow – less sheep on the high fells and a steady move toward cattle which have less impact on the moorland; the river has been freed to meander; tough breeds of cattle now graze the woodland and some exotic plantation trees have been removed. Thus far, proposals to introduce beaver have not been followed but relations to other contiguous estates suggest a large area may come under a wilder form of management with less of the marginally economic usage of traditional farming and forestry. Should there be major shifts in agricultural economics and public support for re-introductions of wild grazers and even the lynx as predator, Ennerdale will be well-placed to take the lead.

Both of these examples involve local people who know and love their land. They also involve a conscious awareness that the land is degraded, unfree and capable of being restored to a wilder state. Participants vary greatly in their ecological understanding and their spiritual relationship to nature where there is a spectrum again - from overtly Pagan and shamanic to traditionally Christian concepts of stewardship. And perceptions of a timescale for progress vary. There are no easy prescriptions.

In some ways, Britain is unique in the scale and number of such locally-born rewilding initiatives. On continental Europe and in the USA, there are large-scale visions that are predominantly top-down, involving corporate conservation agencies, government and even commercial eco-tourist interests. Some of these projects are reviewed in my edited volume of ECOS articles - *Rewilding* (published in 2011), and the shift to corporate involvement commented upon in this volume in my reportage of the 2013 wilderness congress in Salamanca. I have reservations about top-down approaches. Unless they engage participants on-the-ground and foster a right and loving relationship to the land I would not call them rewilding. However, there are signs that such issues of participation and involvement are being dealt with by the larger organisations with ambitions over large tracts of land in Europe.

I would say – let there be no prescription! Several commentators fall into the mindset of recreating the past – for example, past assemblages of wild herbivores (wood bison, moose, wild cattle and wild horse are missing over large forested areas of Europe, and we can add beaver and boar for Britain);

and their predators – such as wolf, lynx and bear. Few forested areas actually contain mature trees over two hundred years of age – for example, in Czech republic which is 30% forested, only a few hundred hectares of primeval forest remain; and in France, equally rich in forest cover, there may be none such. And whatever the tree-cover, without the forest herbivores and their predators, the wild dynamic is absent (I cover these issues in detail in my book *Beyond Conservation*).

So – certainly an ideal rewilding project would re-establish the naturally wild dynamic and would require a large area in which to do so. However, it would be naïve to expect there to be zero-management or human interference. The boundaries of wildland are permeable – not the least to allow human access, but also, outwith the use of extreme fencing, animals wander and would require a management response. Further, the complete guild of herbivore and predator that created the original dynamic cannot now be re-constituted (forest elephants, rhino and sabre-toothed cat are extinct). Added to this is the thorny problem of invasive alien plants and animals that out-compete the natives and how this can or should be managed. This latter problem has no easy solutions and is very relevant to smaller-scale British projects faced with Japanese knotweed, Himalayan balsam and rhododendron. And as I pointed out in *Beyond Conservation* – almost the entire inherited British landscape is populated by aliens – Sitka spruce, engineered rye-grass monocultures, muntjac and Sika deer, non-native rats, brown hares, rabbits and pheasants! And it is doubtless upon these that Britain's feral panthers and pumas are feeding.

It is at this point that I feel the values of traditional conservation, embedded as they are in ecological sciences, begin to fail the rewilding ethos. The future landscape will evolve as a mix of aliens – translocated by whatever follies, and which would prove exhausting to eradicate, if indeed, that is feasible. As I have argued in the pages of ECOS, conservation values are stuck in the old paradigms of science – and they inform and determine much of the legal frameworks. For example, there would be a rewilding case to introduce the smaller Spanish lynx to South West Britain where there are more of its natural prey, the rabbit, than currently in its homeland which was devastated by rabbit haemorrhagic disease – but it would be against the guidelines of the International Union for the Conservation of Nature which advises that only former denizens should be re-introduced. Climate change – both natural and human-induced also alters all of the equation related to past assemblages and their adaptability to a future environment.

It is frustrating, I appreciate, for scientists, academics and even journalists to be met with general principles and non-prescriptive rewilding – where almost anything on any scale from garden to local river-bend to several square miles of mountain could be called a rewilding project, but that is the reality in Britain. The most important things happen in the *interaction* – the *process* of rewilding with its challenges to perception, to communication, to values and to cooperation.

Rewilding Britain (www.rewildingbritain.org.uk ) is a recent organisation aiming to further the development of projects in the UK. Rewilding Europe is a contact point for European initiatives – www.rewildingeurope.com

The former issued this recent summary of what it is to rewild:

In the brief we explore how the following seven rewilding principles can complement and extend existing conservation law and policy.

1. **Restoring natural processes and ecological dynamics** – both abiotic such as river flows, and biotic such as the ecological web and food-chain – through reassembling lost guilds of animals in dynamic landscapes.
2. **A gradated and situated approach**, where the goal is to move up a scale of wildness within the constraints of what is possible
3. **Taking inspiration from the past but not replicating it.** Developing new natural heritage and value that evokes the past but shapes the future.
4. **Creating self-sustaining, resilient eco-systems** including re-connecting habitats and species populations within the wider landscapes.
5. **Working towards the ideal of passive management**, where once restored, we step back and allow dynamic natural processes to shape conservation outcomes.
6. **Creating new natural assets that connect with modern society and economy** and promote innovation, enterprise and investment in and around natural areas, leading to new nature-inspired economies.
7. **Reconnecting policy with popular conservation sentiment** and a recognition that conservation is a cultural dynamic as well as a scientific and technical pursuit.

And much as these principles reflect a considerable movement for conservationists, they still stem from an old paradigm that tacks on 'cultural sentiment' whilst speaking the econometric language of 'natural assets, innovation, enterprise and investment' and hardly acknowledging the nature of the human and the potential for a reciprocal process of rewilding.

271

Lightning Source UK Ltd.
Milton Keynes UK
UKOW06n0346150617
303355UK00001B/59/P

9 780954 706449